GO *for the* GREEN

Leadership Secrets from the Golf Course

THE FRONT NINE

GO *for the* GREEN
Leadership Secrets
from the Golf Course
THE FRONT NINE

Donald A. Sanders, Ph.D.

INSYNC
PRESS

SANFORD • FLORIDA

Copyright © 2001 by Donald A. Sanders

All rights reserved. No part of this publication may be reproduced, stored in a retrieval system, or transmitted in any form or by any means – electronic, mechanical, photocopy, recording, or any other except for brief quotations in printed reviews, without the prior permission of the publisher:

InSync Communications LLC and InSync Press
2445 River Tree Circle
Sanford, Florida 32771
http://www.insynchronicity.com

ISBN: 1-929902-04-2
Library of Congress Catalog Number: 00-103276
Sanders, Donald A., 1943
Go For The Green: Leadership Secrets from the Golf Course/
Donald Sanders

First InSync Press Edition
10 9 8 7 6 5 4 3 2 1

InSync Press books are available at special discounts when purchased in bulk for use in seminars, as premiums or in sales promotions. Special editions or book excerpts can also be created to specification. For details, contact InSync Communications LLC at the address above.

Cover Design by Jonathan Pennell
Book Design/Typesetting by Jonathan Pennell
Printed in the United States of America

For Angie

Table of Contents

Preface xvii

Forward xxi

Glossary of Essential Golf Terms xxxi

Hole #1 – Begin With the Flag:
Secrets from the Golf Course on Vision 1

About Hole #1 1

Introduction 1

Why We Need "The Pin" 2

Stepping Into the Tee Box 3

The Game Without a Target 5

Where's the Goal? How Do We Achieve It? 7

Vision 7

Creating a Vision – Begin With Values 9

A Vision for All Companies 12

The Elements of a Vision Statement 14

The Enemies of Articulating and
      Implementing a Vision 15

Implementing the Vision 26

Aligning to Achieve the Vision 27

How to Play This Hole 29

Hole #2 – Parallel Tracks: Secrets
From the Golf Course on Aligning
to Achieve the Vision 33

About Hole #2 33

Introduction 34

Golf and Alignment 35

Alignment in the Corporation: Seeing
      the Hazards, Assessing the Risks and
      Defining the Plan 37

Barriers to Achieving the Vision 38
Appoint the Guideline Team 46
Establish Corporate Goals 47
Setting Corporate Goals 49
Setting Departmental Goals 50
The Role of Management in Attaining
    the Vision 55
Semi-Final Thoughts on Achieving the Vision 56
How to Play This Hole 57

**Hole #3 – Why We Play: Secrets from the Golf Course
    on Motivation 59**
About Hole #3 59
Introduction 59
Motivation – Touchy-Feely or Good Business? 60
The Question 61
The Demonstration 62
The Great Motivational Myth 64
The Enthusiastic Novice 64
High Enthusiasm, Low Competence
    in the Office 66
The Competent Professional 70
The Manager as Competent Professional 71
Coaching from Jack to Tim 72
The Next Step 80
Why Do We Play? 79
The Lesson From Why We Play 82
Compensation 82
Beyond Compensation 83
The Profit Link 86
The Danger With Bonuses 89
From Herzberg to Golf 90
Why Leaders Care About Motivation 92
The Skills You Need to Motivate 96
A Compelling Vision 99
Implementing Motivational Strategies 101
How to Play This Hole 103

Hole #4 – Wedges, Irons, Drivers, and Putters: Secrets From the Golf Course on Leadership and Communication 105

About Hole #4 105
Introduction 105
Managers Talk, Leaders Communicate 106
"They are all Like Me – And, If They Aren't,
    They Should Be" 107
"My People are Empowered" 109
Effective Behavior – "The Freedom of
    the And" 110
Encode, Send, Decode – A Brief History
    of Recent Communication Theory 112
Challenging Your Personal
    Communication Style 113
Empathy – An Essential Skill of Leadership 114
Beyond Empathy 116
How Many Clubs Are In Your Bag? 116
Hammers and Nails 119
The Four Different Styles of Communication 120
Differentiating Questions for Leaders 122
Why Do We Care About Communication
    Anyway? 122
The Repair Incident 127
Synergistic Communication 126
Communication for Leadership 127
A Final Word on Communication 129
Summary 130
How to Play This Hole 130

Hole #5 – You Can't Improve a Random Process: Secrets from the Golf Course on Process Improvement 133

About Hole #5 133
Introduction 133
End of One Career, Beginning of Another 134
In the Beginning There Was Utter
    Unpredictability 135
The Day I Hit the Squirrel 136
The Lesson of Lessons 137
The Golf Swing and Benchmarking 138
Adapt Yes, Adopt No 139

Standardizing the Swing 140
Predictability Requires Structure 142
Standardizing a Business Process 143
Predictably Unpredictable 145
"Structure" Without Description Breeds
    Variation 146
From the Real to the Ideal 147
Process Standardization 148
The Need for Constant Attention
    to the Process 150
How to Play This Hole 151

Hole #6 – The Key to Improvement:
    Secrets from the Golf Course
    on Keeping an Accurate Score 153
About Hole #6 153
Introduction 153
Golf is a Game of Number (So is Business) 154
Not Just a Score, But an Accurate Score 155
Situational Scoring – How We Often
    (or at least sometimes) Keep Score in Golf 156
Situational Statistics – How We Often Keep
    Score in Business 159
Situational Score Keeping in Practice 160
How to Keep Score 162
The Emphasis on "Lagging Indicators" 163
Metrics to Improve by or "Why Am I
    Shooting a Ninety-Two?" 165
The Macro Metric 167
An Industry Scorecard 168
Measurements Are As Measurements Do 172
How to Play This Hole 175

Hole #7 – In the Rough: Secrets from
    the Golf Course on Judgment,
    Emotional Intelligence, Power, and
    the Nature of Leadership 177
About Hole #7 177
Introduction 177
Judgement in Business – The Mike
    Benson Story 179

In the Rough 182
Leadership EQ:Nature or Nurture 183
Leadership "Course Management" 184
Emotional Intelligence 185
Emotions in the Work Place 185
How We Process Information 186
Leadership and Emotional Intelligence 187
Emotional Intelligence – What It Is and
    What It Isn't 188
"I Don't Have Time to Baby Sit" 191
Recent Developments in Emotional
    Intelligence 192
Influence and Emotional Intelligence 194
The "Why" – Lack of Wisdom 196
Wisdom and Emotional Intelligence 198
Wisdom in the Workplace 199
Power 201
Referent Power and Course Management 204
The Nature of Leadership 205
How to Play This Hole 207

**Hole #8 – Play It Where it Lies: Secrets
    from the Golf Course on Character 211**
About Hole #8 211
Introduction 211
"But I'm Not a Leader" 213
The Character/Competence Debate 215
Personality Is Not Character 215
Play It Where It Lies: Golf and Character 217
Character is Golf's Greatest Lesson 219
Honesty 220
Authenticity 222
Predictability 223
Tenacity and Persistence 229
Courage 231
Concentration 231
Will 235
How to Play This Hole 236

Hole #9 – Improving Your Game:
   Secrets from the Golf Course on
   Personal Change **239**
About Hole #9 239
So, You Want to Be a Leader 239
Mummies 240
Breaking Out 243
The Transition to Leadership 243
Golf, Fear and Personal Change 244
Golf and a Paradigm for Change 246
A Model for Change 247
A Clarifier or Two 248
Why Positive, Purposeful Change is Such
   a Challenge 249
Half a Brain is Worse Than None When
   It Comes to Change 250
The First Step Toward Change:
   Dissatisfaction 250
The Leadership Commitment 252
Aligning the Two Systems 252
Breaking Out of the Comfort Zone 253
The Logic of Change – The Need for
   Autonomy 255
The Emotion of Change – Accepting
   the Risk 259
Commitment: Logic or Emotion? 262
A Model for Change 262
Review Your Current State 264
Develop a Deep Personal Commitment
   to Change 264
Create a Vision 264
Align Internal System Toward Achieving
   the Vision 265
Lead and/or Perfect New Skills 266
Take Action 268
Stay the Course Until the Vision Is Achieved 268
A Final Lesson From Golf on Change 269
Summary 269
How to Play This Hole 270

At the Turn: Mulligans **273**

Bibliography **297**

About the Author

Dr. Don Sanders is a speaker, trainer and consultant who has started and developed his own successful company. A former college teacher, Don left the academic world in 1986 and experienced a high degree of success working with senior executives in companies large and small to improve processes, products, results and profits. Featured in Peters' and Waterman's video, "In Search of Quality," Don is the author of three books on quality management.

He "discovered" golf six years ago, and in this book he marries golf with his other passion, leadership, to provide a rich and compelling case for the fact that we all have undiscovered leadership potential that golf shows us how to uncover and develop.

The Message

The message of this book, distilled into one sentence is this:

Like golf, leadership has a discipline

By discipline I mean that leadership has a basic underlying structure that accommodates some variation from individual to individual. This leadership structure is based on trial and error, on observing what works, on research with literally thousands of men and women. We know what works and what doesn't, we even know why it works, and the obstacles to effective implementation.

Golfers would no more ignore the importance of the alignment to the target as they address the ball or the value of the proper take away during the swing than they would use cut up balls and broken clubs. But we see managers do this all the time. They "wing it;" they assume that one approach is as good as another. They ignore the lessons of successful leaders and pretend that there is no structure to leadership, but there is.

In golf we know there are common elements for an effective swing, a method to successful course management ("bad shots are inevitable, stupid ones are not") and a process for a skillful short game. My goal in this book is to provide the same structure for leadership, to outline what works within the many facets of what we know to be effective ("birdie") leadership. My hope is that, whether you read one chapter at a time and figure out how to implement that facet of leadership or read two or three at a time and plan the implementation of those, you will put your distinct mark on this structure and make it work for you and those you lead.

Preface

"If you are not aware of what is happening to your mind and your body when you are playing, you will never be the best you can be."

— Jack Nicklaus

"How do I become a leader?" "What can I do to increase my leadership effectiveness?" "What is it that I need to do to become more influential in my department?" "How can I become more outgoing and less analytical?" "I know I have the potential to lead, but I just keep getting run over by people who are more assertive; how do I get past this?" "I feel like a bully rather than a leader, how do I get people to willingly follow me?"

These are the kinds of questions that I am asked when I conduct training and when I speak to organizations of all sizes and types. These are the kinds of questions asked of me after a team meeting when someone with a good idea, but without a plan, sees that idea lost in the shuffle of other ideas. These are the kinds of questions on the minds of many who would like to, but who, for personal reasons don't ask. These questions all say "I want to, but I don't know how."

This book was written to furnish answers. It was written to provide a strategy that an individual could use to increase his or her leadership effectiveness. Although the book is well grounded in both research and observation, it is practical rather than theoretical. It is a book about how to be a leader rather than a book "about leadership." It will bring your level of awareness about how you are playing the game of "leadership" to a conscious level, so that, like Jack Nicklaus, you can be the best you can be.

In writing the book, I relied primarily on four sources: first, my own years of running organizations and owning a company; second, fifteen years consulting in small medium and large size companies, almost always with the senior executives of the companies (some who were leaders and some who were not); the input from the participants in my training and speaking engagements; and fourth, resources from both inside and outside "the leadership establishment."

This fourth source is important. Joel Barker pointed out that it is outsiders who pioneer new thoughts on old paradigms, outsiders who, not bound by the constraints of the old paradigm, can say, "Here is an improved strategy for tackling this problem."

And I am an "outsider" in the leadership arena, an "expert without portfolio." So, I not only read the works of the "insiders," people like Bennis, Kouzes and Posner, Tichy, and Blanchard, but I searched beyond this literature for additional ideas on what leaders need to do to be effective.

Thus, I sourced not only Dr. Ken Blanchard who lays the groundwork for the chapters on motivation and communication, but also Edward Deci and "Why We Do What We Do". I read Daniel Goleman on "Emotional Intelligence" for insights on judgment and leadership, Kaplan and Norton ("The Balanced Scorecard") for concepts on aligning an organization (a golfing term) thorough keeping score, and Steven Chandler ("Reinventing Yourself") and Dennis Deaton ("Mind Management") for new breakthroughs on how we can direct the process of personal change and improvement. John Kotter's book on organizational change, "Leading Change" provided an integrated overview to the challenges faced by individuals who seek to bring enduring improvements to organizations.

(Oh yes, and as part of my "research," I read an armload of books on golf. Some of these books were about how to improve your golf game; they ranged from Harvey Pennick to Freddy Couples to Gary McCord. Other books were about the spirit of golf, books like John Updike's *Golf Dreams*, Lee Eisenberg's, *Breaking Eighty* and James Patterson's *Miracle on the 17ᵗʰ Green*. I also had to play more golf, of course, so that I could assess the effectiveness of the strategies described herein.)

Thus, while this is a personal book, like most, it rests on the shoulders of others. It is synergistic; the work of one and the work of many. Some of these made direct contributions.

First and most importantly I want to thank those men and women who, in my years in speaking, training and consulting served as models of effective leadership and who are not mentioned here by name (and who will hopefully recognize themselves from the stories told), also Angie Sanders, who not only worked with me on preparing and editing the manuscript but who introduced me to the game of golf, Connie Power, for feedback on many of the ideas nestled in these pages and Gordon Andrews of NASA for team based support.

Two other individuals were important in this endeavor. Todd Gibbons, of Touchstone Communications, a low handicapper, for suggesting the title *Go for the Green* (I had originally titled it *Everything I Ever Wanted to Know About Leadership I Learned on the Golf Course* — see the improvement?) and Dennis McClellan of InSync Publications for taking a chance on something he believes in.

Foreword

About the Course

The leadership course is exciting and challenging; it provides more than enough opportunity to score well, but it also presents many hazards. If you were to play a course for the first time, you would likely visit the pro shop and, if one is available, pick up a course guide. If one isn't available, then you might find a marshall, or a frequent player of the course and talk to them. The information gathered would help you understand the unique nature of the course, in particular its special features, layout and hazards. Taking the time to learn about the course will not only help you enjoy the course more, but will likely save you strokes. The Forward to this book is your course guide. Hopefully, after reading the forward, you will understand both the opportunities that this book provides to improve your "leadership" game and the hazards that you must have the skills to master on the "leadership course."

Why?

Why another book on leadership? Because there is a need for a practical, readable, applicable primer on leadership for those who want to achieve more in the area of leadership, but don't know how. As a consultant, business owner and speaker over the past fifteen years I have watched great leaders and not so great leaders; but more than this I have seen men and women who might have been great leaders, who truly might have made a significant difference in their companies, fail to seize a leadership opportunity. These years of experience have convinced me of three incontrovertible facts:

>*First, the most costly career mistake in terms of both dollars and opportunities made by most people in business and other organizations today is the failure to develop their leadership abilities;*

>*Second, the most costly error made by most organizations is the failure to develop the leadership required to take those organizations through the coming years of revolutionary transition;*

>*Third, much of what has been written about leadership has stressed process over results. In fact, leaders are not measured by intentions but by results; the path to achieving leadership results can, as a result of recent findings in the areas of business, psychology, and most importantly neurophysiology, be defined and followed.*

There is also one "controvertible" assertion. The golf course provides a wonderful metaphor for learning about leadership. As Gary McCord notes in his introduction to his best selling book on golf, *"Golf for Dummies":*[1]

>*"Don't make the mistake I made. Here's what will happen. You will be up at the end of the practice range swinging away. Sometimes you will hit the ball and sometimes you won't. If you have a fleck of athletic talent and good eye/hand coordination, you'll start to improve. Those whiffs (swings where you miss the ball) will become less frequent, and you will begin to hit the ball higher and farther. Then,*

---

[1] *"Golf for Dummies"*® by Gary McCord with John Huggan. Copyright©1996 IDG Books Worldwide Inc. All rights resereved. Reproduced here by permission of the publisher. For Dummies is a registered trademark of IDG Books Worldwide, Inc.

however, you will 'hit a wall.' That improvement will slow to a trickle and then stop altogether. You will be stuck at whatever level your inborn talent has taken you to. And you will be that golfer for the rest of your life.

Why? Because your technique—or rather lack of it—won't let you get any better. You'll either be good in spite of your technique or bad because of it. It doesn't matter. You'll be swimming at the deep end of a pool filled with Jell-O."

The same is true for leadership. To paraphrase this quote:

"If you have a fleck of natural leadership ability and decent people skills, you may start to improve. Those moments when you absolutely miss the opportunity to influence either individuals or the team will occur with less frequency and you'll begin to believe that you really can be a leader. But sooner or later you will plateau. The improvements you have made in leading others will slow to a trickle and then stop altogether. Your will have reached your level of natural ability as a leader. And that is the maximum level of leadership that you will be able to attain for the rest of your life.

Why? Because your leadership skills, or rather your lack of them, won't let you get any better. You will be good despite your level of character and competence or bad because of them. It doesn't matter. As a leader you will be swimming at the deep end of a pool filled with Jell-O."

And this is how I will use golf metaphors to teach leadership. In both golf and leadership the goal is to continually get better. So, my goal for the reader of this book is simply this. Wherever you are on the leadership ladder, I want to take you up a few rungs and show you how to get to the top. The days of leadership being limited to a select few are gone, today if you want a leadership position, if you want to achieve your leadership potential, you can. This book will show you how.

Identify Your Target, Take Dead Aim

One of the most often used phrases in golf (and in this book) is "Take Dead Aim." Take Dead Aim means just that. It means to select a target or a goal and aim for it. Too seldom in business or life do we do this. Too often in life we Take Broad Aim or we Take No Aim At All. So let me identify a target for you and then I want you to take dead aim. I want to use your imagination to see yourself in that leadership role that has been eluding you. I want you to take a moment as you begin this book to imagine a moment. I want you to imagine that moment in the future when you, through your leadership skills make a significant contribution to the success of your organization. I realize that this exercise is a reach for many of you, but it is critical. You need to know what you want to achieve as a leader in order to become a leader; you need to take dead aim at this target. Don't look at all the reasons you have not achieved what you might, don't look at the traps and water hazards that have kept you from becoming more of a leader; just focus on your target.

Perhaps you have already experienced this moment of leadership success; if you have, you know the satisfaction of achieving the goal. However, if you have not experienced this moment, you will. Leadership is not magic or some collection of inborn character traits. True leadership is a learned behavior. All of us have the ability to provide leadership at some level. The purpose of this book is simple: To increase the leadership ability of everyone who reads the book through the development of the character and competencies required to lead.

Is This Book Just for Golfers?

Having just used a famous golf phrase, let me first answer the most often asked question about this book, *"Is this book just for golfers?"* **The answer is no.** This is a book for leaders and those who aspire to lead. This is a book about leadership and management, about improving productivity through people, about time tested strategies for increasing individual and company-wide performance. The book simply uses golf as a metaphor to help inform, clarify and, occasionally, entertain. If you have never played golf, if you don't know the difference between a wood and an iron, a par and a birdie, a mulligan and a gimme, you can still learn from this book. Of course, if you are a golfer, you may more easily relate to some of the stories, anecdotes and real life descriptions used in the book. (Incidentally, for the golfing purists who believe that the game is somehow reduced in value by extending its lessons from the fairway to the floor, I ask your indulgence in advance. I would argue that the game is there to teach us about life as well as to provide the experience of golfing.

The title of this book, *Go for the Green* was chosen because it truly has a double meaning. In golf, "Go for the Green" means to take aim at the pin, to set your sights on that target and go for it. In business, "Go for the Green" means more than simply seeking greater monetary rewards; it means to achieve a level of leadership that allows you to influence others to achieve organizational and personal success. So, Go for the Green.

Leadership's "Tyranny of the Or"

There is an underlying premise to this book and that is this: since the beginning of the study of management and leadership in the early 1900's there has often been a serious disconnect between theory and practice. Business schools have often focused on the "hard" or management side of business (accounting, scheduling, finance, technology—those things that could be measured and controlled) at the expense of the "soft" or leadership side of business. In doing so, we have produced several generations of managers (by whatever title) who have been well educated in fiscal matters, in how to command and control, plan and budget, who may have received some very rudimentary training in how to solve problems and monitor results, and who may have even learned something either directly or indirectly about how to work effectively with people. But these same people must simply do the best they can to provide leadership when a crisis or opportunity arises because the skills and attributes of leadership have generally not been codified and taught.

So, while the title of the book is "leadership" and the focus is primarily on leadership, we also talk some about management of people, because, at a micro level, the management and the leadership of people go hand in hand. How you manage and lead the people of your organization is one of the most important, if not the most important determinants of, not only personal development, but also productivity and profits.

In other words, my goal has been to write a **practical book,** to provide steps, strategies and concepts to both demystify leadership and to make leadership (as opposed to just management) more widely practiced and more widely available. For all types of organizations, private and public businesses, educational institutions, governmental and non-profit entities, implementing the concepts in this book should be seen as a step toward improving bottom line results.

One of my favorite business books of recent years is Collins and Porras's *"Built to Last."* I was particularly impressed with their concept of the "Tyranny of the Or." This concept says that people and companies often think they have to choose between two competing values, for example, productivity and satisfied employees, or between investment for the long term and short term profitability. Thus we have companies that have selected one value or the other, they are "bottom line, profit driven" or "they are people oriented, customer driven." Collins and Porras effectively argue from their experience with successful companies that these values are not mutually exclusive, that companies can, in fact "have both."

Skills versus Character,
Manager versus Leader

There is a similar dichotomy in the debate over leadership. Some, like Kouzes and Posner, who have written extensively on leadership, say, "Credibility is the foundation of leadership." They are on what I call, the "Who You Are" side of leadership.

Others writers and researchers focus on the "how" side, on leadership skills. They suggest that leadership is manifested in what one does, not who one is. What good does it do to have credibility, they argue, if your people don't follow your lead? This is the "Tyranny of the OR" applied to leadership.

What I am going to suggest in this book is that effective leaders have both. That is, they have a foundation of credibility based on character (Golf's Greatest Lesson) and they have skills to galvanize people into action. These skills, including the abilities to motivate, to passionately communicate a vision, to measure performance, and the persistence to carry through on a plan to make the vision a reality, are critical for effective leadership. In short, successful leaders must have character and competence, they must bridge values and combine them under a banner that is more encompassing, less limiting.

The "Tyranny of the Or" applies equally to definitions of managers and leaders. It is as if people have to decide whether they are one or the other. Are they the ones, as Covey says, who are making sure, as the road gets cut through the jungle, that the supply lines are functioning well, that the road is straight and properly crowned, that the tools are sharp and available (the managers), or are they the ones who climb the tree, survey the land and shout, "wrong jungle" (the leaders).

Covey's assertion betrays the belief held by many authorities on leadership that managing is one thing and leadership quite another. I believe management is a subset of the overall leadership function. In traditional thinking, managers plan, control, organize, budget, and staff. They do all of those jobs that are necessary for operations to function, for the organization to produce results. This traditional thinking suggests that leaders, on the other hand, provide direction, inspire, motivate and align. *My position on management and leadership is this: you can provide inspiration all day, but if you cannot budget and staff (or manage those who budget and staff), the vision won't come into being; you can plan, control, and organize all day, but if you cannot motivate and inspire your people, your plans will go unfulfilled (or perhaps even be sabotaged).*

So, this dichotomy is just one more manifestation of the "Tyranny of the Or." We need a new word, "leaderment" or "managership" or "manager" to clarify the fact that, in today's business climate, you cannot choose either, you must choose both. This is frightening for a lot of people. We are comfortable in our role as manager, we don't want to have to lead. Or (less often) we are comfortable in our role of leadership, we don't want to have to worry about those details of planning and budgeting. I submit, with the pace of change in today's world, you don't have the option, you must learn both—and both can be learned.

The Need for Leadership

This book originally grew out of a conversation that I had with a client over two years ago. I was consulting with a company which was experiencing high turnover in professional ranks while overall white collar productivity was plummeting. The president of this company came to me and said, "I realize that book learning isn't the total answer to the problem, but I just saw one of my top managers chew a subordinate out in public. I have got to begin somewhere. Do you know of any practical, application-oriented book that includes a compendium of chapters on how to implement best leadership and management practices"? He definitely did not want a textbook.

I mentally reviewed my bookshelf: Peter Drucker, brilliant and yet theoretical, Tom Peters, creative, cutting edge, challenging, but simply not practical for the average manager, Ken Blanchard, practical, applicable, but focused on only two or three aspects of management and leadership, Steven Covey, courageous, insightful, people-oriented but difficult to translate into day to day operations. Then there were books such as *Built to Last* by Collins and Porras, the *Customer Centered Company* by Richard Waitely, *Leading Change* by John Kotter and Kouzes and Posner's *"The Leadership Challenge"* and *"Credibility."*

None of these books met the need of providing practical application, of defining and detailing the skills and character development required of managers and leaders that had been identified by this company president. His company, like many US companies was full of two kinds of managers: first, those who had received "battlefield commissions", excellent soldiers who had been promoted based on performance (often during a crisis) to officer rank and then proceeded up through the ranks based primarily on seniority; and second, degreed engineers who had come into the company out of college, been promoted because of technical skills, picked up additional technical skills of a different sort in an MBA program, but really had no broad understanding of leadership, of how to effectively integrate people and analytical skills.

Oh, yes, and this company president was an avid golfer who had completed many "deals" either on the course itself or later on the "19th Hole" following a game.

So, this book is designed to fill that void. It is for those people who are in a management or supervisory role who want to know why and how to improve their skills both as managers and leaders—and to discover this in an interesting and practical format.

The Front Nine

This book, then, responds to his request. It is subtitled, "The Front Nine," because in leadership, as in golf, the deeper you get into the game, the more your realize there is to learn.

Each chapter (or "Hole" on Front Nine) also includes a summary section called "How to Play This Hole." This is the practical application of the concepts taught in the chapter. For example, in the second chapter we will look at strategies for alignment; in this chapter's "How to Play this Hole" we essentially say, "Now that you've read about how important alignment is, here are some strategies to make it happen. Remember, my bias is toward results. In golf, you keep an accurate score on each hole and for each game. You then submit your scores and in return receive a rating called a "handicap." Over time, the goal of every golfer is to improve his game and therefore his or her handicap. The same is true for leaders. Improve your skills and over time you will see the results in terms of your impact on the organization; your leadership "handicap" will improve.

Because the game of golf is used to illustrate many of the critical leadership practices covered in this book, and because all readers may not be totally familiar with the nuances of this wonderful game, we are going to begin with a slightly tongue in cheek glossary of the most commonly used golf terms and then proceed to a very tough hole on developing a vision. This is in keeping with the strategy of all golf course designers, (a sort of sadistic group of individuals) who always like to start you off with a character challenging, skill stretching, and generally intimidating, first hole.

Oh, and by the way, because I have played this course many times, a little word of caution. The most difficult hole to par on this course is not Vision or Alignment. It is not Motivation, Communication or even Judgment. The number one rated hole on this course is "Change."

Glossary of Essential Golf Terms

Note: Because this is a book for both golfers and non-golfers, a glossary of golf terms is provided for the uninitiated. Further, to help clarify concepts, it is provided at the beginning rather than the end of the book. Finally, the terms are in the order of relative importance as used in this book rather than alphabetical order.

Par—A standard score for a hole or for a game. Par is a score that all golfers chase, but few attain (if they count all their strokes). The common expression, "That's par for the course" suggests that par is average. It's not. It is an "A", not a "C." A "birdie" (see below) is really an A+ and an 'eagle" or a "hole in one" is really an "A+" with lots of extra credit.

Bogey—Par plus one. Forget what you thought a bogey was. If this is a par four hole and it takes you five strokes to get the ball from the tee box into the hole, you have "taken a bogey." As noted elsewhere, not all bogies are bad.

Double Bogey—Par plus two. A dispiriting but not really terrible score. Pro's get these occasionally, duffers frequently. Continuing down the line there are also triple bogies and "snowmen" (an eight). We don't talk about these in this book. If their scorecards are any indication, most golfers can't count beyond eight.

Birdie and Eagle—These are mythical scores attained only by the anointed. A birdie is one better than par and an eagle two better. For most golfers, a par is really a birdie, if you think about it.

A Hole in One—This phrase refers to the occasions when a golfer hits his or her first shot from the tee box into the hole located many yards away. The odds of a hole in one are astronomical. No other sport would have the gall to establish a goal that is only attained in something like one every two million shots. Most golfers don't realize it but they have a better chance to win the lotto.

The Iron—A golf club with an iron (well, some metallic version) head (the part you hit the ball with) and a steel or composite (never iron) shaft. Typically numbered 1-9, these clubs are most frequently used after the drive (but not necessarily, some golfers hit their drives with an iron). To further confuse things, some irons are wedges which golfers use to hit the ball out of the sand or when they need lots of loft. But these are usually called wedges and not irons, but this is too fine a point to worry about here.

Wood—A golf club with a titanium, aluminum or composite head (although to be fair, the heads of these clubs used to be made of very hard woods such as persimmon). Shafts of these clubs are today made of graphite or steel or something else that gives you a lot of problems with controlling the flight of the ball after it is hit (if it is hit).

Drive—The first shot out of the tee box (the tee box is the area from which you hit your first shot). In others words, a drive is your tee shot (except, of course, on a par three where your first shot is usually with an iron and is not considered a drive). See how confusing golf can be?

Par 4—Most holes on an eighteen hole golf course are par 4's. They are mixed in with par 3's (shorter distance holes—almost always under two hundred yards) and par 5's (longer holes—almost always at least 480 yards long) so that in the end, the golf course designer can say the average hole is par four so par for this course is 72 (18 holes at an average of par four = 72)

18 x 3 = 54—A multiplier effect of having to take three putts on each hole which most golfers conveniently forget when they decide to spend practice time on the practice range rather than the putting green or chipping area.

Fairway—That part of the area between the tee box and the green that is covered by short grass that is cut in such a way as to allow the golfer to hit from the fairway with some degree of ease. Most golfers prefer to land in the Rough which is higher and more difficult grass that makes the game more challenging.

Green—At the end of the fairway (see above) you will find the green. This is very short, very slick grass (sometimes like a wooden floor) where you must putt the ball into the hole which is placed by the golf leprechauns on the most difficult part of this slick grassy area.

Flag—A flexible cloth or plastic pennant attached to the top of the stick that protrudes from the cup which is in a hole on the green at the end of the fairway where the ball is supposed to go. The flag is supposed to be your target, it is the "bull's-eye" of golf; in reality it only tells you the direction the wind is blowing.

Hazards—The term hazard refers to huge sand and grass traps (also called bunkers) and various bodies of water (ponds, lakes, oceans) that indiscriminately line golf courses and that cause golfers to quit the game because no matter how well they hit the ball it winds up in a hazard.

Read a Green—Figuring out how to hit your putt given critical factors of the green. For example, "If the green is sloping toward the river with the sun setting in the direction opposite the river with fast bent grass greens that were cut this morning on the upper shelf of a two tiered green with the wind from the west, just hit the putt." See the Science of Alchemy.

Trees—Ball magnets that line fairways. Anyone who says that wood has no magnetic properties has never played golf. On links courses, bushes, through natural selection, have developed similar properties.

Squirrels—Targets on the fairway.

Duffers—Amateur golfers (often very amateur) who prove the old adage that ignorance is bliss. These people don't play well and don't care. They still believe that golf is a game to be enjoyed.

Divots—(See *Trees*) Magnetized small holes in the otherwise smooth grass of the fairway and green that attract golf balls. Divots typically cover less than one tenth of one percent of the area of the fairway or green and attract forty percent of the golf balls.

Scratch Golfer—A very good golfer. One whose scores, if not necessarily his playing, indicates that he or she normally shoots "Par" or close to "Par."

Pro—A scratch golfer who gets paid (lots of money if he or she is really good) for playing the game. These are called "touring pro's" because they travel around a lot. There are also club "pro's" who can be either teachers or those members of the club who consistently win the club championship (or who are truly expert at "Bingo, Bango, Bongo").

Handicap—The mathematical difference between what you should shoot and what you do shoot. The lower your handicap, the better you are (at least with a golf club). An "eight handicapper", for example, is a pretty good golfer; a "twenty handicapper" an okay golfer and a "thirty handicapper" one who really enjoys the game. Handicaps are actually physically maintained today in computers through various organizations using a slope value, which nobody really understands. The goal in golf is to always lower your real handicap while maintaining a higher paper handicap so that you can more easily win bets.

"Play It Where It Lies"—One of golf's oldest, most important and most frequently broken rules. It means that the golfer must play his beautiful drive from behind that oak tree that is directly between her and the flag, or that divot that was just created by the foursome in front of her (unless of course, no one is looking, in which case the kicker works better than any wedge—just kidding).

The First Hole—Where we are headed now.

BEGIN WITH THE FLAG
Secrets from the Golf Course on Vision

About Hole #1

As with many courses, the first hole is a challenge. This is a very tough par 4 at 435 yards. You can birdie this hole, first, if you take time to plan your strategy rather than just hitting the ball: and second, if you can avoid the many hazards that line both sides of the fairway and surround the green. These hazards include: "I'm not a charismatic leader, I can't provide a vision," poor planning, lack of commitment, lack of sufficient communication and, most critically, cynicism and obstructionism within the company. Not surprisingly having a vision begins with having a target. So, lets begin by revisiting Harvey Penick.

Introduction

Harvey Penick, one of golf's greatest teachers, was the champion of that famous golf dictum: "Take Dead Aim." *But in business, as in golf, it is not enough to simply take dead aim.* The first requirement is that you have a target, then you must not only aim at your target, but you must have the skills to hit it, and finally you must fully implement those skills in order to hit

Leadership, like golf, begins with a target, with knowing where you are going. Just the word, "leadership" implies that the leader knows where he or she is taking others. And don't just sight in on the target. Follow Harvey Penick's wisdom and take dead aim for the bull's-eye.

your target. The focus on aiming at a general target (the fairway), rather than selecting the specific target to aim at ("four yards left of the bunker"), explains why the American view of leadership is somewhat distorted. We look at those who carried the mantle of a great leader, Jack Kennedy, Martin Luther King, Abraham Lincoln, and we marvel at their words. But words alone, even words that clearly specify a goal ("We will put a man on the moon and bring him home alive by the end of decade") are not sufficient to effect the change that is needed in corporations, departments, divisions, plants and regions today. To effect needed change we need both a well-defined goal and a method to achieve it. The first two chapters of this book outline a plan for defining and achieving a vision.

"Quality is a necessary but not sufficient condition for business success," said David Kearns of Xerox. The same is true for vision. Articulating the vision is obviously the first, the essential, step; but achieving that vision, actually getting the ball into the hole, is the ultimate goal. Transformational leaders like Kearns, J. Willard Marriott (Jr. and Sr.) and Jack Welch are teaching us this—and it is a lesson that golf illustrates well.

Why We Need "The Pin"

Imagine that you wanted to create a great golf team that would be based on the model of other sports such as baseball, football and basketball; that is, a sport based on the specialization of skills. Let's further say that you could only have four players on this team. What would you do?

First, you would go out and find a person who could consistently hit the ball 300 yards off the tee. Then you would find yourself someone who was really good with the mid range irons. Next you would find somebody who could hit the ball well from the rough, the sand, from difficult lies. Finally, you would find yourself an ace with the putter.

Here is the question. With all that excellence, with all that skill and talent, how well would your team do if they didn't know where the flag was? This is the dilemma faced not only by people in organizations, but by organizations themselves. So let's first look at why it is so important to know the location of the pin, then go back and look at how we can improve the opportunity of our players to help us shoot birdies and eagles, not just pars.

Stepping Into the Tee Box

There are few more accurate metaphors in golf for business processes than vision and alignment. As you step into the tee box and look down the fairway toward the flag, you are aware of an unarticulated vision of what you want to achieve and why you want to achieve it—the vision of the ball rolling into the hole producing a par or a birdie, (okay, a bogey) depending on your game. You are intuitively aware, maybe consciously aware, that you have a well defined goal, namely, to get the ball into the cup in a minimum number of strokes. In addition, you have a plan to achieve that goal. You select that part of the fairway where you want your first shot to land and you choose your target for your second shot. You know where you want your ball to land after that second shot so that you can perhaps birdie, but definitely par the hole. Finally, you know that you have to be flexible in achieving the vision. Your first shot may go into the trees or (heaven forbid) into the water. You know that you have to be able to be flexible to achieve your vision and your goals and you must believe that you have the skill, flexibil-

The pin provides the vision of success. We have to have the skills to get there.

ity and determination to prevent one bad shot from keeping you from accomplishing your vision.

In short, golf teaches us both as individuals and organizations that, in order to achieve our goals, we must develop a vision of success, we must develop a plan to achieve that success, we must communicate to ourselves what we need to do in order to achieve our goal and we must marshal all of our skills to successfully put our plan into action. Finally, because randomness (for example, that beautiful chip shot that hits a hard spot and bounces over, not on, the green) is inherent in golf as it is in business, we must understand that flexibility in pursuing the goal is part of the process.

As Total Quality Management (TQM) swept the country in the eighties, some companies tried and succeeded, others tried and failed, and a third group never tried, often based on the experience of those companies who had tried and failed or based on the perception that these same customers who were insisting that they become "quality companies"` were simultaneously beating them down on price. The successful TQM companies integrated the key concepts of TQM (customer focus, variation based measurements, supplier improvement, employee satisfaction) into their business culture while the companies who failed at TQM called the system unworkable (never acknowledging the short term focus and lack of management commitment which were frequently the true root causes of many of these "TQM failures").

There is an analogue for the TQM experience in the recent efforts of many companies to implement the processes of vision and "alignment." Those Fortune 500 companies who have successfully implemented the vision and alignment process, Hewlett Packard, 3-M, Johnson and Johnson, Southwest Airlines, General Electric, Merck, Marriott and a host of smaller companies, have reaped the benefits. But many companies dismiss vision and alignment because, while they are simple concepts, both are extremely difficult to implement (not unlike trying to shoot par on every hole). In addition, the vision and alignment process, like TQM, has become trivialized with a focus on the mechanics of the swing rather than a focus on achieving the vision (birdie, par) and letting the alignment process take you there. So, lets begin by looking at golf as a metaphor for the need for vision and alignment, then look at the process beginning with that most misused of business terms — vision, then work through the development and implementation of a vision process. Finally, let's look at what you have to do to remedy the disconnects, those policies and practices in the organization that make it difficult to achieve the vision.

The Game without a Target

Imagine a golf course without a green, a flag and a cup, a basketball court without a backboard, a hoop and a net, a football field without a goal line, an end zone, or uprights. No game, right? No way of knowing what you are aiming at, no definition of success, no process to link performance and achievement.

Now imagine a company without defined core values, without a defined vision for its future, without corporate goals, without established, defined and well disseminated tactical and strategic plans. Imagine a company without a strategy to galvanize all employees toward achieving the predetermined targets that the executive staff and the board have deemed critical for both short and long term success.

Why is it so difficult to imagine golf without pins, but so easy to imagine organizations without goals?

Why is it that imagining a company without goals and without a coherent and comprehensive strategy to achieve these goals is easier than imagining golf without a flag, basketball without a hoop or football without an end zone? The answer is, of course, that it is easy to imagine because this is how many companies, perhaps even yours, operate.

Golf provides a compelling metaphor for not only the importance of goals, but for the importance of having a strategy to achieve them. In other words, golf presents a compelling metaphor for the need for both vision and alignment.

Of course all sports are goal driven; hockey, for example, has its net as does soccer. Downhill skiing has a time over a specified distance as a goal; track and field has times and distances. In a society as sports oriented as ours, it should be natural to take the metaphor of winning through setting and achieving goals and applying it to the workplace, but it hasn't been.

Oh, there is no doubt that thousands of companies set goals, there is no doubt that thousands of companies spend countless hours meeting, strategizing and planning. Some companies even take the time to say, "what is it that we stand for—what are our core values." There is also little doubt that the employees of many of these companies have little idea about what these values, goals and strategies are, or what they can do to help the company achieve them.

During 1998, Watson Wyatt conducted a worldwide survey of employees. They asked these employees some very basic questions such as, "Do you know your company's goals" and "Do you understand your own job responsibilities?"

While most employees said that they had a very general knowledge of the company's goals and, of course, a general knowledge of their own job responsibilities, forty percent reported that they didn't have enough information to really understand what their role was in attaining the goals of the company and almost sixty percent said they didn't have the skills required to achieve the goals as they understood them. Yes, sixty percent of the employees said that they lacked the skills to help the company achieve its goals! You can't have people aligned to help you achieve your goals when they don't know what these goals are and they don't believe that they have the skills to help the company achieve them.

Where's The Goal?
How Do We Achieve It?

Of all the major sports (defined as those that we can most easily tune into on our televisions on a weekend afternoon) golf is certainly one of the most goal oriented.

Well, you say, what about football's goal line or basketball's basket or baseball's fences or bases. And yes, all of these have potential as metaphors for goals, but none is so strong as the feeling you have when you step into the tee box, look down the fairway to that flag and mentally design a strategy to get there. Golf tells you that not only must you have a goal, but a defined strategy and the skills to get there.

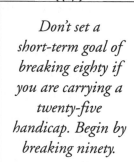

Don't set a short-term goal of breaking eighty if you are carrying a twenty-five handicap. Begin by breaking ninety.

So what we are talking about is not just goals, but an articulated overarching goal (called vision) and a process to assure the achievement of that vision through the focused efforts of all employees. Let's begin by looking at vision, what it is, how it is developed and why many companies don't develop and implement their vision.

Vision

In fifteen years of working with companies to change culture either in terms of increasing customer focus, developing and implementing quality management systems, re-engineering and quality improvement efforts (reduced errors, narrowed variation, employee involvement, reduced cycle times) both the successes and the failures begin with vision and values. We will

*Forget logic!
Forget analysis!
A vision statement
does not have to be
Shakespeare!*

begin by examining the vision process, then back up and look at how values are a critical part of that process.

Forget logic! Forget analysis! Forget thinking that a vision statement has to be Shakespeare! The purposes of a vision statement are simple—to galvanize the company into action, to provide a common goal, to unite everyone in the company in the pursuit of something greater than themselves. Peter Drucker calls today's knowledge workers "volunteers." Most can sell their knowledge any number of different places for about the same amount of money. If you want to attract and keep the best, one of the best strategies is to provide each individual within the company with a vision of being involved in an endeavor greater than themselves. (We will revisit this theme in Chapter 3.)

In order to achieve this goal, a vision must be clear, cogent and compelling. It must reflect unchanging beliefs within the organization (core values of the company) that extend beyond those who currently manage the company, and, it must be embraced by executive staff and translated by these executives into action. A vision must include both a picture of the future, and a forceful rationale as to why the company needs to achieve this goal. In a world where it is difficult for the individual to feel that he or she is making a difference, vision unites the group. A vision statement focuses and galvanizes action.

Sometimes managers will say to me, "Sure, I can articulate my vision." Then they either talk for ten minutes about a special project or tell me some wild dream they have about utilizing technology that doesn't exist yet. This is a hope or a dream, not a vision. The process of creating a vision is a disciplined, creative process that unites a future oriented verbal canvas with goals and a plan—and, depending on the situation, the appropriate amount of urgency.

What is a vision not? A vision is not a strategic plan, but it should lead to a strategic plan. It is not a product or service announcement. It is not "happy words" or flavor of the month motivation. It is not a statement of management change, it is not simply a call to arms, it is not tactical change; but it is the beginning of a process aimed at changing the company.

> *A vision must be clear, cognent and compelling. In order to be a motivator, it must encourage all employees to believe that they are involved, "In an enterprise greater than themselves."*

Finally, as we will mention many times in this chapter, a vision is not the sole province of executive management. A vision process that parallels the method outlined in this chapter can be carried out by managers at any level (or by an individual to galvanize personal action). Certainly plant managers, regional managers, department managers, product managers and divisional managers can create and implement a vision/alignment process. If your company already has a corporate vision, then the vision of your business unit should help achieve it. If there is no corporate vision statement, utilize the process outlined here to galvanize your people into achieving your vision. The presence or absence of a corporate vision statement must not limit you as an individual.

Creating a Vision—Begin with Values

Some golfers walk into the tee box, take out their driver, or whatever club they are going to hit the first shot with, put down their tee, place the ball on the tee, look down the fairway, take their stance, bend their knees slightly and hit the ball. They give less thought to the vagaries of the hole, their own skill levels, or how they are going to achieve their goals, than they give to pulling that "Titleist" out of their pocket.

Don Shula always taught that success begins with beliefs, with a conviction that what you are pursuing hasvalue. Vision statements reflect these beliefs.

Many individuals and companies approach a vision statement the same way, they just start writing. But remember the purpose of a vision. The purpose of a vision is not just to set a goal, it is also to challenge complacency, to shift perspectives, to establish urgency and to galvanize action. In order to achieve this, a vision statement must integrate aspects of strategic planning and it must reflect the deeply held values of the company. Many management schools teach strategic planning, but few teach people how to examine values to determine those that are the true "core values" of your company.

How do you discover the deeply held values of a company? If you are an entrepreneur, just starting out, it is a reflection of your own deeply held beliefs; if you are an established company it is an articulation of what that company really stands for. Values precede vision. To determine values, gather a representative group of employees; executives certainly, but also people from the shop floor, from the offices where the "worker bees" live; bring in people with ten, fifteen, twenty, or thirty years experience and ask them, "What does this company stand for?"

The cynicism that management fears, the comments about "profits at any cost," "money, money, money," or "I work, they play" are not usually heard in these meetings. Rather, these meetings, particularly if the employees know that the company is facing some degree of crisis, are somber. People talk about the pride they had when the company stood for technological excellence, or the days when management could call every worker in the plant by his or her first name, or the self esteem that was built when they were involved in solving problems, or the feeling they had when they worked for a company that was known for innovation, for being the leader in the industry.

The senior executive should lead some of these sessions. Keep in mind that the purpose is to create a list of values that people associate with the company. It is not a complaint session or a question and answer town hall meeting. Whoever chairs the meetings will need to keep the discussion focused on values.

These meetings begin the process of truly defining the "Core Values" of the company. The core values are those enduring values that are linked with the company in the minds of the employees at all levels—from the boardroom to the warehouse, from the executive offices to the shop floor. When the process is completed, the company should have a list of four to seven (no more than seven) fundamental values that are reflective of what the company has traditionally stood for. This list might include:

- Integrity
- Respect for the individual worker
- Unwavering integrity in dealing with customers, suppliers and employees
- Never resting on our laurels
- Innovation
- Excellence in everything we do
- Courage to do the right thing
- Empowered employees
- Customer first
- World Class Customer Service
- Reward based on merit
- Aggressive, confident, industry leaders
- Being on the leading edge of technology
- Making safe (airplanes, brakes and wheels, tires, automobiles, equipment...)
- Individual responsibility
- Profit as a measure of success rather than a goal
- Corporate responsibility
- Environmental stewardship

- Work hard, have fun
- We exist to solve the tough problems
- Excellence leads to profits
- Unequivocal quality in products and service
- The value leader
- Our word is our bond

Obviously, this list could go on and on. But that isn't the idea. The idea is that, in order to create a vision, you have to take time to clarify your values as a company. The company vision must reflect these values, must connect enduring company values to the current situation and targeted goal. Let's look at what such a vision statement might look like.

A Vision for All Companies

The venue for presenting the following example of a vision statement would be an "all hands" meeting (in large companies, this might include televising the presentation at remote sites). The president and the executive staff would be visibly united, the executive staff sitting behind the president or CEO who presents this short vision statement to the employees. The critical issues are: decline in revenues and profits, dramatic plunge in overall customer satisfaction, previous failed initiatives to improve performance, aggressive competition, lack of innovation. Once the presentation is made, copies of the vision are made available to everyone.

Ladies and Gentlemen:

I know we have traveled a similar road before and I can only tell you that time is not our ally. I am committing to you that not only are we going to change, but that we have no choice. Over the past few months, the executive staff and I, with the input of many of you, have reviewed where we are, where we want to be and what we need to do to get there. We have achieved many milestones both as individuals and as a company but much, much more needs to be done. When I look at us today I realize that, with different management and leadership tools, we could have achieved so much more. But yesterday is history and tomorrow is just a hope. Today, right now, is what we have control over and where we must start and focus. I want to share with you the vision of excellence I have for the company and how we will go forward in the future.

I know that things won't be terribly different tomorrow than they are today, but they will be different the day after that and the day after that and the day after that as we begin to work together within the confines of a systematized approach to achieving our goals. I fear that our success over the years has bred complacency. Our competition hasn't enjoyed our success and they are hungry.

This company has always stood for customer value, for fair profits and a reasonable return on investment, and for providing a technologically superior product in a timely manner at a competitive price. We stood for quality of service long before everyone became a "quality" company. We have always put a premium on hiring extraordinary people for every job in the company and turning those people loose so that they could serve our customers and maintain our position as industry leaders.

However, over the past few years, we seem to have forgotten some of those values. Revenues are down by eighteen percent in twelve months, profits by twenty-one percent, rejects are running at more than two percent and we haven't introduced a technologically superior product in more than three years. Worse yet, our customers no longer see a measurable difference between our service and that of the competition. We are hanging on to industry leadership by a thread.

I can't, you can't, allow this to continue. During the next twelve months we must reduce costs by twenty five percent while we simultaneously increase our customer response time by a minimum of thirty percent. We have increased our R & D budget by more than forty percent for next year, and we are investing in process improvement technology to reduce rejects. I didn't pull these figures out of the air. We studied our processes and our people, we can reach these goals with only a minimum initial investment of capital in some technological improvements and with your commitment.

We all know that money alone won't solve these problems. Our very survival is being challenged by national and international competitors. To achieve our goals, to thrive, not merely survive, will take all of us pulling together. We have the talent, of that there is no doubt. It is a question of will and it requires that all of us pull together. The executive committee is united in our course of action. Our goal is simple, we want to win this race by a length, not a nose. We want clear victory, not a photo finish. This is our guidepost.

I know we can do this. Persistence in pursuit of this goal is the key. I want to look back upon this day as a turning point, I want all of us to look back six months from now, a year from now, two years from now and say, 'Look how far we have come.' This approach will bring security for us all.

As I said at the beginning of this speech, time is not our ally. The executive committee has selected this phrase to represent everything I have said here today. When you see the words, "Time is Not Our Ally," I want each of you to remember that it symbolizes the need for us to quickly and wisely implement the ideas I have put forth today.

The Elements of a Vision Statement

This vision statement achieves the purpose of a vision. It articulates core values (customer value, technologically superior product, quality service, fair return on investment); it defines the problems (reductions in revenues, profits, and customer service, an increase in rejects, decline in technology); it sets some targets (new products, better customer service, reduced costs); it defines the urgency of this situation (competition, survival issue); and it galvanizes people (we must all pull together, we have the talent, executive committee united). It contains metaphors (hanging on by a thread, winning by a length) that help clarify the problem and the goal. While it hints at a plan, it doesn't describe the plan, describing the plan would simply take too much time. Remember, the vision statement must be kept short. It is the

Vision statements are short and to the point. They are designed to set a target and briefly explain why we must get there. Think Gettysburg Address rather than filibusters.

Gettysburg Address, not a filibuster. Finally, it should include a "hook," a way to remember the concept without having to remember the whole speech—"Time is Not Our Ally."

This vision sets the stage. It takes about three minutes to make this vision speech. It is simple, direct and unambiguous. People would not walk away from this speech wondering if there is urgency; they know there is urgency.

So why don't more companies use vision to help them set direction and achieve targets?[1] There are many reasons. The most common of these is that it has been tried and failed, failed because the company saw the vision as the solution to a problem, not as a step in the overall process of solving problems. But there are other reasons. In every company there are enemies of the vision. These are the people who are comfortable, very comfortable, for whatever reason, with things just the way they are and the bureaucratic organizations that support mediocrity. So, let's examine some reasons why visions are not realized.

The Enemies of Articulating and Achieving a Vision

When a leader takes the initiative to develop and communicate a vision, it is seldom a two hundred fifty yard drive down the middle of the fairway. Like the trees, divots, bushes and sand that seem to reach out for that tee shot, the leader's vision will encounter unexpected obstacles in achieving the goal. While there are many hazards, the seven primary enemies of articulat-

---

[1]Whenever I talk about vision statements, someone brings up Lou Gerstner. So let's look at Mr. Gerstner and vision.

When Lou Gerstner was brought in as CEO of IBM, he was asked about a vision for the company. He is said to have tersely responded to the effect of, "The last thing IBM needs now is a vision." This may sound like double talk, but I consider this one of the most succinct vision statements on record. In nine words Gerstner laid out a plan that said, "let's get back to basics, let's focus on the customer, let's optimize what IBM does best – and we have no time to waste in getting there." If your company is in as serious condition as IBM was when Gerstner took over, use this approach.

ing and implementing a vision are poor preparation, lack of commitment, interpersonal timidity, insufficient communication, cynicism, obstructionism, and lack of consequences.

Poor Preparation

As suggested in the discussion of core values, a vision statement is not created overnight, it is a work of some thought. The vision is a reflection of long held values, of the core values of the company, of principles that exist outside of the company, that are universal, and of today's reality and tomorrow's goals. To simply sit down and write a vision statement based on the current situation and a dream of what tomorrow should look like, is shortchanging the process. As noted at the beginning of this section, you must forget logic and analysis; writing and communicating the vision statement is a time for setting a bold direction, not timidly endorsing slow sustained growth or reduction in the number of errors made per employee.

Lack of Commitment

If you are a golfer with a twenty-five handicap and you have a vision of being a fifteen within two years, if you have created a plan that calls for you going down to the practice range and putting green a minimum of twice per week, you cannot deviate from your plan the first time the temperature reaches ninety-five degrees. Yet, this is exactly what a lot of leaders do. Deming called this failure to stay with the plan, a lack of "Constancy of Purpose." By that he meant not staying the course, not creating a plan and sticking to it, not following through on public and private commitments—especially when times were tough.

Creating a vision is a critical process. Don't shortchange it by rushing through or ignoring essential steps.

Commitment is a test of leadership. Several years ago I received a call from a CEO of a medium sized distribution company who asked if we could help him develop a quality process for his company. I asked him why he wanted to invest the time, money and energy in the process. "Customers," he responded, "our customers are demanding it." (Incidentally, this is almost always a bad reason. If the leadership of the company doesn't see the inherent value in a change effort, or, as we have discussed above, if there is not a sufficient sense of urgency, visions often fail.)

You can't quit going to the practice range just because it is ninety-five degrees.

So, we responded.

We conducted orientation training, established a Quality Steering Committee, and identified critical measures. We began reviewing processes with employees and holding customer focus groups. We created vision and mission statements with employee input and the president took the message to all his branches personally. Having attended the training, having seen some short term wins and having witnessed the improving morale of his employees, he seemed to be becoming a "believer."

In the fifth month of the engagement, with the process gaining steam and showing results, I received a call from the vice-president of sales (who had been put in charge of the quality process). "Don, I have some bad news," he said. "Sales were down by ten percent last quarter and Steve has blamed it on the quality process even though it is an industry wide problem. As a matter of fact, we are doing a lot better than our competitors who are down fifteen to twenty percent as best as we can tell. But it doesn't make any difference, Steve (the President) cancelled the process."

"You mean he doesn't want to work with us anymore, he is just going to let you run the program in house?" I replied.

"No, that is not what I mean. You guys did a great job but we just had a bad quarter. The whole quality process here is

Golf teaches us to stay the course, to finish the game even if we have had several bad holes. Staying the course, sticking to a commitment is a test of leadership.

done, finished, through, canned. We are back to business as usual."

And that was exactly what happened. Improvement meetings ended abruptly, measurement of critical variables ceased, a new banner of cost cutting was raised. As a result, thousands of dollars were wasted, and hundreds of hours of employee time were needlessly spent in training and meetings. But worse than that, this decision reflected a failed attempt at improvement, a dashing of a lot of hope, the arrogant dumping of an effort by a significant number of people who had bought into the vision; all because of less than expected earnings for one quarter—and they were still profitable! That story is about lack of commitment. Will the people of this company rise to the challenge of the next vision? Maybe, but there will be a lot of "prove it to me" before the involvement becomes real.

There are other stories. For example, the story of a call from a vice president of sales who wanted to know if I could make them a quality company "over the weekend" (seriously), or the story of the process ending words of a vice president to an inside salesman, "I don't care what the vision statement says, your customers will have to wait, I want my customer to get his product first."

Each of these, and there are many others, reflects lack of commitment. Commitment takes courage and courage is required both in carrying out the vision and communicating this vision to the company.

Interpersonal Timidity

Even bold and outgoing managers have trouble articulating a vision. Many managers have said to me, That is not my style, I'm not charismatic, I can't lead the charge." This is because they have somehow linked vision with charisma. But most companies don't have charismatic leaders, and fortunately, courage counts far more than charisma when articulating the vision.

As we will discuss in Chapter 8, it is character, not charisma that is required for leadership. People will test your sincerity and credibility, not your charm and extroversion. The other side of the coin is interpersonal. If you want to be a leader, you must be willing to put your beliefs on the line, you must be willing to demonstrate the courage of your convictions. You must not be afraid to stand up publicly and articulate a vision for the company or the business unit. To be a leader, you must find the grit to put yourself and your values on display. Of course, it is a risk, but it is also part of the job. You must be able to personally communicate the vision to all who need to hear it.

It is not unusual to see a chief executive officer meet with his or her executive team, review the company values and then create a vision statement. So far, so good. But this is where the process often stops. Perhaps this vision statement is printed on glossy paper, perhaps several copies are placed in the foyer, in the employee lounge, out in the warehouse, in the plant and branch offices.

Then the chief executive officer brings his or her management team together and, in most serious tones, reviews the vision and what it means to each of them. The next statement is deadly. "I expect each of you to take vision to your people and explain it to them. Oh, yes Sarah, make sure that it is incorporated into our new employee orientation process and that it is included in the employee handbook and all our promotional materials."

I was called into a company where just this process occurred. The CEO understood intellectually why the vision was important to his company that had lost more than thirty

You can't e-mail a vision statement!

percent of market share and almost all credibility with their customers regarding timeliness of delivery over a period of three years of cutbacks. I was called in after he had read a book on leadership and decided that the company needed a vision statement. He had created the vision by himself and e-mailed it to his managers. He wondered why he hadn't had any response, why, after six months, the vision didn't seem to be having the desired effect. I went to the manufacturing plant to ask people on the floor if they knew what the vision statement for the company said. I encountered anger, lots of anger. "Vision," they asked, "what vision." All we have heard about is what a crummy job we are doing, how our wages are too high for what we do, and how many more layoffs are going to occur if we don't quit making mistakes."

I found out that, not only did they not know the vision, they didn't know the CEO. In six years he had been to the plant twice, and neither time had he bothered to walk the plant, he just met with the plant manager and then headed back to corporate. He didn't know any of his workers. He wondered why his vision statement had not produced results. The reason was simple: you cannot e-mail vision.

Nor can you delegate vision. You can meet with the managers as they meet with their people, but for a vision to be effective, the leader, by whatever title, must take the vision to the people. When you meet with your people you must be prepared to interact, not simply present.

Apathy and Confusion

It is difficult to rank the barriers to implementation of the vision, but surely apathy and confusion are near the top. Some golf courses have a single system of water that meanders through the course creating hazard after hazard for the golfer. It is a left side hazard on one hole, a lake with a one hundred fifty yard carry on another, and a ball-eating stream cutting across the fairway at the two hundred to two forty mark on another. So it is with apathy and confusion; they wander aimlessly through the company creating hazards in every department, division, region and plant.

Apathy and confusion are not unlike the high grass. You have to grip the club a little harder to overcome them.

The root cause of apathy and confusion are changing priorities and poor communication.

Workers in most American companies are inured to change. They have participated in Total Quality Management, Re-engineering, Statistical Process Control, The Excellence Movement, a "Customer-Focused" Process and a "Cost-Cutting" phase (or two). They have been downsized, right-sized and outsourced. During the last fifteen years, they have moved from a perception of long term two way loyalty between the company and the employee to a reality that says, "every man for himself" (and, obviously, "every woman for herself" as well).

The result of all this is not just a resistance to change, but an indifference to change. It is harder today than it was ten years ago to get people involved in change efforts—they have been there before. These people have seen managers come and go, CEO's come and go. They have watched consultants bring the latest and greatest business fashion, come and go and as a result, these employees have become apathetic about anything that smacks of disturbing the status quo.

Part of the problem is that management and leadership saw the various innovations listed above—TQM, Excellence, Customer Focus, SPC and Process Efficiency and Improvement—as separate and distinct programs rather than a potentially integrated approach to improved long term sufficiency. As a result, many people learned that, if they just keep their heads down and don't get involved, this too, shall pass. They are confused

Be creative in posting the vision; relentless in following it.

about the priorities of the company and just want to get on with their day to day business. The only way to reassert control and focus energy to overcome the passive resistance that has developed in many companies is to use a planned and deliberate communication effort in promulgating the vision.

Let's return to our leader who was articulating the vision. When we last left our leader, he had worked hard with a group to create the vision and had presented it at an all hands meeting. This is just the beginning of the communication process. If our leader had seen this as the end of the effort to communicate the vision, it would fail.

To overcome insufficient commun-ication, our hypothetical leader must continuously take the message to his or her employees—time and time again. People who report to the leader must know and understand the vision and must refer to it in meetings, in conversations, when decisions are made. Every employee should see it on the walls and in action as management "walks the talk."

To take communication to the required level you must understand that employees are constantly bombarded by both verbal and nonverbal messages. In *Leading Change,* John Kotter states that the typical employee receives over two million words and numbers in a three-month period. To give the vision adequate airtime, you have to be both creative and dedicated. Does the vision appear when they open their PC's in the morning? Does it become a topic at staff and departmental meetings? Does it appear not just as articles, but as banners or headlines in all corporate publications? In order to be taken seriously, it must be widely and continuously communicated.

It isn't just employees of course, who don't know and understand the vision. The results of a 1996 study by CFO Magazine, Renaissance Solutions, Inc. and Robert Kaplan produced some surprising results related to vision. While more nearly 80% of those responding indicated that having a clear vision statement played a key role in the effectiveness of the company, 30% of senior management, 60% of primary operating managers and 97% of the general employee base did not clearly understand the vision of the company! Communication of the vision statement must begin with senior management and must be clearly communicated to all managers.

The reasons that 97% of employees do not understand this vision is that the managers typically do not take it to their people. Every manager needs to understand the apathy and confusion of the employees. They must be ready to address the two questions that employees want answers to. These questions are: first, "why are we doing this"; and second, "you are asking me to work harder to achieve this vision, what is in it for me?"

When you begin the vision process, when you create and implement a new vision, you are asking people to leave a comfort zone. If you want people to leave this comfort zone you must give them reasons and rewards. You must, with your vision, create a sense of urgency. You must let them know why attaining this vision is important and why their cooperation is essential. People often ask me when I am in a company supporting a vision created by management that sets out a new direction in a time of urgency, "What is in this for me?"

Sometimes the answer is survival. Sometimes it is growth. Sometimes it is the opportunity to make more money and get promoted. But one answer is always applicable: Pride. When you are in a company that is unified in pursuing a coherent, cogent and compelling vision, you can feel, see and hear the pride of the people.

Sufficient communication means that the person delivering the message presents it in

The question you must answer for employees is, "What's in it for me?"

person to as many people as possible, in as many venues as possible. Jack Welch of GE accepts this role, presenting the GE philosophy at some new employee orientations, so that everyone understands that this is important and that each of them is needed in order to make it happen.

Cynicism and Obstructionism —The Need for Consequences

In communicating the vision, you must let everyone know that they are part of the process and you must let them know in very clear terms that obstruction, active defiance, or passive sabotage will not be tolerated.

Then, when the first vivid example of any of these occurs, you must clearly and directly make that individual aware of the issues. If the cynicism and/or obstruction continues, negative consequences must be applied and applied without rancor or favoritism. This person, even the best salesman in the company, the chief operating officer, the head of finance, whoever it is, this individual must be terminated. Terminating obstructionists is called "creating a representative anecdote." Everyone will know that "old Bob" who had been here twenty years and been a loyal supporter of the status quo for lo those twenty years, was let go because he couldn't support the needed changes to take this company, this plant, this department, this division, into the next decade—or whatever the vision calls for.

Before you begin this process, ask yourself the question, "Can I fire those closest to me if they hinder achievement of the vision?"

If you don't do this, if you don't take action, the natural reaction of others is to conclude that the initiative can't be that important. They will seek the level of the cynic or obstructionist and the initiative will fail. In my years of working to improve the processes and cultures of companies, it is this failure to take the steps to implement negative conse-

quences, more than any other single course
of action, that has doomed the vision/align-
ment process to failure.

This is particularly true if the obstructionist is a member of senior management. The
surest way to make a vision fail is to have key
executives behave contrary to the purpose of
the vision. The "words and music" of the vision must be embraced and embodied by top
management (including sales and marketing,

*The surest way to
have a vision fail is
to have key
executives behave
contrary to the
vision.*

who typically have the most to gain by the success of the initiative and who frequently take the longest to get on board). If top
management doesn't personify the importance of the vision, why
should anyone else? Every employee will silently ask: "If they
can get away with not adhering to the vision, why can't I?"

Middle managers, by the nature and pressures of the position, are frequently opposed to change. If middle managers don't
understand the urgency of the vision, if they don't see dedication in their executive team, if they are not rewarded and praised
for contributions to the vision, they will simply resist the change.
In one company in which I was consulting, senior executives
realized this within six months of the introduction of the innovation. They then created a series of "middle manager
roundtable" discussions to listen to the concerns of these managers and to help guide their decision making. Within three
weeks, and after serious give and take, the name of the meetings
was changed to the "leadership roundtable" and advocacy for
the change was firmly incorporated into the process.

If it is difficult enough to rid yourself of obstructionists in a
large corporation, it is almost impossible, in a small or medium
sized, family run, privately held business. In three recent consulting engagements the biggest obstructionists were (1) the
brother of the CEO, (2) the brother-in-law of the president and

If you can't fire, you must isolate them from others and insulate the company from their potential damage.

(3) the husband of the CEO (it is not easy to be in business with your spouse).

In all three cases, there was no way that these people could be fired and still maintain any semblance of family (which was a core value at all three companies). The only viable solution to this problem is to isolate the individual so that he or she cannot damage the initiative. Isolate them from interfering with the process and insulate them from doing damage by influencing others.

Once again, although the examples cited here reflect the behavior of the company president, please remember that this process can occur at any level within the company. Departments, plants, divisions, regions or business units by any other name are organizationally structured to encourage leadership. If you are a manager of a department, division or region, your opportunities for leadership are considerable. If you are not incorporating vision into your leadership activities, you are missing a tremendous opportunity to impact not only your department, but the organization as a whole. Think of the examples provided here as a macro for your micro situation.

Implementing the Vision

As we have stressed, reviewing the values, creating the vision and communicating this vision to the people you lead, is only the first part of the process, and based on my experience, it is the easiest part of the process. Aligning to achieve the vision and following through to achieve the vision is the difficult part. To understand why this is so difficult, let's return to the golf metaphor and an activity which many golfers undertake when they have free time and it's raining (pouring), snowing, roasting outside, namely, watching an instructional video.

Let's say, for example, that you decide to watch Johnny Miller's perceptive and entertaining videotape on *The Swing*. While watching this video, you develop a vision of yourself as a better golfer. Truly, if you could implement the things that Miller is talking about, you could play in the low eighties; this video contains at least ten great ideas on improving your swing that most golfers could benefit from. Then, when the rain stops, you go out and practice Johnny's techniques on the practice range. They seem to be working. The ball is going straighter and longer. You seem to have achieved some degree of predictability.

You decide to take these ideas to the real test, your match with three of your friends next Saturday. As you play, you sense that nothing is really changed. You are pulling the ball, pushing the ball, hitting an occasional great shot, but not really improving your game that much. You shoot an eighty-nine—an average score for you.

Will you go back to that videotape again? Will you revisit your vision? Or will you just fall back to the old patterns and assume that they are good enough, that improvement will happen at its own pace, and watching that Johnny Miller video was an interesting diversion. After all guys like Johnny Miller have played golf since they were seven or eight, they don't know the problems faced by someone like you.

This is the problem with change, particularly with large transformational changes at the corporate level. No matter how well the vision is articulated, if people don't see that there is improvement, both personally and organizationally in the short run, they give up on the effort. They regress to a comfort zone.

Aligning to Achieve the Vision

In order to keep people from regressing to that comfort zone, a comprehensive alignment process is needed. Again, golf provides a wonderful analogy. The hardest thing in golf is not hitting the ball, it is consistently hitting the ball *straight* (or at least where you are aiming). You will hear a lot of golfers say, "Boy I was really hitting the ball well, today, but my score doesn't reflect it." (Sounds a little like, "Revenues are up, but profits are down," doesn't it—and for similar reasons.) When a golfer says "I was hitting the ball well but my score doesn't reflect it, the reason is most often that they are not hitting the ball straight, that they are not aligning the stance and swing with the target, that they are unable to connect their current position with the target through the flight of the ball.

The word "alignment" is one of those consultant jargon terms that I had trouble with for a great many years. Fellow consultants used to tell me, "We are conducting an 'executive alignment session' with Amalgamated Insurance (or whatever) today." And I would think, "Words like alignment are what give consultants a bad reputation."

Then, a couple of years ago, frustrated that my shots were going anywhere but straight (or at least if they went straight, they went straight right or left of my target), I started reading the great American golf teacher quoted at the beginning of this chapter: Harvey Penick.

Now, if you are a golfer and you have never read Harvey Penick, give yourself a gift and read his *Little Red Book*. Penick is slightly opinionated and definitely a gentleman from another era, but he knows golf and one of his favorite sayings is "Take Dead Aim."

Such a simple and obvious phrase, yet most golfers and most businesses don't do it. Like many simple and obvious maxims, "Take Dead Aim"; is a lot easier to say than to implement.

When I was taking my golf lessons some years ago, the teaching pro used to say to me, "Watch those railroad tracks – they run parallel from your feet and the ball to the hole." And he would start talking about aligning my feet with the imaginary

line going from the ball to the hole. I was, to
say the least, confused. Then he put down two
sticks, one running parallel from my feet, the
other on the outside of the tee in the direction of my swing. "If you hit the ball right, it
will go where those two sticks are pointing,"
he said. And he was right. The ball didn't go
where I wanted it to go, it went where the
sticks were pointing. *Ergo*, if I wanted the ball
to go to the target, I had to align with that
target. Golf and business success depend upon
alignment, if you cannot align, you cannot
really succeed at either. Now, I don't want to

*While setting the
vision is
challenging, it is
only 20% of the
battle. The other
80% is in
alignment and
follow through.*

push this metaphor into the ground (so to speak), but alignment does not occur on just each hole, but on each shot, so that
ideally you hit each shot to set up the next one. In this way, the
drive supports the second shot which supports the third shot
which supports the putt into the cup.

Do golfers disagree with the concept of the importance of
alignment on the golf course? Of course not. Then why is there
so much trouble selling the concept of alignment in the corporation? That's the next hole "Parallel Tracks—Secrets from the
Golf Course on Aligning to Achieve the Vision."

How To Play This Hole:

*n order to effectively establish a vision that will establish urgency
and stimulate action, you need to implement the following eight
steps:*

1. Establishing a meaningful vision for a company begins
    with understanding the need. Visions can be developed
    in good times or bad. If the times are bad, it is essential
    that the vision statement develop a sense of urgency
    among employees.

2. In order to draft the vision statement itself, begin with a review of the closely held values of the company (or department, region, plant etc.). Involve employees in the process, especially those with long terms of employment (10, 20, 30 years and more).

3. Narrow the list of values generated to more than three, but less than seven. Use this to define what the company stands for in the vision statement.

4. One person should write the initial draft; if it is not the person who is going to deliver the message and communicate it to the company or department, then that individual needs to rewrite it in his or her own words maintaining the commitment to core values.

5. A vision statement should be clear, cogent, compelling and concise. Minimally, it needs to include the following elements: a picture of the future, a review of what the company stands for, a target to be achieved, a description of problems being faced, and a powerful rationale as to why the vision must be achieved (*urgency*). Remember: communicating a vision is an opportunity to galvanize action.

6. The enemies of vision are poor preparation, interpersonal timidity, lack of commitment and insufficient communication and obstructionism (including subtle sabotage and cynicism). Lack of commitment will ruin all other efforts to achieve the vision. Obstructionism must be dealt with directly and forcefully or the company will often seek out the level of the obstructionist. It is critical that the leader take immediate and convincing action (including termination) against any employee who knowingly blocks progress toward achieving the vision.

7. You cannot "Take Dead Aim" if you don't have a target to aim at. The company, department or divisional vision will provide that target.

8. If you cannot align your company to achieve the vision, it will not achieve its full potential. In fact, it probably won't happen at all. How to align for success is the focus of the next chapter.

GOLF TEACHES US THAT

DEFINING A

VISION FOR SUCCESS

IS THE

FIRST CRITICAL STEP IN

ACHIEVING SUCCESS.

PARALLEL TRACKS

Secrets from the Golf Course
on Aligning to Achieve the Vision

About Hole #2

Rated number 4 in difficulty, aligning to achieve the vision is a very difficult hole to par. This 513 yard par 5 has an extremely narrow fairway that is lined by trees and deep rough on both sides. To par this hole not only takes a good drive; it takes excellence in all areas of the game—and a disciplined approach to playing the hole. "Just going for it" on this hole typically produces at least a double bogey. Hazards are everywhere on this hole and include: " we don't have time to plan,""alignment is just another business buzzword", "you can pursue your vision, but our basic structure of promoting and rewarding people isn't changing", "we've tried goals before", "we've had a small win, let's get back to normal", "goals are just for corporate", "nothing happens when we don't achieve goals", "goals take all the flexibility and creativity out of managing (or selling, or engineering, or manufacturing, or scheduling, or…) and the biggest of them all, "If I can just wait this out and manage like I always have, I'll be positioned for promotion when this vision thing is over."

> *In a visionary company, the leader ensures that the structure and systems support achieving the vision.*

Introduction

"The companies that will be the winners in the twentieth century," says George Bailey of Watson Wyatt, "will be those that succeed in aligning the goals, behaviors and skills of their employees with their business strategy."

Vision without alignment, without systems, won't achieve the desired results. People may get enthused, they may feel empowered, but without a defined system, the results will be disappointing. In **Built to Last**, *Collins and Porras take great pains to distinguish the difference between a visionary leader and a visionary company. That is, between the on again, off again commitment of employees to the vision of a charismatic leader and the long term covenant that is created between leaders and employees when structure supports vision.*

The message of this chapter can be summed up in a single sentence: There is no point in creating a vision that meets the criteria covered in Chapter 1 if you do not simultaneously develop and implement a company wide structure to encourage every employee, every stakeholder in the company, to achieve this vision—and if you don't stay the course. As a matter of fact, you are often better off not starting such a process unless you are committed to carrying it through. As noted in the first chapter, starting the process, creating urgency, getting buy-in and mustering the energy of the followers creates enormous cynicism about the possibility of improvement if the leader loses energy on the vision, switches focus, leaves the company, or acts contrary to the vision in day to day operations. Think of the vision process in these terms: twenty percent of the effort is in writing and communicating the vision; eighty percent of the effort is in aligning and then implementing the alignment to achieve the vision.

Golf and Alignment

Not surprisingly, golf teaches us the importance of aligning all systems in order to succeed. Golf teaches us that there is structure to success. Golf teaches us that achieving par, or whatever is a good score for us, is not a random process. Golf teaches us that there is a structure essential to achieving the vision of success you have while standing in the tee box. This structure combines skills, attitude, planning and follow through. Each shot in golf combines these elements under a process we call alignment. In order to score well on any given hole, the golfer must repeat the process of alignment several times. In order to score well for eighteen holes, this process must be repeated over and over for every hole. Every golfer knows this instinctively and experientially; if you don't align, you don't succeed.

> *Do not begin the vision/alignment process unless you are committed to staying the course.*

A parallel system exists in business; if the company doesn't align it won't achieve its potential. The difference is, that when we fail to achieve our vision in golf, it costs us wasted strokes, perhaps a double bogey when we had planned on par. In business, not achieving our vision can cost anywhere from millions to loss of the company.

Yet, according to surveys, this is exactly what most companies do. In the study by CFO, Renaissance and Kaplan cited in the first chapter, strategic planning was not linked to achieving the vision in nearly 70% of the companies surveyed. So let's look at what golf teaches us about aligning strategy and vision.

Looking Down the Fairway:
Anticipating the Hazards, Planning to Succeed

In most books and articles, an innovation or new idea is described and then the barriers to implementing that change effort typically follow. In this chapter we are going to reverse this approach and look at barriers first and the process second so that the reader, while considering how the process might fit in his or her company is simultaneously thinking, "How do I overcome the barriers?"

Imagine yourself standing in the tee box of a very difficult five hundred twenty-five yard par 5 dogleg right with pines at the bend. As you survey the expanse between you and the pin, two thoughts simultaneously compete for your attention—the distance and the hazards.

In terms of distance, you know that, on your best day, you can't reach the green in two if you play the fairway. You also know that the green is large and the pin placement favorable for a two putt if you can reach the green in three. (Par for you is very good on this hole.)

As your mind is calculating distances it is also taking into account the hazards, those special challenges afforded by the course designer. You look down the fairway and note the trap on the right, about two hundred twenty yards. You also see a lake on your right at about three hundred yards; the lake juts out into the fairway and only has a carry of about seventy yards. You've played the course before and you know there is a ravine of some sort at about four hundred twenty yards.

How does this knowledge affect your thinking? Hitting it in the rough is going to almost assuredly cost you a stroke, hitting into the trees or sand, could cost you a chance at par. You plan your strategy.

"I can hit my three wood about two twenty down the right. I could hit my driver two fifty, but I give up a lot of accuracy and I might wind up in the trap. So I'll hit my three about two ten to two twenty and then hit my five iron about one hundred sixty yards. I know I can carry that lake on the fly. That will leave me a soft seven on to the green. I love that seven iron, I know I can put it on the green from there. If my seven is working, I'll get close and I can sink that putt. If not, I'll still have my par."

Or you might consciously or unconsciously run a risk assessment. "I am playing with Ed today and he never, never takes a risk. He can't reach this green in two either, if I can carry the trees on the second shot, I can cut eighty yards off this hole. I could do that and go one up, but the downside is that, if I wind up in the trees instead of hitting over them, it is almost a sure double and maybe a triple."

So goes the thinking. Golfers know that execution is the difficult part. But the point is that, in golf, we see the barriers and anticipate them, we analyze risks and make appropriate decisions. We make plans to avoid the barriers and even have contingency plans should our skills not live up to our planning, "If I hit that seven fat, I'll still be able to chip close and I might still get my par." And risk

> *Golf teaches us that there is a structure to success. Good golf is not random and neither is successful leadership.*

assessment: "six long or seven short, seven normally, but today I haven't been hitting it well, worse that can happen is that I wind up in the sand behind the pin." The same kind of thinking is needed in aligning to achieve vision.

Alignment in the Corporation: Seeing the Hazards, Assessing the Risks, and Defining the Plan

In business we frequently forget to look at the barriers to achieving our vision and the risks that we may have to take to achieve that vision. We look down the fairway and see only success. We have a vision of landing on the "green" of our vision and putting for birdie, maybe even an eagle and we don't bother to look at all the sand, water, hills, valleys, trees, bushes and other obstacles that lay in wait for our best efforts. But these hazards do exist, they are called policies, procedures, cultural norms, compensation systems, offices, cubicles, tactical and strategic planning, job descriptions, reward systems, status, departments, divisions – the list goes on and on – and seldom are they all aligned to help you achieve your vision. As a matter of fact, some of them, like compensation systems, are often directly opposed to helping you achieve your goals.

In order to achieve the vision, the leader must, as must the golfer, take a realistic look at these barriers and define a plan as to how to achieve the vision knowing that these obstacles exist. Like the experienced golfer, the effective leader will determine both what is needed to avoid the obstacles and how to play the game if "a shot lands in the water." So, lets look at some of these barriers and how they work to hinder you, rather than assist you, in your efforts to achieve your vision.

Barriers to Achieving the Vision

In Chapter 1 we examined some of the more common barriers to achieving the vision. We suggested that conditions such as cynicism, obstructionism, poor planning and interpersonal timidity can derail a visionary effort if not dealt with directly. In this chapter we are going to examine systemic and structural issues, issues related to often unarticulated but widely accepted cultural beliefs that prevent a great vision from being achieved. Some of these cultural/systemic barriers are compensation, hiring and promotional policies, the performance appraisal system, succession planning and corporate support functions such as Human Resources, Information Technology, and Accounting.

Compensation and Reward Systems

As we will see in Chapter 3 which focuses on Motivation, compensation is one driver of behavior. Please understand, compensation is not the driver of behavior, it is one driver of behavior, probably twenty-thirty percent of the overall motivational package of a given individual.

Aligning compensation with vision is a challenging task. Consider, for example, the automobile dealership that announced a vision of "Customers—First, Last and Always," and continued to pay their service writers on a commission basis and reward their mechanics for work completed under the standard time allotted for that job. The message was confusing. Do we continue to try and sell more and focus on efficiency rather than effectiveness or do we really put the customer first?

Eventually this company selected a combination of four alternative measures as part of bonus system: first, customer satisfaction as measured by lack of complaints; second, percentage of cars returned because what the customer brought the car in for the first time had not been repaired properly; third, "atta boys" or customer compliments; and fourth, overall profitability. This program produced a dramatic increase in customer satisfaction as measured in customer surveys and, not surprisingly, resulted in both increased revenue and margins.

> *One of the more challenging tasks of a leader is to align compensation polices with the vision.*

Another example of misplaced emphasis is the "Dealer Satisfaction" ratings issued when you buy a new or used car at many dealerships. The last time I bought a car I was told by the salesman that it was critical that I give him all "Excellents," if not, he would lose his job (cynically I thought "or not get your bonus"). The point is, with that kind of pressure, how accurate is the feedback that either the dealer or General Motors is getting?

Hiring and Promotional Policies

Most golfers play with a matched set of clubs. They play with Cobras or Titleists or Taylor Mades or Pings. These golf clubs, used time and time again help them achieve their vision of shooting par, improving their game or winning a championship. The golfer becomes comfortable with his or her clubs and only changes them when there is a demonstrable improvement in technology (or if an excuse is needed for why he or she can't get off that plateau.)

If you play Taylor Made clubs and someone handed you a Titleist or King Cobra, you wouldn't want to immediately use this club in competition. Maybe on the range, but not in a match until you were comfortable with the club.

Why? Because it doesn't have the balance, fit and feel of your other clubs. It may be offset or cavity backed; it may have a rifle shaft or a graphite shaft. However, it won't "feel" right and this new club won't help you score well, it will hinder your efforts to achieve your vision. It is unlikely that you would play this club out of choice.

Then why would you hire or promote someone who doesn't share the vision that you have promulgated? Why would you hire or promote someone who doesn't fit, who has a negative view about the vision, who will "cost you strokes."

Yet, this is exactly what we find in many companies. Gloria is promoted because she has been with the company for twelve years and has powerful connections. Al is hired because his brother-in-law knows the vice-president. Christa is moved into a regional manager role because she has exceeded her sales quota by fifty percent for three years running.

You wouldn't want to play with mismatched clubs, why would you want to promote someone who will "cost you strokes" in terms of achieving the vision.

But are they part of a matched set? Do they share the vision? If they don't share the vision, if they are not seen as part of the change team, promoting Gloria or Christa and hiring Al sends a powerful message to all employees that the vision does not apply company-wide, and it certainly does not apply to superstars, friends of friends or politically connected people who know how to play the game.

Alignment must be a company-wide effort. If it is to succeed, all departments, particularly the traditional support functions of Human Resources, Information Systems and Accounting must be part of the alignment. Each of these departments must examine the policies and procedures that they implement on a regular basis and ask two questions. The first of these is: Why do we conduct this process this way, what is the underlying thought process behind this procedure?" The second question is: "Do these policies and procedures help us achieve the vision—if not, how can we change them so they do?"

Human Resources in particular must develop criteria for promotion that are based on contributing to the achievement of the vision. In many HR departments, policies and procedures have developed over time to support a culture that most employees are only vaguely aware of. For example, in many companies where I consult promotion to senior management positions comes only after a stint in the sales department—the unspoken cultural message is: "If you can't sell, you can't lead this company."

Ignore HR at your peril. The polices and procedures of the Human Resource function must be integrally aligned with the vision – and they must be enforced.

I worked with another company where the president consciously weeded out from management anyone who was not identified as a "driver or dominant" in one of the quadrant behavioral analysis systems. His reasoning was that only "high D's" (his style, of course) had the drive, determination and toughness to survive in a highly competitive industry. (In essence, he loaded his golf bag with "Big Bertha" drivers and wondered why he couldn't chip or putt.) What he did with this and other similar beliefs was to establish a culture of focus on task and immediate results at the expense of systems, customer satisfaction, long term strategic thinking and employee development. His attempts at setting and achieving an all encompassing vision failed because the skill sets he needed in order to succeed were not the master (or often even the secondary) skills of those he had consciously selected to run the company.

Meanwhile, of course, talented people who were not high in the dominant/driver quadrant chose to take their intelligence, motivation, commitment and skills to companies where these assets were valued.

Performance Appraisal

There are so many problems with performance appraisal as commonly carried out in this country that it is hard to include it as a barriers to vision as well. In most companies in the United States, performance appraisal is an annual attempt of the supervisor to tell the supervised where he or she needs to improve, after which the person is told how much or how little of a raise he or she will receive this year. The process of performance appraisal is our annual "great de-motivator" and it needs to be replaced by a process that is proactive, and formative, rather than reactive and summative. Performance appraisal must not be whimsically and (in the employee's eyes) mysteriously tied to compensation.

In particular, the leadership team that is carrying out the initial steps in aligning to achieve the vision must include the performance appraisal process as an instrument for attaining the vision. For example, if the vision focuses totally or partially on customer service, the performance appraisal system should include customer service orientation (internal or external). If the vision focuses totally or partially on reducing internal inefficiencies and cutting costs, the performance appraisal system should include a mechanism for assessing contribution to this effort.

In short, like taking the proper stance that will allow you to hit your target on the fairway or the green, aligning the performance appraisal system is an early and necessary step in achieving the goal.

Succession Planning

Succession planning, which an alarming number of companies don't do, is another key alignment strategy. It is obviously related to the hiring and promotional policies outlined above, but it takes it a step further into the planning phase. Every manager should know who is going to take his place when the next promotion occurs. She should be grooming this replacement with the thought, "If I don't have a replacement I am not promotable," rather than "If there is someone who can take my place, I am expendable." In visionary companies the former attitude holds and the people selected in the succession plan are those who have advanced the vision.

Accounting and Information Technology

Accounting procedures that served management may not serve leadership. The focus of accounting has too often been on providing data and reports and not often enough about breaking barriers to customer service. Information Technology (the old MIS department) often drives processes in companies today because we have become so computer dependent. Some of the software packages in use are customer focused, many are not. Many of these packages are designed to help manage costs, inventories and operations rather than streamline and improve customer service. Chapters could be written on both of these areas, suffice to say here, for a vision to be successful, all functions of the company must be reviewed for alignment. If the policies and procedures of these functions are not aligned, align them.

In visionary companies, those who have actively supported the vision are the ones who are promoted.

The Alignment Process: A Strategic Approach

On the practice range at the club I belong to in Houston, there are a number of white plastic "arrows". These arrows are cut from 1" x 2" material and are about 36" in length. If you place them perpendicular to your feet and parallel with your target line, they make an amazing difference in the accuracy of your shots. Placing one three or four inches beyond the ball as a swing line further increases the accuracy of your shots. Using these arrows helps you better align body and swing to the target. It helps you ensure that all aspects of the swing are working together in order to achieve your objective. This is the purpose of the strategic alignment process.

There are many variations on the theme of strategic alignment, including:

1. Analyzing the external environment (competitiveness, technology)
2. Analyzing the internal environment (balance sheet, sales)
3. Analyzing competencies (capability assessment)
4. Reviewing company paradigms (about the market, about our company)
5. Conducting a Strategic Assessment (issues, what goes wrong)
6. Setting Corporate Goals and Objectives (write mission, goals, objectives)
7. Developing Action Plans
8. Developing Budgets to Support the Action Plan (operating budget, cash flow, investment needs)
9. Establishing a system to monitor progress

The vision/alignment approach presented here is equally encompassing, but simpler in design and execution. It includes the following steps:

1. Create the Vision
2. Appoint the Guidance Team

3. Establish Corporate Goals
4. Develop Departmental Goals and Objectives
5. Develop Departmental Action Plans and Timelines
6. Specify the Roles and Responsibilities of Employees in Achieving the Objectives and Thus the Vision
7. Empower Employees to Act in Accordance with the Vision

THE VISION/ALIGNMENT MODEL

A Vision Statement

Which is Supported by:

A Guidance Team

Which Develops Strategy and Defines
Corporate Goals (Overarching)

Which are Supported by:

Divisional/Departmental Goals

Which are Achieved Through:

Action Plans and Timelines

Which Drive:

Individual Employee Behavior

Which Results in:

Achieving the Vision

(IF, and only IF, The Barriers Have Been Removed)

(Note: There is an assumption here that the current system can be revised to meet the needs of the vision. As often as not, it can't be; if the current system will not allow achievement of the vision, the primary corporate goal must be to restructure to achieve the vision. For example, when Intel realized that memory had become a commodity business and that foreign competition was beating them on price, Andy Grove courageously moved the company into microprocessors. For Intel, the primary corporate goal would have been to move the company from memory to microprocessors. Everything else would have followed from that goal.)

This is obviously a "top down" approach and it certainly isn't the only approach that is effective in achieving a vision. It is heavily biased toward a planned, integrated, strategic implementation. Some leaders are too random, too impulsive to implement this methodology. However, in my experience it is the one that provides the best opportunity for the company to achieve the vision. If you are a department manager, a regional or plant manager, or in some other position where you want to create and implement a vision, simply scale down the vision/alignment model to meet your needs.

Appoint the Guidance Team

Chapter One is devoted to Creating the Vision, so let's begin by looking at how we can ensure continuity of the vision through the operations of a guidance team.

The leader, except in departments and small companies, is seldom able to manage the day to day implementation of the vision. In order to establish and maintain the alignment structure, a guidance team must be appointed.

Guidance teams should be kept small, no more than nine people (unless yours is a very large company where twelve-fifteen may be needed). This team reports directly to the leader and meets with the leader on a weekly or bi-weekly basis to report progress. Members should include at least one executive who reports directly to the president/CEO, principal line managers who are committed to the process and at least one, but no more than two, employee(s) who are seen by others as having high credibility and commitment to the company. Leadership and management (see below) must be represented on this team.

Once established, this team must be provided with training in the essential skills of effective teamwork. It is an investment of time that pays large dividends when tough decisions must be made. This team ensures that the vision is implemented in every department and at every level within the company. In addition, this team initiates and monitors the goals process.

Establish Corporate Goals

The "Goals Process" in most companies has about the same degree of credibility as some current well known political figures. Mention the word goal and you are greeted with a yawn or a smirk or maybe even a smile. They have seen goals before and the goals didn't change anything. Oh, maybe there was an initial rush

> *In larger companies, the leader needs the active help of a guidance team to make the vision a reality.*

of excitement and a few people took them seriously, but no one was rewarded for achieving them and, more importantly, nobody lost any compensation or stature because they were not achieved. And that is the problem with goals. Before I begin the process of outlining how a goal should be written and how it should be achieved, let me share with you a classic example of negative goals-driven behavior.

I was on a plane flying back from Los Angeles to Houston. I distinctly remember it being mid to late October as the summer is finally starting to wind down in Houston.

Seated in the row in front of me were two men with rather loud voices. Often, when I am on a plane, particularly if it is after six or seven at night, I try to relax with fiction. It is quire likely that I was reading a novel by James Lee Burke, but I just as well may have been re-reading John Updike's wonderful collection of golf articles: Golf Dreams. (If you love golf I recommend this book highly).

At any rate, these two men in front of me were talking about the customer they had just visited and they were so loud it was hard to read my book. (It was obvious that their natural ebullience – they were salespeople – had been significantly enhanced with the assistance of Jim Beam or Jack Daniels, or one of those guys.) As I heard their conversation I understood that they were selling hardware in the $200,000 to $500,000 range. This is the gist of their conversation.

One said, "You know I have to post date this order. I can't sell it before January 1 or Bill will really increase my goals for next year. I made my $20 million (sales goal) in August and have tried to slow it down ever since, the bonus isn't worth the stress."

The other replied, "Yeah, I made mine in September and feel the same way. I am letting the small orders dribble in, but we are going to have to call Marsha and have her help us with the paperwork on this order so that the customer gets the product in early January and we aren't killed with ridiculous increases in our goals for next year."

What kind of thinking encourages this kind of behavior? It is looking at goals as the golden egg rather than the goose. In pursuing the golden egg, many companies inadvertently kill the goose. Quotas are to goals as the score for one hole is the score for the round.

I know that the topic of goals is a droll issue. It is for many of us, boring, unexciting and even deathly. But it doesn't have to be. A goal, well conceived, well written and properly supported throughout the organization, can actually energize and focus eighty percent of the people in your organization.

(I say eighty percent of the people in your company because there is research that shows that twenty-percent of the population is not only not motivated by goals at all, but, in fact, are de-motivated by them. These people are motivated by solving problems, not by achieving goals. In other words, when they go to the golf course their goal is to avoid a bogey, not to shoot par. Literally, their focus is not so much on the flag as it is how to get out of the haz-

Quotas are to goals as the score for one hole is to the score for the round.

ards. So remember these people when you set your goals; for them, turn the goal around and make it into a problem to be solved.

Having made a bow to the problem solvers, let's return to goals.)

If you are an executive or a manager and your company or department does not have goals, you aren't really managing with purpose. Imagine a golf course without a flag and cup. Managers say to me, "How can I motivate my people?" And I say to them, "Do you have a cup and a flag? Do you have a plan to get

> *Stretch targets can change routine tasks into challenging ones. Everyone needs a cup to knock that ball into.*

there so they know if they are headed for an eagle or a double bogey?"

Would you play golf without that cup to knock the ball in? Would you play if the greens were flat and targetless? Of course not! Then why do you expect your people to be excited about working without a target, without a goal, without a plan as to how to achieve it?

Work can be routine without a target, it can be exciting with one.

In a truly aligned company, all the functions of the company work in concert to achieve the goals of the company— financial, customer service, human resources, engineering, manufacturing, distribution, administration, operations, sales —everyone works towards achieving the vision by setting and achieving their own goals.

Remember, in business as in golf, you can look at the target and plan for a win, or look at the target and hope for a win. Planning is the better alternative.

Setting Corporate Goals

The company, plant or division has established its vision and appointed its guidance team, how does it set goals that help achieve the vision? The first step is to define large overarching corporate goals. These corporate goals will not change dramatically from year to year. Corporate goals are measurable by adding up the successes of the goals and objectives that support them, but are not measurable by themselves. They often reflect enduring company values such as:

- Continuously improve the service provided to our customers
- Create value added relationships with our suppliers
- Involve all employees in appropriate levels of decision making
- Reduce the overall cost of operations
- Increase the return of investment for all shareholders
- Create an atmosphere of loyalty and trust among all employees

As you can see, these goals are very broad, very general. These goals may not even change from year to year. What they do is to give the regions, divisions, departments and employees a knowledge of what the leadership of the company thinks is important. They essentially give the departments something to peg their goals and objectives to.

Setting Departmental Goals

Departmental goals begin the process of more closely focusing in on the target. Departmental goals follow the tried and true "SMART" formula:

S— Specific
M—Measurable
A—Attainable
R—Relevant
T—Time Oriented

That is, goals should be:

Specific

Corporate or company wide goals can be general, but departmental goals should be more focused. They should leave no doubt about exactly what the target is. A good example of a specific goal is: "Achieve a 12% reduction in the cost of purchased supplies by October 31, 2001." There is little ambiguity in this goal. It is very specific.

Measurable

Ideally, goals should have a measurement system built in. For example, reduce time to respond to an order by forty-five percent, reduce lost customers by 50%, or as the Japanese did in the eighties, improve quality (some acceptable unit of measure such as defects per hundred cars) by 100% (or more). Not to belabor the obvious, but how do you know if you achieved it if you don't establish a measurable target. That is what you do in golf. You set yourself a target of reaching 85 or 80 or playing par golf ten times or more during the coming year. Do you know if you have attained it, sure you do; you have a measurable goal.

Attainable

Is 85 attainable? Can I reasonably reach that goal? Of course I can. With diligence, practice, concentration and enough time to play (twice a week) I can reach that goal. Do not set random goals. Do not pull some magic number out of the air (e.g., reduce scrap by 100%). Know your process and what it is capable of (If I am shooting 90 now, 85 is reachable, 78 probably isn't unless I want to give up another important goal—a happy homelife). Do not choose a number just to please the boss. Attainable means "with a little stretch and by doing things differently, we can reach this goal." Attainable goals that are easy to achieve do not generate employee energy. Remember, attainable means you can reach it if you do

Golf teaches us the importance of having measurable goals. Set a goal of breaking 80 and keep an accurate score!

things differently, if you make improvements to the system, if you change paradigms that have impeded progress in the past.

Relevant

There are thousands of goals you could choose. Using the SMART system, choose a goal that relates to the achievement of the vision as supported by the first layer of goals, the corporate goals. If at all possible, make it not only relevant to the goals but relevant to the employees, something that they can see and feel and sense, something that will bring pride to them when it is achieved. Irrelevant goals will not help you achieve your vision.

Time-Related

This simply means that the goal will be achieved by a certain date. Time-related is really a part of attainable, it must be achieved within a certain time frame. It has often been said that a goal without a measurement system is just a dream and a goal without a deadline is just a wish. To be effective give your goal a time by which it should be achieved.

Examples

This is a personal goal of mine, written at the end of 1998 when the best I had ever scored on a course rated at 20 or better had been 95 (remember, you of the golf elite, I only started playing in 1993). At any rate, excuses aside, my written goal was:

> *"By December 31, 1999, shoot a score of 87 or better on a course with a slope of at least twenty."*

This goal meets the SMART criteria: it is measurable (87), it is attainable (I shot a ninety on July 29) it is relevant (to my vision of myself as a good golfer and my goal of having a 15 or better handicap so I can play those Scottish courses) and it is time-related (it will be accomplished by December 31, 1999).

Here are two examples of departmental goals that support the Corporate Goal of reducing the cost of operations by 10% company-wide. This plant had been running full bore (all three shifts) for a couple of years and, as a result, had not given the time to periodic maintenance that was required to keep the machines (and the plant) running (a classic case of short-term thinking).

By the end of the 1999 fiscal year, the cost of equipment repairs due to improper or uncompleted preventive maintenance will be reduced from the $261,387 incurred in 1998 to less than $ 80,000.

By the end of the 1999 fiscal year, unplanned machine downtime will be reduced from 1998's two hundred twelve days to fewer than seventy days.

That is all there is to it. Enough of these and you are on your way to achieving your vision.

Objectives

The next question is, "How do you achieve your goals?" This is where objectives enter the picture. The problem with objectives is that they became trivialized during the heyday of the MBO (Management by Objectives) movement and still have a bad reputation because of it. During the early seventies, while the Japanese were perfecting the use of teams, customer satisfaction, Statistical Process Control, and quality in general, American management and employees spent hours creating detailed lists of objectives for each employee to complete. For the most part, it was a waste of time. People spent so much time on their measurement of achieving their objectives that they often couldn't get their work done. In addition, these objectives were so specific that the employee had little time to get her work done, and when she did, it certainly wasn't fulfilling.

(This seems to happen a lot in this country. We take a good idea, take it to an unintended extreme and wonder why it didn't work. MBWA (Managing by Wandering Around) is another example of this as is TQM which was and is a great idea that often became trivialized by a focus on the bureaucracy to make it happen rather than by focusing on the processes of continuous improvement and customer satisfaction that are at the core of Total Quality Management. Let's hope the same thing doesn't happen to leadership.)

So the question is, how do you write meaningful objectives that will drive behavior without trivializing day to day work production?

Let's return to our departmental goal:

"By the end of the 1999 fiscal year, the cost of equipment repairs due to improper or uncompleted preventive maintenance will be reduced from the $261,387 incurred in 1998 to less than $80,000."

Objectives to attain this goal might include;

"Complete a review of machines that have not received a complete PM over the last 18 months by November 1."

"Ensure that all machines are scheduled for their PM by November 15."

An Action Plan to Ensure Achievement of the Objective

Does this mean that you wind up with a lot of objectives? Yes, this is what alignment is all about. It isn't developing and communicating the vision, as difficult as that is, it is easier than organizing to achieve the vision. If the vision process is to be successful, you must "get into the weeds."

Once the objective is decided, it is assigned to an individual who puts together a series of steps to achieve the objective and a timeline showing the estimated times for completion of these steps. At this point, the individual can be evaluated as to how well the objective is being achieved.

The Role of Management in Attaining the Vision

In the Forward to this book, we looked at "The Tyranny of the Or" in relationship to managers and leaders. The "Tyranny of the Or" says that you must choose management or leadership. The "Perspective of the And" says that you can have both, you can be both. In truth, successfully implementing a vision requires both leadership and management. (This is critically important on the Guidance Team.) In Chapter One, we looked at the potential role of middle managers to block the path to the vision. In Chapter 7, we are going to revisit this concept from the perspective of chaos vs. linear thinking and realize that all leaders must at some times be managers and all managers, leaders.

In the 1950's, through the 1980's business schools and businesses taught management (think of what MBA suggests: advanced skills in how to administer businesses, where's the MBL?). Managers are taught to plan, organize, budget and control. Are managers needed in a vision process? The answer is not only yes, it is an emphatic yes. You cannot achieve a vision without effective management of the process. This is why it is so critical in the early stages of the vision/alignment process not only to weed out the cynics and the obstructionists, but to deeply involve those who will administer the process and ensure the attainment of the short term wins that will drive the process.

Do not neglect the people critical to implementation of the plan requisite to attaining the vision. Involve them, listen to them, reward them for helping to achieve the vision.

Some Semi-Final Thoughts
on Achieving the Vision

In my experience, more visions have failed than succeeded, not completely failed, but failed to achieve the total package. Visions fail because leadership doesn't anticipate the barriers outlined in these first two chapters, because they don't deal firmly with cynics and obstructionists, because they switch focus or lose focus after a few initial minor wins. Visions fail because leaders don't anchor wins in the structure of the company, because they don't really empower others to help achieve the vision, because they celebrate too early, because leaders retire, get promoted, leave for a better position, or (rarely) get fired. Visions fail because leaders neglect to create a structure to achieve the vision, because it takes time to change the culture of a company, because they do not continuously communicate the importance of the vision to the employees of the company and most frequently, because of lack of consistency between the behavior of leadership and management in implementing the vision and the promise that was made to stay the course.

It is difficult to shoot par (actually for some of us it is hard to shoot 85). It is even more difficult to shoot par day in and day out every day of the year. Think about all those things you need to do to shoot par (or to simply improve your game from an average score of 85 to an average score of 79) the continuous practice, the single minded focus, the concentration on each shot, continually working to overcome that slice, the knowledge of what it is that you are supposed to do in any situation. Think about all these requirements and the others that you need to implement and you will understand why implementing a vision is so difficult.

Most importantly you cannot give up after you bogey the first three holes and double bogey the fourth. You cannot relax if you birdie the first three holes and eagle the fourth. You must literally, finish the course.

And Finally

For those of you who ask: "Is this the only way to achieve a vision, isn't this process extremely structured?" I have an answer. I have seen CEO's ignore structure. I have seen them create chaos in order to achieve a vision; I have seen them pound on tables, swear and threaten and demand results. I have seen them fire at will and create fear and havoc.

> *Failure to achieve the vision is almost always a failure of the leader.*

The cost in morale, turnover, rework and productivity is seldom worth whatever is gained. Structure doesn't have to be boring and unimaginative. The greatest moments on the golf course are often those moments of creative shot making where your years of practice and skill development allow you to make a planned shot others can't make. This is the philosophy that should drive the structure of achieving the vision.

How To Play This Hole:

In order to achieve a vision, whether it is company, plant, region, or department wide, several steps must be taken. Among these are:

1. Develop a comprehensive plan to include everyone involved in the vision in the achievement of the vision.

2. The plan needs to evolve into a systematic structure that includes every facet of operations, from the planning function, through customer service, to the customers themselves.

3. Anticipate the barriers to achieving your vision, analyze the risks involved and make the appropriate decisions.

4. Examine and align internal systems and processes with the vision. Pay special attention to compensation and reward systems, hiring and promotional policies, performance appraisal, succession planning, and accounting and information systems.

5. Implement an alignment model that integrates all elements of your plan.

6. Set SMART goals.

7. Use the SMART goals to drive objectives and behaviors further removed from the process.

8. Anchor short term wins in the structure of the company in order to achieve long term victories.

9. Don't quit.

GOLF TEACHES US THAT, TO BE SUCCESSFUL, YOU MUST NOT ONLY HAVE A TARGET, BUT A CONSCIOUS PLAN TO ATTAIN IT. YOU MUST ALIGN YOUR VISION WITH YOUR STRATEGY IN ORDER TO ACHIEVE THE VISION.

WHY WE PLAY

Management Secrets from the Golf Course on Motivation

About Hole #3

Motivation is a challenging but "par-able" hole. It is a 534 yard par 5 where everyone plays from the "tips." It is the longest hole of the course. It is a sharp dogleg left with a 160 yard carry over water. Hazards such as "Too much to do to have time to motivate," "that soft stuff has no place in business," "They get a paycheck, don't they," and "If they can't motivate themselves, I don't want them in my department," litter the course. Even though it is a long hole, knowledge and strategy can carry you through to par.

Introduction

One of those ancient Chinese proverbs that, for me, is of undetermined origin, has been translated, "A leader without followers is just a person going for a walk." We have examined vision and alignment, the question now becomes, "What else can we do to ensure that people embrace and achieve the vision, not just because they have to, but because they want to?"

Again, the ability to motivate is one of those significant differences between managers and leaders; it is the difference between those who push and those who pull, between those who cajole and those who guide. The manager will organize to en-

> *A leader without followers is just a person out for a walk.*

force compliance, the leader will motivate to exceed compliance.

If you have been in a supervisory position for any amount of time, you know the immense variation in what might best be called, "psychological make-up." The easy way to deal with this variation is to insist that everyone receive the same treatment. This is, as Covey says, "efficient, but not effective." It is not unlike asking the person who is five foot seven and the person who is six foot five to wear the same clothes, often clothing designed for someone six foot even. The result is that the clothes fit no one except the occasional six footer.

Motivation—"Touchy-Feely" or Good Business?

So, while it may be easier to deny that we need motivation, while it may be easier to say that, in this company, "one size fits all," the truth is that leaders understand that the strength of diverse personalities can be harnessed through effective motivational strategies. Further, they understand that the time spent in implementing these strategies is a classic investment strategy: invest now for greater payback in the future.

> *Motivation is about the relationship of trust that leads to customer retention and greater profitability.*

One of the prime rules of leadership is that it is the job of the leader to provide for the employees what they cannot provide for themselves. Couple this with the fact that the research indicates that only ten percent of the population are true self starters, and you have a strong rationale for providing motivation to those you lead.

The difficulty with motivation is that there is so much to know. Maslow and Herzberg contributed insight into motivation forty years ago that is still valid today; Dr. Kenneth Blanchard has worked for thirty years to define a system that looks at the individual in terms of both competence and confidence, and more recently, Dr. Edward Deci has answered the question of "Why We Do What We Do" in a book by that same name.

This chapter provides an overview to all of this. We begin by visiting two extremes of performance, look at some fundamentals of interpersonal effectiveness and then review a comprehensive strategy for motivating people to perform at their highest level. While we do this, we focus on the fact that motivation is not some "touchy-feely" exercise. Research leaves no doubt about the fact that *people who feel good about what they do and how they are treated perform at higher levels.* Motivation is not about something out of sensitivity train-

People who feel good about themselves, their jobs and how they are treated, perform at higher levels.

ing, it is not about being "nice" or soft, it is about productivity. Motivation is about the employer/employee relationship of loyalty and trust that leads to customer retention and greater profitability. Managers who say, "I don't have time to motivate" are really saying, "I am satisfied with making seventy percent of what I could make." We'll look at this in greater depth later in the chapter.

The Question

Some leaders intuitively sense the need for motivation and understand that there is a high correlation between productivity and motivation. Their question is: *"How do you motivate when you have such wide variation within the people being lead?"* The process begins by identifying some basic levels of what Blanchard calls confidence and competence and continues through the appropriate application of targeted recognition, feedback and correction. To understand the basics of motivation, lets look at an exercise in identifying types of employees in terms of confidence and competence and then move from there to the story of my friend Jack and his initiation into the fraternal order of golfers.

The Demonstration

The following few paragraphs describe an exercise that I use when teaching motivational concepts to groups of managers (incidentally, I have yet to see the term "leader" on anyone's business card, people are still plant managers, department managers, regional managers, etc.). For the purpose of this exercise, imagine that you are in the audience and that I am presenting from a raised stage. On the stage I have put down a practice putting green – a ten foot long, 30 inch wide strip of Astroturf with a cup at the end. You can see the stage without obstruction as my presentation begins:

"You see, we have different types of people working for us in terms of motivation, but we often treat them the same. With this exercise I want to demonstrate two basic types of employees and why it is that applying the same techniques to both won't produce the desired results. I need two volunteers – first, a golfer who is a 10 handicapper or less (I point to the audience and select a volunteer who comes up to the stage). Now I need someone who is a twenty-five handicapper or more or someone who never played golf at all (again, a volunteer comes up to the stage — these people are typically volunteered by someone else).

Okay, Michelle, (a "7 handicap") I have two putters here, a center shafted and a heel shafted; you have your choice of which one you want to hit (she selects the center shafted). Now go ahead and get a feel of this green and the putter - hit two or three.

"Now, Michelle, I have five golf balls here. Let's see how you do (Michelle putts in three of the five.) Okay Michelle, now let's see how you can do with motivation. I pull out a realistic looking (plastic) pistol. Let's say I aimed this at your head – how would you do?"

Michelle tries and gets two balls in the hole.

"Well, that type of motivation didn't work so well, so let's move from the stick to the carrot, let's try a performance bonus." (I take a twenty-dollar bill out of my pocket.) "What if I offered you twenty dollars if you could get all five in?"

Michelle experiences a dramatic improvement in concentration. She knocks in four out of five (occasionally I lose my twenty). "I see, Michelle, you are more motivated by money than fear. Now, let's talk to Mike over here."

> *One of the great myths of motivation is that, if you can only find the right combination of carrot and stick, you can motivate anyone.*

"All right, Mike, you have a thirty-one handicap, right?" (Mike: "Well it used to be a nineteen, but I stopped playing for about ten years.") "So which putter do you prefer?"

Mike also selects the center shafted and practices hitting a couple.

"Okay, we are going to do the same thing with you that we did with Michelle. Let's see you get these five balls in the cup."

Mike practices and sinks only one of his shots.

"Well Mike, the goal is to get all of those little white balls in that cup. Do you need some motivation? I have motivation." I pull out the plastic pistol. (Usually the audience is starting to give Mike some words of encouragement at this point.) "Now get those five balls in the cup."

Mike says, "I'll try," and gets one ball in the cup.

"Mike, I see you are not motivated by fear. Are you money motivated?"

Mike empathetically answers that he is. I place a twenty dollar bill on the table and say, "This twenty is yours if you can get all five balls in the cup."

This time Mike misses on all five shots.

I comment, "Mike, I guess you are not as money motivated as you think." (Actually, my money was really safe; Mike didn't have the necessary skills.)

The point of this demonstration? Applying motivation without understanding individual competence and, confidence, won't produce the desired results.

The Great Motivation Myth

Applying "motivation" without a proper understanding of the individual's competence and confidence levels won't produce the desired results.

One of the great myths of motivation is that, **if we can only find that right combination of carrot and stick, we can motivate others.** The putting demonstration shows this to be false. No matter how much fear we engender, nor how many rewards we proffer, carrots and sticks have limited impact on individual motivation — particularly over the long term. So, what does? Blanchard's Situational Leadership© model affords insight into this process. Let's look at the experience of two golfers to better understand the basics of effective motivation in business.

The Enthusiastic Novice

A friend of mine started playing golf again last week after a twenty-five year lay-off (Jack is not a young man) and when he was playing twenty-five years ago he wasn't particularly good.

It is fascinating for me to watch him play. Fortunately for him he is a senior vice president in a fairly successful firm so his first four times playing were at beautiful and challenging tracks like the Desert Inn's course in Las Vegas and Indian Wells outside of Palm Springs where the Bob Hope Open is played (not bad places for anyone to be playing golf).

I want you to know that Jack is enthusiastic. He can't wait to play. He knows that he isn't all that good, but he went out and spent more than a thousand dollars on clubs and he just loves to get out there and smash that ball around. If he shoots 110 on a par 70 course, great. If he shoots 120, great. If he should happen to shoot 105, he would be ecstatic. He lives for that moment when he hits that one drive right down the middle of the fairway or sinks that twenty foot putt, or gets it out of the trap and onto the green (the first time).

You have to see Jack to believe him. Jack is terrible, but it doesn't matter because he is still in that honeymoon phase with golf. He loves it. He will get up at 5:00 in the morning to be on the course and would gladly play four or five times a week if he had the time. He hits the ball in the woods and he laughs, he hits his brand new Pinnacle in the water and yells, "Mulligan!"

If he hits it out of bounds, he simply tees it up again and hits another one. If he skulls three straight shots from one side of the green to the other, he simply smiles and mumbles, "I'm gaining on it." He doesn't worry about playing by the rules because he doesn't know the rules-although he is slowly learning (or more accurately, being informed) about the ancient and honorable laws that govern the game.

Jack doesn't throw his clubs or curse his luck; he is committed to getting better and knows that, in order to do this, he will have to play, practice, play, practice. He also knows that to expedite the process of improvement, Jack will have to take some lessons from an established pro - and knowing Jack, he will - and soon.

Jack is what Ken Blanchard calls an "enthusiastic beginner." He has a lot of enthusiasm and energy, but his skill level, his golf competence level, is relatively low. He doesn't yet know that it is not enough to be able to

The enthusiastic beginner has lots of enthusiasm and energy but a relatively low level of competence.

hit his seven iron well, but that he has to be able to hit it from an uphill, downhill or sidehill lie or a combination of two of these lies and that he not only has to be able to hit it for distance, but for predictable distance.

Jack doesn't know yet that sand comes in an infinite variety of weights and that greens vary from those as smooth as a table top to those that feel like some shag carpet from the sixties. But to him, as an enthusiastic beginner, it doesn't matter — he just loves to get to the course or the range and begin swinging away. Golf teaches us how to motivate the enthusiastic beginner, to motivate that person toward excellence, not just eagerness. But, before we look at how to motivate the enthusiastic beginner, lets remember:

ENTHUSIASTIC BEGINNERS ARE NOT LIMITED TO THE GOLF COURSE

High Enthusiasm, Low Competence in the Office

If you have been a manager for any amount of time, you have supervised enthusiastic beginners. These are the ones who come in the door smiling, who can't wait for that first tough assignment, who know they have a lot to learn (and are willing to learn it), who volunteer for everything but don't contribute a lot, who sometimes appear like puppy dogs in their desire to please. The most typical of these is the new employee.

The New Employee

Enthusiastic beginners are not defined by age, gender or education, but by attitude and competence. You might have a recent college graduate settle down in a department where she knows that her experience is limited and her education insufficient to really contribute to the company, but she is a willing learner who is not offended when she finds herself "in the woods" because, after all, she tried hard to hit the ball further than her skills would allow. Her enthusiasm goes beyond attitude to behavior, she comes in early, stays late, and generally lets you know that she will take on any assignment.

Enthusiastic beginners are defined by attitude and competence.

She doesn't know that office politics reflect as much variation as green side bunkers, that excellence is often related not only to performance, but to perception, and that patience is often the key to promotion.

Like Jack, this person knows that, either through on the job training or through externally provided training, she has a lot to learn and is willing to make the effort to learn what she needs. After all, she is an enthusiastic beginner. But, like Jack, she doesn't know yet about all the sidehill lies and "bunker fried eggs" that await even the most talented.

The Transfer

You might also have someone transfer in from another department, where he was burned out by routine duties and is looking to learn again, looking for a challenge, looking for a second chance. This person, no matter their education or their experience with this company or a previous one, is really an "enthusiastic beginner."

The New Manager

There is a third enthusiastic beginner that is frequently found in business. This is the new manager or leader. If you are now or have been a manager or supervisor, think back to your early months in the position. You were excited, you wanted to make a difference; you probably had a model in your mind of what the ideal supervisor or manager should be like or should not be like.

However, if you were like most of us when you got that first management position, you had little formal people skills, just an intuitive sense of how to hit the ball, that is, how to work with people and how to stay organized. (Actually, if you were representative of a lot of managers, you were probably promoted to a manager position because you were superior as a doer — that is, you were the best salesperson so they made you a sales manager, you were the best engineer so they made you the manager of the design engineering group. This is a little like taking Tiger Woods and making him manager of the tour — but that is another story, one only indirectly related to motivation.)

The point is, when you first became a manager, you probably had little formal training, but lots of enthusiasm. Even though you had little formal training, you wanted to make a difference, you wanted to prove to others that this was the right decision, so you jumped in with both feet and sixty hour weeks.

You likely looked back at managers that you wanted to emulate and those that you didn't. You may have looked at those managers you considered successful and tried to adopt some of their behaviors into yours, you may have thought back into your past and remembered incidents that taught you what you did and didn't want to be as a supervisor.

For example, when I was working weekends in a supermarket during college I was given the assignment one weekend of totally rearranging the warehouse by myself. At the end of the first day of a two day project when I was about one third of the way through the entire inventory and had taken great pains to do the job right, I was told by the store manager, "If *you* can't do this in my time frame, I will find someone who can." I stopped doing it right, made it look good ("fronted" the material for appear-

"If you can't do it, I will find someone who can," is a major, major demotivator for most people.

ance), reported that I was finished at noon the next day, was praised for my initiative and industriousness—I am sure this manager thought that his "motivation" was successful—and I resolved never to say to anyone, "If you can't do it I will find someone who can." We all learn from negative as well as positive models.

Most of us have stories like this, stories that reflect the use of "demotivators" or short term motivators such as inducing fear, pounding on the desk, swearing, shouting, humiliation and other techniques which are often consciously used as a tactic for effect. However, as we will see later in this chapter use of these techniques often results in exactly the opposite behavior that we want to encourage, often produces short term compliance but long term sabotage or even outright rebellion.

Years later and with some wisdom and experience, I can now appreciate that Jim, the store manager, (I still remember his name) was young, around thirty-one or thirty-two and that this was his first store to manage. Obviously he himself was an enthusiastic beginner, trying to get results to impress his bosses. He was like many novice golfers, thinking they can score well by hitting the ball with their driver as hard as they can; having no understanding of the subtleties of the game. But Jim was only one of many managers that I have experienced over the years, and from all of them I have learned something.

As a matter of fact, what happens to us over time, assuming that we didn't have one of those rare but treasured corporate mentors to guide us through the process, to teach us what managing was all about, is that we begin a process of self teaching, a process of trial and error, incredible highs when things work well and determination to improve when things don't. In fact, as a new manager you were a lot like my friend, Jack, and every day was excitement and personal challenge. Every day was a learning experience, and, as you skulled that managerial ball back and forth over the green you likely thought to yourself — "I'm gaining on it."

The Newly Promoted or Hired Customer

One final enthusiastic beginner that is becoming more and more common as downsizing and mergers continue is the newly hired or promoted customer. You may have encountered these enthusiastic beginners who are customers, who often know less about the product and the process than you do and who are determined to make a name for themselves by making the boss happy—often by cutting costs on products like yours. While it is not in the scope of this book to talk about how to handle and coach this person, recognizing them for their enthusiasm rather than becoming frustrated at their lack of competence is more than half of the battle when it comes to working effectively with them.

The Competent Professional

Now, contrast my friend Jack, as a golfer, with Tim, one of the sixty-seven or so serious members of the "Men's Golf Association" at the club I belong to (there is a similarly dedicated group of women, the "Women's Golf Association", but I don't know any of them as well as the men. We don't want to take this any further.) At any rate these men will often play three times on the weekend during the summer (they must all be single) and if there is a tournament coming up, it is not unusual to find them practicing for about thirty hours (yes, thirty hours—as I said, they must all be single) during the week prior to the tournament. These men are all nine handicappers or better. Tim is one of them.

In times like these, with so many mergers and acquisitions as well as downsizings, we are often dealing with enthusiastic beginners at the customer or supplier site rather than more experienced contacts.

Unlike Jack, Tim does get mad if he hits one in the woods, and he doesn't even consider taking a mulligan, much less a 12 inch "gimme" and a ball in the water is sometimes followed by a club in the water (just the shallow part). He might carry a "ball retriever" in his bag, but wouldn't be caught dead with an "Alien Wedge." Tim not only knows the rules of golf, he can use them to his advantage and quote the rules to obtain benefit, somewhat like a parliamentarian uses "Robert's Rules of Order."

A ninety is disastrous for Tim (or any of these guys), an eighty barely tolerable (and they are, of course, playing from the "tips"). Tim expects the ball to go down the middle and he expects to get out of the sand in one. Sinking a twenty foot putt brings joy, but not ecstasy, and he is upset if his second shot doesn't give him a shot at a birdie (or a "tweeter" as he calls it). With all the heightened expectations and the resultant high level of stress, Tim still tells you that he loves the game. But the truth of the matter is that Tim has been an eight handicap for over two years. At forty-three, he wants to put himself into an even more elite group of golfers by pulling that handicap down to five (or less).

The Manager as Competent Professional

If you are a senior manager, you know that you also have this type of competent and committed individual working for you in a management capacity. They are the professional managers. The professional manager exhibits both competence and confidence, just like the touring professional golfer.

If you are a senior manager, if you are a vice president, executive vice president and/or any one of those "O" people (CEO, CFO, CIO, CLO, COO, CQO) you depend on the "Tim's" in your organization—as a matter of fact you may be in your position because, in your company, you were one of the "Tim's".

The competent professional is characterized by both competence and commitment.

Like our novice beginner, the competent professional is defined by a certain set of characteristics. They are usually good at problem solving, at dealing with conflict, at providing structure and producing results. They have mastered (or at least are comfortable with) one or two clubs and can use them with skill. In almost any situation they exude confidence; they are the ones you want to rely on when you need that twenty foot putt or that buried lie lifted from the sand and not only on the green but near the pin. They have often been mentored by other professionals, have read extensively on management and leadership and have had considerable training in areas such as communication, time management, delegation, project management and goal setting. Sometimes, rarely, they have had none of this training, they are simply naturals at managing others to obtain results — not unlike my nephew Roland, who, at the age of fifteen shot an eighty-two the first time he ever played the game of golf (a major demotivator for me!).

Coaching from Jack to Tim

Obviously, not everyone is a Jack or a Tim. Between the nine handicapper and the thirty handicapper are 10 handicappers, and 20 handicappers, the fifteen handicapper and the twenty-five. Again, if you are a manager you can probably see the range in your direct reports from the enthusiastic, but unskilled, to the competent and committed, and many in between.

Would we expect Jack to consistently shoot an 80? Not without considerable coaching, experience and training. Would we expect Tim, an eight handicapper, to take an 18 on a par four? Not unless he is related to Kevin Costner in "Tin Cup" or John Daly at Bay Hill.

The metaphor makes the weakness of treating everyone the same in terms of motivation obvious, yet this is often exactly what many managers do. Yes, there is a dramatic difference between Jack and Tim, and you will likely also find a similar difference on your staff — perhaps between Sharon and Suzanne.

Obviously the issue of motivation is much more complex than simply identifying the current status of each of the people you supervise - although this is an important and critical step. As a matter of fact, it is such an important step that one of the first things you can do to improve the performance of your people is to identify where they fit on a continuum from enthusiastic beginner to competent professional.

In order to do this you may want to create a quadrant on which you place your people in their most time intensive roles or you might want to use a more detailed graph such as the Blanchard Situational Leadership© model that shows leadership styles appropriate to different levels of employee development. Whichever method you use, if you are going to consciously motivate your people to higher productivity, it needs to be structured, not random. The first step in the process is to identify where they are and what they need at a basic level. The four basic levels of performance and the leadership needs of each are briefly described below.[1]

> *Enthusiastic beginners need coaching, direction and follow up. Do not ignore them.*

The Enthusiastic Beginner

Because the enthusiastic beginner is low on skill and high on commitment, this individual needs highly directive behavior from his or her manager. Highly directive behaviors include planning and organizing work in advance, en-

---

[1]For a more detailed treatment of this concept, see Blanchard's "Leadership and the One Minute Manager."

suring that the employee knows what is expected in advance of the job, defining timeliness, following up to ensure that these timelines are met, providing instruction in specific job tasks, and setting goals and objectives.

It is a mistake to assume that the enthusiastic beginner can be left alone and succeed. Coaching the enthusiastic beginner is definitely one of those situations where the time has to be invested before the job to make sure that it is done right, or you wind up coaching anyway after the job is done wrong. In short, enthusiastic beginners need highly directive coaching from their managers; they need to know the "what" and the "how" of the job. Motivation for the enthusiastic beginner is related to making them feel successful by providing sufficient direction and then letting them know they were successful at the task.

The "Tween"

People, like golfers, don't progress on a direct line from enthusiastic beginner to competent professional. There are usually at least two stages in between. These stages might better be described as plateaus, because there is definitely a leveling out of performance and/or motivation – and it takes a while to proceed to the next level. As the employee begins to understand that the job is far more complex than he realized, enthusiasm often wanes. The individual now knows that a lot more is expected of him than he first thought. This stage is often called "conscious incompetence," it is where the employee is aware of how much there is to learn.

I think that the concept of the "tween" comes from the Hobbit. Tweens were those aged twenty to thirty, not yet adults, but certainly not teenagers. They were in between, thus, "tween". (If you have had a child go through this age, you know how accurate this description is.)

Jack, my golfing friend, is a "tween" in terms of golf. The last time we talked he was beginning to feel the effects of this stage. He related how frustrating it was not to be able to hit the ball straight, how he was tired of hitting the ball fat, then thin, and how aggravating it was to hit the ball back and forth across the green. He has started lobbing the ball out of the sand (with his hand) and taking a penalty in order to save strokes. He had signed up for lessons, which, by the way, is exactly what beginners need. Like the enthusiastic beginner in business, the enthusiastic beginner in golf needs a highly directive approach. If they don't get significant instruction from a pro, they will continue to experience frustration and lack of skill development. They need this time with the pro in order to improve the time spent actually playing the game.

In order for an employee to progress from Enthusiastic Beginner to Tween, coaching is needed. But not just any coaching, the manager (the employee's pro) must be highly directive with the Tween at this stage.

After playing golf for about two years I decided I needed some more lessons. I signed up for one of those three day golf schools in Florida where they promise a small student/teacher ratio and lots of on course instruction. I was lumped in with a group of seven high handicappers and a teaching pro who was, to say the least, laissez-faire. He took us out to the practice range and told us to hit with our natural swing, that if we continued to practice and aim at the target, success would come. Occasionally he would give direction and on the last day we had a video made of our swing and he dissected it for us in front of the group (so that we could all learn from the "efforts" of others). I left there disillusioned about golf schools and a worse golfer than when I went. His failure to be more directive increased a general dissatisfaction I was having with the game. I went to improve, not to

"Tween" is the stage at which many golfers quit the game – mentally, physically, emotionally or all three.

return a worse golfer than when I left. (This instructor also taught me a lesson about "nice." This teaching pro was the quintessential nice guy. Everybody liked him; but nice wasn't what we needed to improve at this stage—direction was.)

"Tween" is the stage where a lot of golfers, who announced that they loved the game when they started, find themselves after six or eight months of regular play. This is a time when a lot of golfers quit. It is also a time when a lot of employees, who walked in the door full of enthusiasm four months ago, quit. For many, this is because they can't face a challenge by themselves, and they don't know what to do to advance to the next stage, so, they get stuck here. These employees frequently "retire on active duty" and turn their criticism outward, blaming the management of the company, the systems of the company, their direct supervisor, anyone but themselves, for their failure to progress. This stage of indifference, of facing personal failure and not knowing what to do about it, is a critical stage of growth for the employee/manager relationship. The issue for the manager is: Can you get them through this stage?

You can if you continue to use the highly directive coaching behaviors detailed above and begin to combine this coaching with reinforcement techniques such as encouraging, supporting, listening, explaining why, and involving the person in some decisions based on their (limited) experience. This means moving from highly directive to partially directive and highly supportive behaviors. You cannot choose one or the other; you cannot choose to be either highly directive or highly supportive. Like the golfer at this stage, the employee needs both. The best strategies to implement directive and supportive coaching at this stage are to encourage the individual to participate in joint problem solving and to listen carefully to their concerns and ideas, providing very direct feedback on both. If you can coach them through this stage they will become:

The Developing Employee

At this stage, the employee is aware that she has learned new skills, but her motivation, her enthusiasm, is not predictable. Some days it is high, some days it is low. She knows that she has learned new skills, but she is now consciously aware of how much more there is to learn. Because she now understands how much more there is to learn, she continues to experience frustration, particularly when she is unable to complete a project in a predetermined time. At this point she is apt to say something like, "Am I ever going to learn how to do this?"

As the coach of this individual, you have to move from the highly directive approach to one that is less directive and more supportive. This includes activities such as: providing more assurance, giving recognition when you catch her doing something right, spending more time listening and discussing the problems she is having, and helping her objectively look at aspects of the job that are frustrating her such as timeliness, procedures and her own skill level.

Increase the skill levels of the developing employee so that her confidence improves or face the fact that both performance and attitude will decline.

Your goal at this stage is to increase her skill level so that her confidence and motivation improve. This is a time when you want her to take over a small project that you help her plan and problem solve, but allow her to actually manage. It is a time when you want to ask her to share with you how she thinks she did and what she would do differently if she had the project to do again. Your goal is to take her to a level of performance where she is unconsciously competent in her job.

The Self-Reliant Professional

The final stage in this developmental sequence is self-reliance. At this level, the employee is both competent to do the task and enthusiastic about doing it. You can now rely on this person's perspective on the job and on problems to be solved. The employee is basically autonomous and your role is to encourage the employee to take the lead in setting personal and departmental goals and in solving problems.

However, having a professional, an autonomously operating, highly competent and motivated person does not mean that you become an observer. Remember Ken Blanchard's dictum that "Feedback is the breakfast of champions." You need to recognize and reinforce this individual, you need to make him aware of your appreciation for his contributions to the company and you need to provide new opportunities and new challenges so that he stays motivated. One of the best strategies is to encourage him to become the coach of an "enthusiastic beginner" and take this beginner through this same developmental process that he went through.

The process is cyclic and task specific. The new engineer who moved through the stages to become a competent professional, begins again as an enthusiastic beginner when he is promoted to quality manager.

The process, of course, is cyclic. The professional engineer who spent five years being mentored to truly learn his craft gets promoted to manager of design engineering and starts all over as an Enthusiastic Beginner. The accountant who began her career out of college in public accounting gets promoted to Senior Manager and finds herself with five direct reports right out of college. Even as president, a mentor may be preparing you to lead the board. These are skills that every manager needs and the process of mentoring the new employee or manager from highly directive, low supportive then to high directive, high supportive, next to high supportive, low directive, and finally to low directive and low supportive is a process that needs to be continuously repeated in order to increase the professionalism of all employees.

The Next Step

The model above might be considered a macro model of motivation. It delineates specific coaching behaviors that are needed in order to help an employee progress through sequential stages of development.

But this global understanding of what each person needs is just the beginning of the process of motivating people, it is the first shot, your drive. To be truly effective you need to understand the "short game" or the "micro game"of motivation as well. If this point is so obvious, why is it so often ignored by managers? If, in order to take each employee to the next level of performance, you must structure and implement an individualized process of recognition, reinforcement and feedback, why is it not done?

The objections to this practice of developing an individualized motivational plan for employees can be summarized by these three: First, "I don't have time to do this kind of planning;" second, "I don't know how to do it even if I did have time;" and third, "I've tried this stuff before and nothing really changes."

In motivation, as in most management activities, doing nothing is doing something. It is the abrogation of the leadership opportunity.

Thus, the goals of the remainder of this chapter are to deal with these very real objections in order to ensure that, over time, performance improves. But the bottom line is this: How long will it take Jack to get to the level of Tim without taking lessons? How is Tim going to get off the eight handicap plateau he is on without direction? The classic management dictum that "doing nothing is doing something" applies; so, let's begin with what you can do and then move on to how you can do this in a time effective process so that you don't lose time in providing motivation, but actually gain it.

Why Do We Play?

To begin this process, let's return to the game of golf and answer the question: Why do you even bother to play this silly game of chasing the little white, dimpled ball around that huge green pasture, a game which Ralph Nader has characterized as requiring extraordinary "manual/visual integration" (hand/eye coordination to the rest of us). So, why do we play golf?

Much of it has to do with who we are when we golf and what golf tells us about ourselves. As Lanny Watkins says, we play golf "because golf mirrors our personality," or as Ben Hogan remarked, "Golf...is the best of all games: the most demanding, the most interesting and the most rewarding." More philosophically, (try this one on for yourself), Hale Irwin calls golf a game where "performance is the outward manifestation of who (the golfer), in his heart, really is."

But is there something else, something on the motivational side (and related to business) that also answers the question: "Why do we play golf?" Psychologists say that we play golf because it contains the compulsion-developing element called "intermittent positive reinforcement." What does this mean? It means that when we hit the perfect two hundred sixty yard drive or the wedge shot that lands twelve feet above the pin and rolls back to just eighteen inches away, or we hit that four iron one hundred ninety yards, splitting the seven yards of air separating two trees, or when we sink that twenty-two foot putt from the fringe with a perfect read and perfect touch, it means that when we hit these shots we are motivated to come back again because they are so, well, so pleasurable. And they are.

Those six or seven (well maybe four or five, okay, two or three) great shots each round bring us back again, particularly if one of them occurs on the seventeenth or eighteenth hole which, almost invariably, they do. That perfect drive or beautiful, splitting wedge shot brings us back for more because they instill in us the belief that we can hit these shots again and again, no matter that the other eighty times we hit the ball it was nothing to write home about. As Gary McCord says, "Golf teases you with brilliant moments of shot making, and then, in the next moment, it wilts your knees with swift failure."

In addition to this, golf is the cleverest of all motivators because it keeps raising the bar. What was a great shot two years ago doesn't seem so great now that you are trying to learn how NOT to hit the ball straight, but to bend it around a solid object such as a tree or a liquid object such as a lake. Thus, in golf, we accept the fact that we are always going to have to try to improve. We aren't satisfied with what we used to shoot (until we reach 70 or so, then we start to long for what we used to shoot).

In golf, there is the long game, the short game, the shorter game, and the shortest game. In golf there is hitting from the fairway, hitting from the tee, hitting from the sand, hitting from the rough, hitting the uphill lie, downhill lie, hitting the straight shot (the most important skill of all) and hitting crooked (an advanced skill and one that appeals to leaders – it is going around the system and you have to be very adept and very confident in order to do it). And, of course, there is diagnosing, knowing what shot this particular situation calls for.

Now, each of these is a discrete skill in and out of itself. You may be able to hit the ball very well from a flat lie on the fairway, but what happens when you hit that beautiful drive two hundred and fifty yards and it winds up just to the left of the fairway on a slight uphill incline? Of course, it changes your shot. Now you have to take more club because the ball is going to go higher, play the ball off your left toe and swing at 75% because you need to keep your balance.

"*The more I practice, the luckier I become.*"

The professionals, as we all know, not only can do all of this well, but they can do some

Somehow the myth of money as the major motivator maintains credibility.

of it incredibly well. A bunker, for example, never intimidated Gary Player. If he couldn't get down in two from a trap (and he often holed the ball from the bunker), he became angry with himself. As a matter of fact, some competitors grumbled that he was too good from the sand and must have some special technique — and he did. It was called practice. I don't know if he was the first, but he is quoted as saying in regard to his bunker play, "The more I practice, the luckier I become."

The Lesson From Why We Play

There is a profound leadership lesson in all of this. The lesson is that effective leaders are able to diagnose the needs of their people and help them "make the shot." They are not the coach who is striding up and down the sidelines shouting orders and berating people. They are the coaches who have a complete motivational toolbox and use these tools to improve performance for a given employee in a given situation. They know that success builds upon success and that, for each employee they must continually raise the bar. They understand that each employee needs to understand that he or she is never through with the challenge of learning.

To begin the review of individual motivators and motivational skills, let's begin with the one that most employers (and many employees) believe is the key to motivation: compensation.

Compensation

There is a surprising discrepancy between management's perception of the importance of compensation and the employee's perception of the importance of compensation. In a recent study, employers cited lack of compensation as the number one reason that employees left their jobs. However, exit interviews with these same employees indicated that their reasons for leaving had more to do with their relationship with their manager than compensation. These employees were far more concerned with the fact that their managers didn't listen to them and that their perspectives on improvement weren't sought out than with what they were being paid. Edward Deci's seminal work on individual motivation, *"Why We Do What We Do"*, demonstrates that when compensation is used as a controlling device ("If you do this I will reward you") it can actually decrease intrinsic motivation. But the myth of money as a major motivator somehow maintains credibility. So, let's look at golf.

Does anyone pay you to play golf? What an absurd idea. Nobody is going to pay you to play golf until you become a professional – and even then, many professionals, even with today's purses, labor quietly for little or no gain after expenses.

Let me ask the question again. Does anyone pay you to play golf? *Au contraire*, you pay to play golf and you often pay big. Fifty or sixty dollars for some municipal courses, one hundred to two hundred (and up) for private courses and you can't even get the tee time you want and let's not even talk about the thousands who trek to courses such as Pebble Beach.

Study after study has indicated that money is an important indicator of how much the employee is valued by the company. Employees need to make what others who do similar work make. And, of course, beyond that, significant bonuses act as a motivator. But money is not *the* motivator. There are other motivators of equal or greater value.

Beyond Compensation

Some twenty-six million Americans play golf (if you don't believe this figure, just try and get an early morning tee time on a Sunday in April — even at your home course) and the vast majority of these twenty-six million pay to do it. Why?

Golf lets us know exactly what is expected of us. Not how to achieve it, not someone standing over our shoulder to say how to hit the ball, but just what the expectation is and how well we are doing in achieving it.

Why? Because golf is the perfect game. Because you are challenged at every hole no matter your skill level. Because, in golf, there is a continuing opportunity to improve. Because you have a grading system that measures your improvement. Because of the concept of par, that is, what you should achieve on each hole and for the entire round is a reach for most of us — a cause to stretch our capabilities. Because feedback and reinforcement are part of the game and this feedback is immediate. If we hit that great shot, even if we are alone on the course, we know it, we experience the joy of having done something well, we are reinforced. If we hit a poor shot, we also receive immediate feedback.

Golf is the perfect game because perfect (or nearly perfect) shots, give us a vision of what we can achieve. They are intrinsically motivating. Golf is the perfect game because, and I cannot tell you how critical this is as a motivator, golf lets us know exactly what is expected of us, not how we are to achieve it, just what it is. Golf lets us know what par is for the hole, and by extension, what is truly excellent in terms of birdies or perhaps even eagles.

There are other reasons as well. camaraderie and companionship, trophies and individual rivalries, the incredible beauty and variety of golf courses.

I believe that, if the majority of golfers could articulate why they play golf, if they could look inside to see what it is that makes them set the alarm for five A.M. on a Saturday after a rough week at the office, they would probably identify some of the following:

Challenge
Opportunity to Improve
Immediacy of Feedback and Environment
Vision of What We Can Become
Camaraderie and Environment
Clarity of the Goal
The Thrill of Achievement
Intrinsic Motivation

And here is the lesson for business. I have worked with many companies and with many managers over the past fifteen years and the most frequent comments I have heard from managers regarding motivation are these three:

1. "I have very little control over their salaries (in some cases, no control). How can I motivate my people?"

2. "I am a full time manager but I also have full time responsibilities other than managing people. I am a doer and not just a supervisor, even if I had the inclination to motivate my people, I don't have time and besides, what difference does it make, some stay, some go, some like security, some like change. Off the record the company pays me for results, not for having happy and satisfied employees. So why spend time and effort on motivation?"

3. "Why do I have to motivate them? They get a paycheck don't they?"

You see these questions beg the issue; they are valid but irrelevant responses. Let me show you why.

First, I want to tell you a story of a balloonist who suddenly and unexpectedly suffered damage to his balloon during a cross country race. As quickly as he could, he put his balloon down on the ground. A passing motorist, seeing the descending balloon and gondola, stopped his car on the side of the road and ran to the balloon.

Upon reaching the balloon, the balloonist asked the man, "Where am I?"

To which the man replied, "Well sir, you are in the middle of a corn field."

And the balloonist asked, "Tell me sir, are you a manager?"

And the man replied, not a little proudly, "Yes, but how did you know?"

And the balloonist replied, "Because your response was at one and the same time totally accurate and absolutely irrelevant."

And so it is with the manager who says "they get a paycheck, don't they. This attitude that the manager does not have to motivate his or her employees ignores the real issue — the demonstrable link between satisfied employees, satisfied customers, and profitability. Saying, as many managers do, "I don't have time for that touchy-feely stuff," is not unlike saying, "I don't have time to manage my budget" in terms of its importance to the company's success.

The Profit Link

Some years ago I was working with a Fortune 500 company whose profitability had been impressive for two years running after a new CEO came in. Then the profits started falling, and falling, and falling more steeply. Why? The reason, we determined, was the CEO's style of operation. He was an intimidator. He was physically large and extremely bright, an engineer by training. He consciously chose to motivate through intimidation using a financially based carrot and stick attitude ("if you do, you get.... if you don't you lose..."). He consciously used his size and intelligence to cower grown men and women into submission. High ranking, experienced staff members would walk out of a meeting with the CEO and right into the rest room because they were so physically upset by one of his tirades. One high ranking manager described it: "After twelve minutes of non stop reaming and threats, my stomach felt like I had been on a little boat in a big ocean in very rough seas for two hours."

Intimidation worked for two years. Profits went up and up. Stockholders were happy. The board was happy, but the employees were not. Then the economy started improving. Suddenly there were other opportunities in other companies. Top people, talented people, began to go elsewhere (remember Drucker's observation that today's knowledge workers are "volunteers," i.e., the talented ones in today's economy can work where they want). Serious holes began to open in corporate staff and line positions. Positions that were not easy to fill because of the reputation of the CEO had somehow been "leaked" to prospective applicants. When new people did come in, their average tenure was three months. Turnover increased, profits fell.

> *The question is not whether you have the time, but how you are going to make the time.*

What happened to the CEO? The board removed him after two dismal years. But, his perceived ability to make a company profitable survived the down years. He went through two more companies. I lost touch.

And the company? They learned. They brought in a new CEO who understood the need for balance between task and people and the company reemerged as a star in their industry. Today, the point is nearly inarguable. The terminology is irrelevant. Whether it is called providing motivation, leadership, vision, or some other term, leaders must establish environments where each employee is encouraged to perform at his or her highest level. The question is not do you have time, but how are you going to make time.

Now, let's return to golf and to the lessons for motivation in the game of golf. As noted above, it is naive to dismiss pay.

Money is a motivator, but it is not the end all and be all of motivation. Like other forms of extrinsic motivation (threats, fear, intimidation) money has a short term directional effect on behavior (the one who is motivated goes in the direction of the one doing the motivating). Please do not misunderstand, compensation *is* a motivator, one of the tools in your managerial bag, and like any motivator it has to be used judiciously. In today's environment, it is critical that the compensation of a worker is equal to or greater than what the compensation is for the same type of work at a different company.

Extra money, extra compensation, whether it is in the form of overtime, or shared returns in the profitability of the company also works as a major motivator as long as you understand that people will choose money until they realize that they are losing personal antinomy in doing so.

When Gordon Bethune became president of Continental Airlines, he focused all employees' attention on the need to improve on-time arrivals (the most critical factor in airline customer satisfaction outside of the assumed level of safety) by offering a $65 per month bonus for all employees of Continental if they could improve enough to finish in the top 5 airlines nationwide in on time arrival according to DOT figures.

Because they were losing about five million dollars per month on delays, the figure of 2.5 million dollars was selected as giving half of the profits from the improvement back to the employees, this approach seemed eminently reasonable. And, of course it worked. Please note that no one publicly said, "Well, that's their job anyway" or "Don't we pay them enough as it is?" No, they simply identified the critical variable, measured it and rewarded all employees (not just office employes, executives, or pilots) for the improved performance. That is how it must be done. The most frequently heard complaint in terms of compensation plans is, "Why should I work my butt off so that seven executives can get huge bonuses?"

Every company must deal with this issue its own way, but studies indicate that, all other things being equal, a philosophy of "when the company does well financially, we all do well financially," results in greater involvement of the employees in their jobs and less employee turnover if the bonus is managed in such a way as to not detract from intrinsic motivation.

The Danger With Bonuses

The danger with bonuses, commissions, profit sharing and the like is that they are less effective when seen as entitlement, as an expectation. At this point it often not only loses its effect, if taken away, it frequently has a very negative effect on motivation.

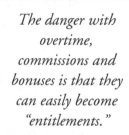

As an example of this, I was consulting in a company where the average hourly worker was putting in 12-18 hours of overtime per week. At fifteen hours, these workers were nearly doubling their regular paycheck. After two years of this they began to feel like it wasn't going away. The company was doing well, orders were continuing to roll in, the future looked bright. So, predictably, as most of us do, these workers began living up to or, (as

The danger with overtime, commissions and bonuses is that they can easily become "entitlements."

conscientious Americans do) over their income. New cars and trucks were bought. Large screen TV's, appliances and stereos were purchased, rooms were added to houses.

And then there was an accident at the plant. The cause of the accident? An investigation determined that the root cause was fatigue. Suddenly, management reconsidered its policy on overtime. Over a period of about two months, new workers were hired and overtime was all but eliminated. Now the old workforce was hostile. In their minds, they were entitled to that pay, they didn't mind working those hours. One accident with one worker did not call for a 40-50% reduction in pay. Soon, there were productivity issues, quiet slow downs, then a strike. Most of the workers had found second jobs and were working the same if not more hours. It took two years for that plant to return to the productivity it had enjoyed before the accident.

The moral? Money is a motivator, no doubt about it. Targeted compensation programs can produce dramatic results in a short period of time because they focus the energy of people on a specific issue whether that issue is customer service, productivity, on time arrivals, or elimination of service or manufacturing defects. But its returns are often short lived. Plateaus in performance follow periods of targeted compensation as the easy fixes are taken care of. Now management is faced with a new challenge – how do we continue to improve?

Managers often say to me, "She would leave me for an extra fifty cents an hour." And regrettably, in some industries, under some circumstances, this is true. But not in most cases, not in most industries. They won't leave for a dollar an hour, or two dollars an hour, not if you take the lessons of golf and apply them to the workplace.

From Herzberg to Golf

When Fredrick Herzberg first did his classic study of motivation in the early fifties, money was less important, less an indicator of value and self worth than it is today; nevertheless, his research and all the replicating studies that have been done since then suggest that business and golf have a lot in common.

The manager who says, "I can't motivate them because I don't control their salaries," is not unlike the twenty handicapper who says, "I can't drive the ball more than two hundred twenty yards – I'll never break ninety."

I have conducted hundred of workshops on motivation. Not "rah rah" motivation, but workshops on how to increase performance through providing motivation on the job. As a part of

Table 1: Motivators in Golf and Business.

Motivators in Golf

Scoring Well on Each Hole and Total Score

Score Better than Handicap

Score Worse than Handicap

The Immediate Feedback from Each Shot

The Opportunity Presented Each Time
the Ball is Addressed

The Challenge of Playing the Ball From the Sand,
Rough, or a Downhill Lie

Playing with Friends, Camaraderie

Winning

Lessons—The Sense of Deliberate Improvement

Improved Score "Great Shot, That'll Play,
I'd Take That Shot"

Ball in trees, rough, challenging position

Motivators in Business

Feedback/Reinforcement

Sense of Accomplishment

Opportunity for Improvement

Immediate Feedback

Challenge, Opportunity, Excitement

Opportunity to Develop New Skills

And, Opportunity to Prove Ourselves

Good Working Environment

Success, Achievement, Recognition

Training, Learning New Skills

Goal – Feedback, Recognition – Immediate

these workshops one of my favorite exercises is to ask the participants to list each of their top five job-related motivators and "demotivators." I then list these on the board or flip chart. There is a predictable level of consistency in the responses.

Time and time again the universal number one response is "money." In answer to the question, "What are your top five motivators at work?" people respond first with, "money, more money, increase in salary, bigger paycheck, share of the profits, bonuses, greater compensation," etc. (it is amazing how many ways this can be said).

But immediately following the many terms for compensation is a long list of personal motivators. These are motivators that, like golf, reach into the interpersonal realm of intrinsic motivation, of setting up the conditions where an individual is motivated by inner drive and the joy that comes from meaningful work conducted in an environment that encourages the use of their talents. Following money, the list quickly moves to psychological incentives such as: challenge, opportunity, recognition, respect, promotions, feedback, empowerment, being listened to, ability to make decisions, learning new things, working with others in a team environment, choice.

The list is strikingly close to the reasons that people mention for playing golf.

In short, and obviously, golf teaches us not only what motivates people to work intrinsically at a high level, but also why these incentives are so critical. Golf, most games for that matter, is based on incentives. It is why we say we "play golf" rather than "work at golf." It is no different in the world of work. People who have the motivators listed above typically love their jobs —they are motivated to improve on a regular basis.

What is the cost to the company of using these motivators? Perhaps it costs something for training, but what is the cost of feedback or recognition? Nothing. What is the cost of providing challenge, opportunity, and empowerment? Nothing in terms of dollars, something in terms of the manager's time, but even here it is an investment with a significant return waiting on that investment – and a significant loss possible without the investment.

All of this, the research, the studies, personal experience, the analogy of why we play golf, suggests that the motivators needed by people in order to increase their involvement in their jobs is fairly universal and definitely well defined. This leads us to the second question, "Why do you as a manager care about motivation anyway?"

> *In the era of "volunteer workers" it is more important than ever to know and meet the motivational needs of all employees. To ignore this fact is to invite the financial and systemic costs of high turnover.*

Why Leaders Care About Motivation

In today's business environment, after a decade of layoffs, downsizing, right-sizing, reengineering, mergers, and acquisitions, this is a reasonable question. Fifteen years ago, in a narrowly defined hierarchy where a manager typically supervised ten to twenty people directly, the manager might easily be held responsible for the performance of his or her direct reports. Today, managers often "supervise" thirty or forty people. Supervisory relationships are more fluid. Reporting relationships are often project-specific or muddied by the impact of self directed teams and "temporary" staff. The truth is that all of these changes have pushed the individual employee further from fulfillment of important psychological needs. Yet, because of the structure of companies today, meeting these needs is more important than ever even though many companies and individuals within the company don't realize it — yet.

Have you ever, as a manager, supervisor, vice president, or in any other position where you are responsible for the output of those reporting to you, said one or more of the following:

"They get their motivation every two weeks in their pay-check."

"I get paid for producing results, for the bottom line, not for motivating people."

"That touchy/feely stuff is for HR and training, not for me. By the time they get to this level they shouldn't need motivation. I believe in all that stuff, I just simply don't have time."

If you have made these statements, or statements similar in tone and meaning, you are leaving money on the table – yes, *motivation is an economic issue.* Motivation is not about soft skills, charm school, your "feminine" side (even for women) or any of the other rationalizations that people use for not stepping out of their comfort zones of focusing on task at the expense of maintaining the "people machine" carrying out the task.

No, motivation purely and simply is about results; it is about productivity. It is about the investment of time in order to produce a return on the investment you have in your most expensive (for many companies) asset, your employees. There is considerable support for this statement, one from the world of psychology, the other from the world of business. Let's look first at the psychology of motivation and results.

In his best selling book, *The Psychology of Self-Esteem*, Dr. Nathaniel Branden established a strong correlation between self-esteem and productivity. In other words, **people who feel good about themselves produce greater results.** Now, while it is true that you, as a manager, cannot give self esteem to anyone (I remember first becoming a manager and working with my new secretary to help her feel better about her competence. I praised, I recognized, I coached, I provided feedback, I even increased her pay. But all to no avail, she would see the negative in any situation, every silver lining had a cloud. However, while you cannot truly "motivate" anyone, you can set up the condi-

tions where self-esteem and intrinsic motivation can emerge.
How? You likely have already guessed, by using the motivators
that are listed in Table 1.

As a manager you also care about motivation because of a proven correlation between profitability, customer satisfaction and
employee satisfaction. In other words, not
surprisingly, satisfied employees generate
more profitability for the company than do
dissatisfied employees. In the book *"The Loyalty Effect,"* Frederick Reichheld makes a compelling case for the bottom line contributions
of satisfied employees to both revenue and
profitability. He strongly suggests that employee oriented elements in a company including loyalty to the employee, use of moti-

*It is more difficult to
implement a
comprehensive plan
of employee
motivation than it is
to design a new
product – it may
also be more critical.*

vational strategies, and organizational alignment are all directly
linked to productivity, and therefore to profitability. He further
states that the goal of the organization in terms of profitability
should not be low cost per unit, but "low cost as a percentage of
revenues."

So, is this motivation fluff? Is it "touchy-feely nonsense"?
Is it baby sitting? Hardly. As a matter of fact, it is a lot more
difficult to correctly implement a comprehensive, integrated,
effective plan of employee motivation than it is to make the
product, develop spreadsheets or read the results. The number
of variables is just much greater. That's why this hole is a par 5,
that's why it is a tough hole. As a matter of fact, that's why so
many managers call it touchy-feely and charm school stuff—
they don't know how to do it and they don't want to do it. It is
a lot easier to just tell people what to do (and a lot less effective
in the long term) than it is to set up the conditions where someone is motivated to do the project. Managers need skills and
their own motivation on why it needs to be done.

The Skills You Need to Motivate

So, let's return to the concept of discrete motivational skills that can be used by the individual manager.

There is a famous golf school that advertises something to the effect that "the game is played on a course, why try to learn it on a driving range?" But this begs the question.

Anyone who has ever tried knows that you cannot learn to play golf on a golf course. In truth, you develop your skills on the practice range, putting green and chipping area and you "implement these skills on the course."

If you are a manager, you need to first understand the discrete skills that you need to know in order to help your people "achieve (or better) par" and then help them to improve using these skills and finally, monitor them (keep score) to see how well they are doing.

The following is a list of those discreet skills. As you read through the list begin to answer the question; "With which of the people I manage could I best use this skill?"

1. **Feedback**—Acknowledgment (written or verbal) of contribution to the organization. Usually of two types:

   A. **Recognition**–Acknowledging actions or contributions that are perceived as unique or special (See it and say it specifically, sincerely and immediately.).

   B. **Reinforcement** – To encourage someone for something done in order to increase the likelihood that the behavior will be repeated.

2. **Challenge**—Challenge is also of two types: first, challenging someone by giving her increased responsibility; or second, providing an unfamiliar task that causes her to stretch her skills. Curtis Strange once said, "Sometimes, in order to win, you have to put yourself in a position to lose." There is so much in that quote about

challenge. In golf, challenge is a subtle but persistent theme. You can also challenge an individual with a promotion (Remember that this will put the individual into the enthusiastic beginner role again and she will need a highly directive approach).

3. **Achievement**—Oriented goals-that relate to the strategic goals of the organization. These goals are cooperatively established and regularly reviewed for accomplishment.

4. **Respect**—A major motivator for almost all employees is being respected. This takes the operational forms of being actively listened to, having their ideas considered (and never ridiculed), being talked to as an equal, and never, never, either directly or indirectly, being put down or having their sense of personal dignity affronted. Respect does not mean always having their ideas accepted. Publicly or privately humiliating an employee destroys respect not just between the manager and the employee, but between the manager and most employees.

5. **Personal Autonomy**—The need for having some control over our own lives is a constant struggle for many people. For this reason, providing some of this control is a major motivator. You can help motivate people through increased personal autonomy by giving them the freedom to explore new avenues, by backing off on some unnecessary control mechanism, by showing appreciation for the divergent thought or creative solution. (Of course this cannot always be done in today's business climate, but where it can, it will increase the intrinsic motivation of people and thus increase loyalty and productivity.)

6. **Meaningful Work**—A high value for many people is that their work makes a contribution to "something."

This something could be to improve a process, it could be to increase customer satisfaction, it could be to help the company become more profitable or to promote the protection of the environment. Few people want to spend their days reworking what others have already done or shuffling papers with no purpose. One of the strategies that you can quickly implement to increase motivation is to involve people in meaningful work or to explain to them why the company is dependent upon them for the work that they do.

Related to this is the need to be involved in an enterprise greater than themselves. Vision statements provide a rationale for being involved in a truly meaningful task.

7. **Empowerment**—This overused word of the nineties does not mean "turning over the asylum to the inmates" as one manager said. It does mean giving employees expanded decision making authority within defined limits dictated by demonstrated competency and risk analysis. (I asked one group of Customer Service Representatives [CSR's] if they were empowered. "Yes," they replied, "we can solve customer problems up to $50.00." Customers, on the other hand were reporting frustration because CSR's could not help them solve problems. Fifty dollars didn't even cover the cost of a hotshot shipment of product. With additional training and risk analysis this was raised to $500.00. Customers were happier and turnover went down. CSR's were truly empowered.) Every company has opportunities to empower. Empower in stages; let people show you that they can handle the responsibility and extend it. But remember, once extended, the price of taking it back is

Empowerment is not "turning the asylum over to the inmates."

enormous, so make sure that they can handle it before you truly empower.

8. **Awareness and Use of Personal Motivators** ("Via Spegas")—I have a client and friend who learned to play golf two years ago. She decided that she wanted to play in a league with other company employees. So she learned the rudiments of the game and started playing. This particular league played a course on which one hole featured a 120 yard carry over water from the women's tees. Four weeks in a row she failed to carry the water. Finally, on the fifth week, she promised herself a pair of moderately expensive women's pumps (Via Spegas) if she carried the water. As she stepped up to the tee, her only thought was Via Spegas, which she repeated almost like a mantra as she swung at the ball. It carried the water, of course, and the next day she bought herself that pair of shoes. You cannot, of course, as a manager, buy everyone shoes, but you can understand their individual motivation.

A Compelling Vision

These eight techniques, providing feedback in the form of recognition and reinforcement, providing an atmosphere of challenge, encouraging people to achieve, giving respect to all employees, providing some personal autonomy, letting people know why the work is important, understanding personal motivators and providing a structure where empowerment and personal responsibility are the norm, will motivate your employees, but there is another strategy that we learn from golf that acts as a company wide motivator, a catalyst for change at all levels of the organization. It is called vision. Golfers are motivated by the vision of the perfect drive, the six iron shot that rolls within four inches of the cup, the twenty foot putt that miraculously finds its way to the hole. Vision is a motivator.

We discussed vision from the leader's point of view in Chapter One. Vision is important, not just for the structure it provides for the strategic and planning side of the business, but for the impact it has on the employees, on the person hearing the statement of vision. As we mentioned in Chapter 1, the vision must provide the listener with more than just revenue and net after tax information. In sharing a vision, tell compelling stories of how you were challenged as a manager, what you went through, how it changed you. Tell stories of how the company grew, of how you grew, of how others have grown. For example:

Most of the successful entrepreneurs I have worked with began with a compelling vision, even if this vision was not articulated on paper, they had a mental image of where they were going and this picture drove their performance.

On the "New" course at the Raveneaux Country Club in Houston, the twelfth is a three hundred ninety two-yard sharp dogleg right par four. The right side of the fairway is guarded by an ancient oak and some large pines that, during the summer, fully cover one third of that fairway at about one hundred ninety-five yards from the tee box. Your best shot is to fly the ball by the left side of that oak and sit it down in the middle of the fairway. Hit it any further to the right and you are in deep rough or OB (Out of bounds). Hit it to the left and it adds yardage to your second shot. I will always remember the three consecutive days when I intentionally put my tee shot forty yards beyond that tree and then put my six iron shot on the green for an easy par.

That story tells more about my golf game than my handicap ever could. I would hope that it would be an inspirational story for those golfers who learn the game in their forties with a handicap beyond calculation. We all have stories as a manager. We all have stories of the companies we work for. These stories help the employee have a personal vision of his or her role within the company.

One company where I consulted started out as a one man operation in East Texas in the early forties. Roads were not plentiful at the time and, when customers called for products to be delivered to the oilfields, the founder would drive the roads to Lufkin and carry the merchandise the rest of the way on horseback. That story was told time and time again to establish in all employees a service mentality that set the tone for the company then and continues to set the tone today. Every employee who works for this company knows these stories—they used to be told by the "old man" himself during orientation, and during moments when employees gathered for special events. These stories, more than any amount of lecturing, said, "we stand for customer service." They were, and continue to be, effective company-wide motivators.

Implementing Motivational Strategies

One of the most frequently heard refrains of trainers is a paraphrase of Albert Einstein's words on change. It is usually rendered, "The definition of insanity is to keep doing what you have been doing and expect different results." Certainly this is true. However, by this definition, most of us are insane because we find ourselves in comfort zones in any number of areas that are hard to break out of. For most of us, one of those comfort zones is how we manage our people. We look at our managerial strategies and say, "well, I am not doing so poorly, after all, we are producing results." So, without a crisis and without honest feedback from our people (and frankly, often without honest feedback from our supervisors) about how we are doing, we don't see any dramatic reason to change.

Golf doesn't let you get away with this type of thinking. Golf gives you scores, a handicap and a vision for improvement. As golfers, we

The question for most managers today is "how do I make the time to save time through motivation; where do I begin?

are always seeking to improve. I submit to you that this is a model for leadership. I suggest that, for most of us, if we knew our real score as a manager, and our handicap against what we should be doing we would be shocked into changing the way we play the game.

One of the distinguishing characteristics between a manager and a leader is that the leader is not afraid to leave that comfort zone, is not afraid to challenge assumptions, is not afraid to change. If you want to begin the process of motivating your people, do it consciously and in a planned orderly fashion.

The problem for most managers is that they don't think they have the time. Most managers today are doers, not just managers, they have their own work responsibilities as well as their managerial responsibilities. How do you make the time to better manage?

The solution is to begin with your most motivated and competent people. Take every opportunity to recognize good work, to show appreciation, to provide autonomy, to be respectful. Work with them to assume responsibilities that you currently have. Use a low directive, high supportive approach to delegate to these people some of the projects that are taking a lot of your time. They, too, are too busy? Involve them in selecting others in the department that might help them, by relieving them of some of their responsibilities. This is "trickle down motivation." Everyone gets more involved in meaningful work and you get more time to meet with people to recognize, reinforce, challenge and share your vision. Implementing this process is a powerful tool for change in your department, plant, region, or company but it takes the willingness to change.

This chapter has focused on the "what of change," what it is that you need to do to motivate. Our next chapter, Drivers, Wedges, Irons, and Putters, focuses on the "How."

How to Play This Hole

In order to establish a comprehensive motivational strategy for your business unit you will need to implement the following steps:

1. Diagnose the competence and motivational stage of employees for their major tasks (just two or three or this task will overwhelm you).

2. Begin with the employee to whom something of yours can be delegated thus freeing up more of your time to spend with others who need greater direction.

3. Analyze the motivational needs of each of your direct reports. Develop and implement a plan to provide these motivators.

4. Don't make the assumption that the competent, long time professional worker doesn't need feedback in the form of recognition and reinforcement.

5. Understand that compensation is a "necessary but not sufficient condition" for high motivation. A paycheck is an expectation for work completed, not a motivator to exceed expectations.

6. Realize that psychological incentives such as recognition, challenge, opportunity to improve, meaningful work, and willingness to listen cost nothing, but produce dramatic returns. Use them often.

7. Let people know you have a personal direction and vision. Ensure that they know they are involved in an enterprise greater than themselves.

8. Leave your comfort zone (See Hole #9—Change). Reach out with these motivational strategies even if it is a "stretch" for you. Begin slowly. Stay the course.

Golf Teaches Us That
Motivation Isn't Just
About Money.
It Is About Challenge,
Feedback, the Opportunity to
Improve, Being a Part of
Something Greater Than
Ourselves, and Ever More
Demanding Goals.

4

WEDGES, IRONS, DRIVERS AND PUTTERS

Secrets from the Golf Course on Leadership and Communication

About Hole #4

Whereas most of the holes on the leadership course are relatively flat, this par four, 382 yard hole is characterized by wide fairways with undulating hills and tiered traps. If you can play uphill, downhill and sidehill lies well, if you can use a variety of clubs in different situations, this hole is relatively easy to par. If you can't, this hole, the hole we call communication, will break your game.

Introduction

Motivation and communication are inextricably linked. You cannot motivate without the proper communication and leaders who don't consider the impact of their communication on the motivation of others cannot be considered true leaders. A short while ago I visited a small "cottage industry" rug factory in Vermont. For the first time, seeing the master weaver work

> *The abilities to communicate and motivate are inextricably linked.*

the loom, I understood not only the importance of color in the weave, but the importance of strength; the self reinforcing nature of the interlocking strands. Communication and motivation are interlocking strands for the leader. Woven correctly they reinforce, woven poorly or not woven at all, simple strands. So this chapter builds on the previous one and the concepts are interlocking. As you move through this chapter, think of how the communication concepts presented here are critical to the implementation of the motivational concepts reviewed in Chapter 3.

Managers Talk, Leaders Communicate

There are fewer more overworked terms in the leader's lexicon than communication, nor, with the exception of judgement, is there any skill more critical. Most surveys suggest that somewhere between 75 and 90 percent of the job of leading people involves communication, so not working at improving this skill is self-defeating, something like trying to break eighty with only a driver in your bag. To put it more directly, lack of communication skills undermines the vision, the alignment, the goals, and the overall effectiveness of a leader. If you are not currently as effective as you would like to be in terms of communication, don't despair; like nearly every other major concept articulated in this book, communication skills can be learned, honed, and improved upon. In a phrase, "Managers talk, Leaders communicate." So, let's begin by visiting two extremes of communication, look at some fundamentals of being interpersonally effective in verbal communication and then examine some of the advanced communication skills needed for effective leadership. Let's begin by looking at the two extremes of communication— the overly assertive and the laissez-faire communicator.

"They Are All Like Me—And, If They Aren't, They Should Be"

A vice president of a major division within a large chemical company once said to me about his employees, "They are all like me—and if they aren't, they should be." I had been called in because a 360° assessment of his leadership style had indicated that people thought he was a poor communicator and because, relative to other divisions, his was suffering more than double the turnover in highly talented, relatively young professionals. We were sitting in his twenty-sixth floor office (he, of course, sitting in his high backed leather chair behind his desk) having a discussion about his leadership style. I explained to Mike that one of the results of the survey I had recently completed was that his people thought he was not an effective communicator.

He sat forward in his chair, hands gripping the edge of the desk. "What do they mean I am not an effective communicator," he exploded. "I am out there in the halls and in the plant all the time. I am constantly telling people what is going on, I tell them what to do and how to do it. I tell them about directives from corporate and I tell them about how we are doing in terms of our measurements. If they don't hear me out there, I bring them in here and tell 'em again. If they don't hear me in this office, I suggest they look elsewhere. My division will perform!"

"It isn't the telling side of communication that people are concerned about."

Anyone who has ever experienced the role of either internal or external consultant to a very powerful top executive has had this moment. I thought of Covey's admonition about exercising integrity in the moment of choice. I decided to pull out the driver and swing away, hoping to hit that two hundred fifty yard green right on the fringe and roll it up to the pin. "Mike," I said, "I know that you really don't understand why this survey was necessary and I am sure you are frustrated at having to spend this time with me right now when there are other problems that need your immediate attention. I want to clearly say to you that it isn't the *telling* side of communication people are concerned about, you do that very well. It is the listening side of the communication equation that is the issue."

Mike was a very large fellow. He stood up from behind his desk, raised his hands, pointed his thumbs toward his chest and shouted , "Listen to them? Listen to them? **I am the boss, they will learn to deal with me, not the other way around"** his hands jerking back and forth with thumbs outstretched as he repeated, "I am the boss. I am the boss."

You don't hit every green in one (or even two), not every roll of the dice pays off, not every consulting engagement is successful. A week later Mike's boss told me that they were going to try to work with Mike internally. Other than his exceptionally high turnover rate, his division was very successful. As a matter of fact, if you looked at profitability only as a difference between cost to produce and the selling price of the product, his was one of the most profitable divisions in the company.

However, the chemical engineers and chemists that he was churning through represented an investment of about $115,000 each (recruiting costs, relocation costs, mentoring costs, salaries) over two years at the time of this engagement—and they were losing this investment all too regularly. There was a significant gap in experience levels in his staff. There were long termers who had found a way to work within his style (and who were building up their retirement benefits), and there were these bright, energetic youngsters with less than two years of experience who were still optimistic that the situation would improve—somehow. There were few employees with between two and nine years of experience. There was no up and coming leadership; those with leadership potential had decided to go elsewhere, to companies, departments and divisions who didn't equate leadership with position power.

What an opportunity Mike missed because he didn't want to learn how to hit a downhill lie. He could have taken his strength and built on it to achieve more, but he was blocked by an unwillingness to learn and an ego that defined power as obedience and being influenced as weakness. But his lost opportunity was no greater than that of the other extreme—the laissez faire manager.

> *"If I don't nurture and grow these people who will be our leaders of tomorrow?"*

"My People are Empowered"

About two years after Mike, I was asked by a president of a national staffing company to work with a regional vice president who was having trouble meeting corporate goals in terms of both recruiting and placements. Gloria's problem was just the opposite of Mike's. She was a great listener, would empathize with the problems faced by staff in sales and recruiting, would work with people to come up with ideas; but she wouldn't hold their feet to the fire, she wouldn't demand results. "I am working with adults," she told me. "They are empowered to do their jobs. If I stand around demanding, they will never learn responsibility. I know that this takes time, but if I don't nurture and grow these people, who will be our leaders of tomorrow?"

Well, not Gloria. She was as stuck in a management and communication paradigm as ineffective as Mike's and she was equally unwilling to examine and change this paradigm. (It never ceases to amaze me that, even with their jobs and careers on the line, some people are unwilling to change. The threat of change is more intimidating for some than the loss of a career. In Chapter 9—The Change Model, we will examine this phenomena and provide a workable solution.) Everybody loved working for Gloria. She had virtually no turnover even though she should have disciplined at least five low and non-performers. After six months of worse than average performance, and no indications that the trend was about to change, Gloria, who had been with the company for more than fifteen years, was given a nice little package and let go.

In Michael Sharra's Pulitzer prize winning novel of the battle of Gettysburg, *The Killer Angels*, Generals Robert E. Lee and James Longstreet are discussing the order of battle. Lee notes concern for Longstreet's safety. Longstreet responds, "You can't lead from the rear." This sums up the styles of both Mike and

"You cannot lead from the rear of the battle."

Gloria. Mike's was the classic "stick" style of leadership. Sticks are applied to prod rather than lead, Gloria's hands off approach reflected "like me" leadership over "respect me" leadership. Her method was not leadership but rather an abdication of leadership. Like Mike, she was standing behind the troops rather than leading from the front.

Effective Balance—"The Freedom of the And"

Mike and Gloria were the exceptions; they are representative of those "stuck in a paradigm" and unwilling to grow. There have also been numerous successes over the years in changing communication style. Alan, a Vice President of Sales who changed from a driving, dominant, telling (sometimes shouting) "flaming expressive" style to one that was more balanced and predictable, thus increasing the profitability of his department twofold in two years. Steve, who stopped "managing by e-mail" and got out of his office and began talking to people, thus receiving two promotions in two years. Linda, who continually coached herself to listen and respond to the ideas of her talented group of network engineers and thus moved from supervisor to vice president in a little less than four years.

Over the past few years we have heard a lot about the directive approach as being passe, about the need for a more democratic approach, about the importance of empowerment, about coaching being a less directive and more effective approach to leadership (this type of coaching is obviously not modeled after those coaches who rant and rave and shout at the players and referees from the sideline). During these same years, we have witnessed the failure of many management and leadership teams to address the basic needs of their people. Again, seeking an appropriate model for leadership, most of us are captured by the "tyranny of the or" when we should be examining the "freedom of the and." We have been made to think that we have to choose between people oriented and task oriented when in fact the best leaders choose both.

Effective leadership is not about getting stuck with a single club in your hand that you must use for every shot. It is about carrying a multitude of clubs and knowing when they are to be used. It's about having that driver when, as Robert Lutz, president and chief operating officer of Chrysler noted, "You need to be aggressive about change, to grab the bull by the horns and get something done." It is also about knowing how to use that wedge when you are in a meeting with four peers and you realize that influence is more valuable than power in this situation.

Today, many companies have shifted empowerment down to the lowest levels of the organization. On the positive side, this definitely gets more people involved in the process—it is a motivator. On the negative side the quality of decision making is often diluted. Some decisions, for example, are based on compromise, rather than on principle or even what is the best for the company. All of which is to say that today more than ever, to be an effective leader, you need more than one club in your bag.

Effective leadership is about carrying multiple "clubs" and knowing how and when to use each one.

Encode, Send, Decode—A Brief History of Recent Communication Theory

When learning the game of golf, the novice typically begins on flat ground. Hitting the ball from a flat surface is difficult enough—to try to learn how to hit a golf ball on a slope would challenge even the most gifted athlete. The same is true of communication. We learn the model of the sender, the message, the medium and the receiver as the essence of communication in Communication 101. And this model is accurate—to a degree. If we simply look at a model of communication in an ideal world, an engineering model, if you will, there is a sender who determines and sends the message, a medium in which the message is sent (e.g. verbal, written, electronic, behavioral, visual) and someone to receive the message.

However, nearly all "ideal" (this will get some calls) engineering models experience difficulty when humans start to "mess" with them. The Communication Model is no exception. As we progressed in our education, we learned that problems can exist in all three of these communication phases. It looked good on a flow chart, and was fine for machines, but it didn't seem to work so well with the added variable of people.

Thus, in Management 501 we learned that encoding a message didn't guarantee that the message would be properly decoded, no matter the medium, no matter how clearly sent. We learned that, in order to be effective in verbal communication, we had to ensure through paraphrasing that the recipient had indeed received the message we were attempting to send. Ah, remember paraphrasing?

The skill of paraphrasing came out of the work of the National Training Labs in the '60's and '70's and, for a while, was effective. Paraphrasing then became trivialized as everyone learned to say, "So, what I hear you saying is …" (to the point of silliness). What typically followed this phrase, of course, would usually more closely resemble what the person wanted to hear than what had actually been sent. Language patterns develop characteristic responses over time. Paraphrasing, and in particular the phrase, "What I hear you saying is…" developed an extremely negative response pattern within about three years of general use and this potentially excellent tool for clarifying communication fell out of practice.

In the eighties, management communication, as taught in most training classes, was expanded to include concepts such as listening with empathy, sharing thoughts and rationales, asking for the employees' input about problems and maintaining the self-esteem of the employee in difficult situations. Each of these is an important skill. And, of these skills, none is more important for the leader than the skill of empathetic listening (we don't have a good word for this—it goes beyond being listened to, to truly being heard—a basic human need). I realize that this sounds "wimpy." Did Patton, listen and clarify? Probably not, but Patton was one of those "one hundredth of one percenters" as leaders, and for most of us is not the ideal model of leadership.

Challenging Your Personal Communication Style

The communication emphasis from the mid eighties to the late nineties has been on non-verbal and linguistic patterning. We now know, of course that communication is as much what you do as what you say; over ninety percent of any face to face communication is "non-verbal." As we will see later in this book (Chapter 9—Golf and Change), leadership means having the courage to do the uncomfortable—often the opposite of what we would normally do. If you are not achieving your personal goals of leadership, examine your style of verbal and nonverbal communication and increase your effectiveness through breaking out of a box that limits your effectiveness.

IF YOU NORMALLY:	THEN:
Talk	Listen more
Take a long time to make a decision	Make and live with snap decisions on occasion
Listen	Talk when it is uncomfortable for you
Assume you know what someone is saying	Clarify
Treat people as machines	Treat people as people
Take power	Empower
Decide without information	Seek information before deciding
Drive decisions through personal power	Involve others in determining "the how."
Shy away from confrontation	Confront with confidence
Get annoyed at listening	Ask assertive questions to "controllers"

Empathy—An Essential Skill of Leadership

As noted in Chapter 3 (Motivation) Edward Deci convincingly argues in his paradigm breaking book on motivation, "*Why We Do What We Do*", that, under normal circumstances, people place a high value on personal autonomy, on doing things for their own reasons: not someone else's, not the system's, not the company's. Thus, Deci suggests, the point of communication for the leader becomes one of helping the follower see that the interests of the individual are in line with the interests of the leader, the system, the company, or any other entity. If this is done poorly, it is seen as coercion and manipulation, resulting in a "hardening of the attitudes" and intransigence rather than cooperation. However, when done consciously and with an awareness of individual needs, this is one of, if not the most effective tools a leader can have. We alluded to it earlier in the chapter; the skill is called empathy.

Empathy is simply taking time to understand something of the emotions that another person is experiencing and then identifying those emotions as a part of the communication process. For example, actively trying to understand why a person is upset, and then indicating that you understand that they are upset (even if you don't agree), and then refraining from giving them a solution or telling them that this, too, shall pass, is exhibiting empathy. Empathy is an invaluable skill in calming down emotionally charged employees.

Communicating with empathy is hard work. It is far easier to simply tell someone what to do or to tell someone that feelings have no place in business. However, in communication, as in most other leadership skills, it is the discipline that results in effectiveness. Simply telling people what to do breeds compliance, not cooperation. Using empathy creates trust and credibility, critical interpersonal attributes for the leader. We will return to empathy as a skill of emotional intelligence in Chapter 7.

Of course empathy isn't the only important communication tool. Certainly the skill of sharing your thoughts and rationale about a decision is also valuable if you want "buy in" to your ideas. Sharing thoughts and rationales increases the likelihood that the listener can build on your ideas and thus multiply the value of those ideas. There are entire books written on the skills of communication, but if you will only begin to use empathy; if, in moments of crisis and confrontation you can take a few seconds to imagine what the

> *The point of communication is one of helping the individual see that the interests of that individual are in line with the interests of the leader, the system, and the organization.*

other person must be experiencing, you can dramatically increase your effectiveness as a leader.

Beyond Empathy

Now let's return to the golf course for some other ideas on leadership and communication.

Leadership, like golf has changed not only from the days of Old Tom Morris, but from the heyday of Arnold Palmer, and communication, in both style and intent, is one of the key variables in this process of change. Think of the word "driver" today and you probably think of an oversized metal "wood" with a name connoting size such as "Great Big Bertha" or "Burner Bubble." (Okay, by the time this is read, maybe we will all be using standard size drivers again, because in golf equipment, as in leadership skills, yesterday's technology won't solve today's challenges.)

So, today, turning the corner of the millennium, communication has moved beyond even skills such as empathy and providing rationales. It has come to stand for a wide array of skills that can be used in a variety of situations according to the demands of that situation. Communication today is about versatility in using skills, not just the knowledge of the skills themselves.

How Many Clubs Are In Your Bag?

Think about this before you answer it. If you are not a golfer, think of it metaphorically. The question is, "How many clubs do you carry in your bag?" Many of us carry up to fourteen (the maximum allowed by the rules), maybe even including that "Alien Wedge!"

Now, let's categorize those clubs. If you are like most golfers you carry woods, long and short irons, two or three wedges, and a putter (your ball retriever doesn't count). Depending on preferences, you can have a mix of these. Some people carry two different putters, a one iron instead of a driver, or a seven wood instead of a five iron or some other club.

The point is becoming glaringly obvious. Why do you have all those clubs? Of course, you have all those clubs because different situations on the course call for different types of shots, which are typically best hit with different types of clubs – unless, of course, you are Tiger Woods.

> *You carry a multitude of golf clubs because different situations call for the use of different clubs. It is the same with communication.*

A digression with a message. Perhaps you saw the golf match that was shown on television Christmas day in 1997. The match (it was a match rather than "stroke play") featured Tiger Woods and three or four of his friends. It was a charity event and every time Tiger won a hole, his friends would take a club away from him. They begun by taking away his woods, then his long irons and his putter, it didn't make any difference, he won anyway – he is in that one-one hundredth of one percent. So, if you are in that one hundredth of one percent, if you are so natural and intuitive and well practiced in the art of communication that your people will *willingly* follow you anywhere, you can ignore the rest of this chapter. But, if you are not in that category, read on.

So, let's return to the average or even above average golfer. Picture yourself on the golf course. Now imagine yourself with a bag that has not fourteen, or twelve or even seven clubs. You don't have five clubs or even three; you have, in fact, only two clubs. Now let's name the clubs; let's say that you have only a driver and a putter. Could you play par golf with these two clubs? How about bogey golf? Could you break one hundred? Unless you are a truly outstanding and versatile golfer, you couldn't break one hundred with only a driver and a putter (I sometimes have trouble doing it with all fourteen.)

This is another one of those lessons from the golf course that is at one and the same time obvious and profound; yet, it is one of those lessons that is often ignored. We will examine why it is ignored later in the chapter. However, the multiple club metaphor really is a clarifier. As a leader, having the ability to deal with different people differently in different situations is like having specialty golf clubs in your bag. In other words, for one individual in one situation you may need a "driver", for another individual in another situation you may need a "wedge", and for a third individual in yet a third situation you may need a "putter."

As we noted in Chapter 3 (Motivation) the individual differences of the people you lead are as great as those found on any golf course. So not only do you need skill with irons in general, with practice and over time, you must develop advanced skills with a five or six iron depending on the situation. These situations may require that you give your five iron a full swing or a three quarter swing, that you hit a fade or a draw. However, being situation responsive in terms of communication takes awareness and practice and most managers haven't taken the time to master the discipline and thus have missed the opportunity to lead. The fact that most managers don't have communication versatility is borne out by the research.

There is a fifty/fifty chance that you carry only one "club" in your "communication" bag.

Dr. Ken Blanchard's studies conclusively prove that, if you are in a management position, there is a better than fifty/fifty chance that you carry only one club in your managerial bag; there is less than a twenty-five percent chance that you have two clubs in this bag, less than a five percent chance that you have three clubs, and less than a one percent chance than you have four clubs in this bag! (Incidentally, versatility with four club types [e.g. drivers, irons, wedges, putters] is all we really need for leading; if we had fourteen different types of clubs, we would look like chameleons to our people.)

So the vast majority of us have either two clubs or one club in our managerial bag.

Hammers and Nails

What does this mean? Remember Abraham Maslow's famous quote: "If the only tool that you have is a hammer, you tend to treat every problem as a nail." This is exactly the problem that is faced by most managers because they carry only one or two clubs. Remember, true leadership is more influence than power. You can't achieve influence with limited versatility with only one "communication club." (As we all know, you can create compliance through coercion if you have only one club and it is a driver—but why would you want to play the game with only one club?)

Let's return to the golf course to explain why versatility in communication is so important. Again, visualize yourself standing inside the tips looking down the fairway of a four hundred ten yard par four. The hole has trees down both sides of this spotted brown fairway, with water about two hundred sixty yards out on the left. There are two large bunkers on this hole, one to the right of the green and a greenside bunker in front with a four foot bank butting up to the green. The pin placement is challenging, it is on the front of the sloping green, about eight yards in front of the bunker.

As you look down the fairway, you make a mental plan of how you are going to play this hole. You decide that you are going to go for a par because it is really a little too long for you to go for birdie. So, let's look in our bag and take out our first club. What is it going to be? Sure, you need a driver, or if your driver hasn't been working, maybe your three wood or a two iron.

Now you have hit that first shot and it is gorgeous, it is a "home run" drive for you. Two hundred fifty yards at least and just to the right of the center of the fairway (you even missed the water). As you walk toward your ball, you look at the hole again. The yard markers indicate that you have about one hundred sixty yards to go and so you decide to overclub and take a three quarter swing, that bunker looks like it covers the entire course. You take out your six iron.

You hit your six iron fat and sure enough it lands on the edge of the bunker and rolls in. But you aren't worried because not only do you have a sand wedge in your bag, you are good with it, very good. So you approach your ball with confidence, take your favorite wedge and set the ball down six feet below the hole. Taking your putter from your bag, you tap in this six footer for your (sandy) par, congratulate yourself, take your buddies' money and start thinking about the next hole.

What made this par possible? Good drive, fair iron shot, great sand wedge and a good steady putt. You even got into trouble (that second shot into the sand) and saved your par because you were so adept at the use of the wedge and because your confidence in the wedge kept you from becoming rattled. (Remember Johnny Miller's adage: "The toughest shot in golf is the shot after the bad shot.")

> *The one club in our bag usually reflects our own personal style of operating and has little to do with the types of people we are managing.*

The Four Different Styles of Communication

And the business lesson here? Obviously it is that too few of us carry more than one club in our communication bag. This one club or communication style is not the same for all of us, but it usually comes in one of four types: the dominant or "I will tell you how it is going to be and you do it" club, the reflective or "let me think about this and tell you how to do it" club, the friendly or "let's talk about it and decide the best way to do it" club or the social "let's work together to accomplish this task" club.

Actually, these four basic styles of interactions are not unlike the four different types of clubs that you have in your bag. That is, you have "woods" that may vary from the number one to the number nine, but are still woods, you have your irons, your wedges and your putter. Each of these clubs is unique. Each of these clubs is designed with a specific purpose. Each of these clubs is appropriate for that purpose and inappropriate for any other (would you putt with a driver or drive with a wedge?).

I don't want to carry this metaphor too far, but if you are basically the "social" (let's work together to get the task accomplished) type of manager, you may vary from very strongly set in your way (3 iron) to someone who combines the power of a long iron with the utility of a short iron (8 iron) in using this style—and you will have different degrees of versatility with that one club. But, based on the averages, if you are good with that iron, you are probably only middling with your putter and you may not be able to drive at all. I hope you see the analogy, because like most analogies, at some point in runs out of gas and that point is here.

The lesson is this: Most of us carry only one club in our bag and that is the club that fits us best. We use it in nearly all situations because that is where we are most comfortable. As we said at the beginning, many managers take the unspoken, often unknown position, "Everybody is like me, and if they are not, they should be. Therefore, my club will work with anyone." But any amount of reflection shows us the limitations of this type of thinking. With so many different personalities, so many differ-

The differentiating question is: "What Do Your People Do When You Are Not There?"

ent circumstances, so many different opportunities, one club simply won't do.

If you are like most people who would be leaders, then, you have one and maybe two clubs in your bag. What is the club? It is almost invariably a projection of your own beliefs and values, often unacknowledged, that often unconsciously says to the world, "I have worked this out, if you will just do as I say, everything will be okay." Whoa, Don," you say, "I have done pretty well for myself just being myself, I don't need any other clubs. I have done quite well with my driver, my iron, my putter or my wedge, thank you."

Differentiating Questions for Leaders

And I say to you, you have done well, you are a manager, a vice president, a senior vice president, maybe you are the president of your company, but there are two questions that you need to answer. The first and most critical question that I would ask you is: "What do your people do when you are not there?" If you are at an off site sales meeting, what are your people doing while you are gone – and why? Right now, this minute, if you are not there with them, is your team working as hard as they would if you were there, because if they aren't, you need more leadership clubs in your bag.

If they are working, are they working out of fear or out of pride? Because, if they are working out of fear, you also need more leadership clubs in your bag. If they are working out of pride, I will guarantee that you have more than one club in your bag, you are probably one of those with two or three—perhaps four.

The second question is this: "What opportunities have you missed because you have treated every employee and every situation with the same "club," the same set of responses? Who have you lost that you might have kept, what have you not achieved as a company, division or department that you might have achieved? What opportunities have you missed because not all employees respond to the same type of leadership? What possibilities have passed you by because of lack of skill and versatility in communication?

I have a friend who has been playing golf for more than fifteen years. For that past ten years he has carried a fifteen to twenty handicap in no small part because he won't examine his stroke and he won't take lessons. Does he enjoy the game? Yes. Would he enjoy it more if he saw progress in his score, if he could regularly hit that green in two, if he could score more pars and bogeys and fewer doubles and triples? Definitely. The same is true for many managers. Improve your communication and enjoy the game at a different level—the leadership level.

Why Do We Care About Communication Style Anyway?

Leaders execute; they use communi-cation skills to transform vision into reality.

There are reasons for improving communication that go beyond our own need to improve for improvement's sake. In business, as in golf, substance is measured to some degree by results. As Warren Bennis says, "Leadership is the capacity to translate vision into reality." It is not the job of the leader to do the work; it is the job of the leader to assure that the work gets done. It is not the job of the leader to make every decision, it is the job of the leader to ensure that the best decision gets made. It is not the job of the leader to micro manage results; it is the job of the leader to ensure that goals are achieved. To accomplish these things requires "interpersonal flexibility" and communication skills. It is truer today than it was yesterday and it will be even more important tomorrow than it is today. Before downsizing, re-engineering and right sizing, most companies had a nice hierarchical flow and a leader or manager, by whatever name, typically supervised twelve to twenty-four people.

Today managers often supervise sixty or more people and may be responsible for the work of additional people with indirect, dotted line responsibilities. In addition to this, managers are also likely to be personally responsible for some type of product development – whether this is the product itself, reports, numbers, something. In order to be successful at this you need even more clubs in your bag. You simply cannot be effective with that many people and this many responsibilities if you cannot adapt your natural strengths to meet the needs of the situation and the people.

You'll notice I use the term "effective". We all know the basic definition. Efficient is getting things done right, effective is getting the right things done right. But effective to leaders means more than that. Let's go back to golf.

What is an effective shot? In our example above, your two hundred fifty yard drive was an effective shot because it put you in a position for a successful follow on shot. This first shot was effective. But what about your second shot, the six iron that you hit "fat"? Fortunately you are good with the wedge, or that shot, even though it covered one hundred fifty yards, would not have been effective. If you had hit your first shot three hundred yards, or hit that six iron one hundred and seventy, but either of them was in the high grass, was the first shot effective?

"Sure," some of you say, "if you can kick it."

But I am going to assert this. You are only truly effective when your people work as hard when you are not there as they do when you are. You are only truly effective when your people are past dependency on your continuous input and are able to make decisions without fear. You are only effective when goals are achieved without your having to continually drive your people toward their accomplishment. You are only effective when people stay with you because they feel part of something greater than themselves in your division, department, branch, plant or company. You are only effective when you can assess the level of competence and confidence of your people and work with them to take to increasing levels of both.

Let me share a final story from my experience in business that illustrates "one club" management and then move from here to an outline of the four communication modalities that you need to be an effective leader.

The Repair Incident

We were consulting at a chemical plant outside of a major city along the Eastern Seaboard. If you have ever visited any of the large chemical or petrochemical processing plants along the Eastern shoreline, the Gulf Coast, or California, you know the problems faced. These plants are essentially composed of four elements, miles and miles of piping, hundreds of individual vessels and, controlling the flow of product, valves of all shapes, sizes and types, and, of course, the people who run them.

The workforce at this plant, as at many plants of this type, was experienced, knowledgeable and unionized, providing a degree of specialization in many areas. The plant had been recently purchased but much of the old management team and employees had been kept on. There was a history of worker/management animosity. We had been called in because of an incident that cost the company

One club management cost the company millions of dollars.

not only hundreds of thousands of dollars, but many upset customers. This is a summary of the incident as it was related to us by the plant management who came in after the investigation was completed:

During routine maintenance, an experienced crew pulled a valve, repacked it and reinstalled it in the line. While they were re-packing the valve, they noted that the valve was severely worn and should probably be replaced. They noted this on their report. Within three weeks, the valve began to leak product, not enough to shut down operations, but enough that the valve had to be pulled again. When the crew pulled the valve, they reported to their supervisor that, in their opinion, this valve was beyond repair and needed to be replaced. The supervisor told the men in no uncertain terms that the budget did not allow for a replacement valve. They were to repair this one.

One of the maintenance men said something to the effect of "you don't understand" and the supervisor retorted that he understood quite well and that their job was to pull and repair the valve and put it back in the line. They asked to talk to the assistant plant manager. He came down and they told him that the valve was beyond repair, that it needed to be replaced. He replied that it was not scheduled for replacement and that they simply needed to do a better job of repairing and re-packing the valve and put it back in the line.

Which they did – professionally, I might add, as there was an investigation after the incident. Yes, the incident. The valve blew four days later necessitating a total plant shut down and costing the company a minimum of a quarter of a million dollars.

Synergistic communication is the result of being versatile in effectively using a variety of communication skills.

Both the supervisor and the assistant plant manager were "one club" managers. They had their drivers and could consistently hit the ball two hundred forty yards; they were consistent but by no means outstanding with that driver. Senior management depended on them to get things done with that driver. They had both been promoted to their level of supervision because they were perceived as no nonsense, "we'll get the job done" managers. In many situations, they looked effective. But were they? Obviously not. If they had had a communication "wedge or a putter," this plant would not have had this incident. Stories like this are legion in almost every company. Why? Because we get promoted for our strengths and only at the next level do we typically find that this strength is not sufficient to carry us through. But this is often the only communication tool we have so we try to use it in every situation instead of developing a degree of comfort with different styles of communication that are more effective in other situations.

Synergistic Communication

The goal of communication should be that the product of the interaction is greater than the individual input of either party. I call this synergistic communication and it is the result of versatility in communication skills, active, empathetic listening, and most importantly, a willingness to acknowledge that the two people communicating have more information related to solving a problem than either one of them individually. Leaders are synergistic communicators. The skills can be learned and the attitude can be developed.

So, what are the skills of an effective leader? What is required of a versatile communicator? As with most everything else (including golf scores), the people that you supervise have a continuum of needs that range from requiring considerable direction to being able to autonomously seek improvement.

Communication for Leadership

Remember that leadership is about obtaining more from individuals and groups in terms of performance than they would have provided without your influence. It is about involving people in something that they recognize as greater than themselves. How is this done? Through modeling the appropriate behavior ("walk the talk"). Through vision and alignment, through preparation and goals, through determination and perseverance, and, in no small part through communication. If you would be a leader you must learn how to communicate.

For a minute, imagine you are a club pro and you have each of the four types of golfers mentioned in the chapter on Motivation (Remember the enthusiastic beginner, the "Tween" and the others?) come to you for help. How do you help them improve? Simply put, you adjust your communication style to their level of competence and confidence.

Blanchard suggests that each one of these styles needs individualized responses that are related to how skilled they are and how motivated they are to play. For the enthusiastic beginner, one who is highly motivated but short on skills, the golf pro would provide abundance of highly directive, highly corrective feedback. He would encourage and provide reinforcement, but his primary goal would be to help this individual do the job right. The experienced, low handicap player would need less direction and more support; less "standing over the shoulder" and more, "what do you think is wrong with your swing?"

In brief, these four styles are used depending on the competence and confidence of the employee. Your job as a supervisor is much like that of a physician. You diagnose the need, provide the right type of treatment, and, as needed, follow up. The four different types of "treatment" are:

1. **For the Enthusiastic Beginner**—Highly directive feedback, a high degree of control of the situation, considerable supervision. Remember these people are enthusiastic, they just don't have a high degree of competence.

2. **For the "Tween"**—This person is more competent than the beginner, but also in greater need of support. This person requires coaching, which is both supportive and directive. Because they have gained some competence, this person can be consulted on what he or she thinks.

This process encourages self reliance, but the coach retains decision making authority.

3. **For the "Developing Employee"**—This person is able to take on more responsibility and therefore, needs support to become more confident in his or her skills. The leader draws out the best ideas of this employee and shares responsibility for decision making with this employee. The basic process at this stage of development is to support the subordinate and to facilitate their growth to the next stage.

4. **For the "Self-Reliant Employee"**—Delegation is the order of the day for this employee who is both competent and confident. You can trust the individual to make high quality decisions and to work independently on this task or in this area.

The leader knows that passion and compassion can exist side by side.

Please understand that each of these leadership approaches depends on the situation, not just the person. An individual may be a "Self-Reliant Employee" in one area and a "Tween" in another. When he or she gets promoted, the process of coaching that person begins anew. (I have used Blanchard's model here because it is research based, well developed and available in depth in any one of a number of publications [e.g., "Leadership and the One Minute Manager"] and through public and private seminars.)

A Final Word on Communication

There is no doubt that formal communication skills are important. Skills such as listening, empathy and situational communication are essential for leadership. But leaders also know that there is nothing more important in leadership than the message communicated by "who you are." In Chapter 8 we will discuss character, and its role in leadership. Part of that character has to be a passion for your beliefs; a passion expressed as much by how you say things as what you say. Too many of us hold back for fear of being judged. The leader doesn't worry about this. The leader knows that passion and compassion can exist side by side. The leader knows that deeply held and strongly articulated personally held beliefs are essential to moving people to achieve something greater than themselves. When it is appropriate, don't hold back. Use changes in tempo, changes in inflection, changes in body language, changes in intensity, to leave no doubt that this issue is one in which you passionately believe.

Summary

Communication is to leadership as the swing is to golf; everyone can do it, but few do it well. There are managers who achieve far less than they could because they believe that most others are like them in terms of style. You cannot lead from the rear of the battle. A dominant, telling style and a laissez-faire "you're empowered" style, emphasize pushing, not pulling. The leader needs versatility in his or her communication style, needs to adjust his or her style to the needs of the individual and the situation. The best leaders respect the autonomy of those they lead. They use paraphrasing and empathy to help align the work of the individual with the vision and goals of the organization. They continually challenge their own style of communication in order to improve. Managers talk and leaders communicate. Believe passionately in what you do and who you are. Let others know that you truly care about the important issues.

How to Play This Hole

1. Analyze your beliefs about communication. What is the message you send? How do you treat others?

2. Analyze your behaviors in communicating with others. Do you expect others to flex to your style? Do you tell more than ask? Do you wait quietly for others to draw out your good ideas? Whatever your natural style, examine it and become more versatile. If you tell more than ask, learn to ask. If you wait around for someone to draw out your ideas, practice being more assertive in presenting these ideas.

3. Develop basic skills such as paraphrasing and empathetic listening. Acknowledge that emotion plays a major part in business. Channel those emotions rather than ignoring them.

4. Remember the "Freedom of the And." You can be both people oriented and task oriented. You can get the job done and take care of the people at the same time.

5. Look at the clubs in your "communication bag." Resolve to be more flexible. Learn to effectively use a variety of clubs under different circumstances. Learn the three quarter swing, not just the full swing. As on the golf course, different situations call for different distances, different clubs and different types of effort.

6. Practice synergistic communication. Remember, those you lead have information you need and you have information they need. The goal is for the decisions made to be better together than they could have been if either of you had made them separately.

7. Be Passionate! Care! Put aside that voice inside of you that says "Play it safe." People long for leaders who not only believe, but who are willing to put those beliefs on the line. Focus on winning, don't worry about losing. The only thing you really have control over is who you are and what you stand for. Be passionate about it!

GOLF TEACHES US
THAT SUCCESS COMES FROM BEING
SKILLED WITH ALL TYPES OF CLUBS.
GOLF TEACHES US THAT WHATEVER
THE ORDER—DRIVER, PUTTER, IRON,
WEDGE OR PUTTER, DRIVER,WEDGE,
IRON—YOU MUST BE ABLE TO TAKE
ADVANTAGE OF THE OPPORTUNITIES
OF EACH SHOT BY
EFFECTIVELY USING THE RIGHT CLUB.
GOLF TEACHES US
THAT YOU CAN'T WIN WITH ONLY
ONE CLUB IN YOUR BAG.

YOU CAN'T IMPROVE A RANDOM PROCESS

Secrets from the Golf Course on Process Improvement

About Hole #5

This is a relatively easy hole for anyone who consistently hits the ball straight. It is a 185 yard par three. The green on this hole is surrounded by bunkers, and the fairway is relatively narrow and lined with trees on both sides. If you hit it straight and get a pretty good drive, a birdie is a real possibility. However, if you put your first shot into the trees or putt wildly past the hole, a double bogey is a distinct possibility.

Introduction

One of the characteristics of leaders is the ability to fly in the face of conventional wisdom, to identify problems and to achieve results. Managers manage a process. Leaders suggest a better way to achieve the same result. Managers put out fires, leaders keep them from starting. Unlike many of the lessons from the

> *The manager accepts the status quo, the leader challenges it.*

golf course in this book, this one, on process improvement, looks like a managerial issue. It is not.

One of the significant differences between the role of the manager and the role of the leader on a day to day basis is that, while the manager accepts the status quo, the leader challenges it. To improve any company, the processes of that company must have a degree of predictability. It is the job of the leader to bring that level of predictability to processes so that the manager can better manage them. Bringing predictability to processes requires all the skills of the leader in terms of listening, influencing, and using the wide variety of clubs in the leader's bag.

End of One Career, Beginning of Another

As I wrote earlier, I came to golf late. I was in my forties when I realized that chasing that little white ball could be a challenge. I was a typical American kid of the fifties and sixties. I grew up on baseball and football. I played Little League, Pony League, and Babe Ruth League; I played Junior Varsity, American Legion and Varsity baseball and continued to play fast and slow pitch baseball/softball into my mid-thirties when, predictably, one sunny Sunday afternoon I was trying to throw out a runner at the plate from center field. As I let the ball go as I had thousands of times on what should have been a rope (okay, a sagging clothes line) to the catcher, I felt something in my arm go "pop" and the ball wound up rolling to second base. End of baseball career.

However, even as this baseball phase of my life came to a painful close, I continued to carry with me the arrogance of so many baseball players for golf. "Look, how hard can it be to hit a ball that is not only stationary, but sitting up on a nice field of grass. I mean, if you can hit a ninety mile an hour fast ball or a sinking curve that looks like a balloon leaving the pitcher's hand

and then turns into a zigzagging grape as it approaches the strike zone, then surely, you can hit this little white ball that isn't moving."

And boy, was I wrong. I probably played twenty rounds of golf between the ages of twenty-five and forty-five and never really enjoyed it, except for the sense of incredible peace that can occur on a golf course when you take the time to enjoy the extraordinary sense of beauty that most golf courses offer.

When I got married in my forties (not for the first time, I must admit – I mean the first time in my forties, but not the first time in my life), my wife Angie imposed two conditions. First, that I would learn how to ski (on frozen ice – called snow – that barely clings to the surface of treacherous slopes, not nice, smooth water, mind you) and that I would learn how to play golf.

At this point, many, many, many men ask the question, "You married a woman who set, as a condition of marriage, that you would learn to play golf? Does this woman have a sister?"

Yes, but she doesn't play golf. I found the request to learn to play golf acceptable and we were married. The baseball days were over and the golf days began.

"When you're hot, you're hot, when you're not, everyone is watching."
– Lee Janzen

In the Beginning There Was Utter Unpredictability

Being the dutiful husband that I was, I started to play golf with my wife. After all, I knew how to hit a ball. Hadn't I been hitting baseballs all my life, a conservative estimate of a hundred thousand times (I played a lot when I was a kid). So, I played golf, some days I played well (I scored one hundred and ten) and some days I played poorly (I quit keeping score), but one thing was for sure: everything that I would do on the golf course would be totally unpredictable. Sometimes my drives would be as straight as an arrow and two hundred forty yards down the middle; other times they would be in the trees, in the high grass, in the water (especially the water) six feet from the tee, or worst case scenario, the ball would still be sitting on the tee after a full swing. As we all know, this is especially galling on the first hole with twelve other golfers looking on. (Actually, if this is not already, it should be one of Murphy's laws: "Your worst drive of the day will be the one you hit or try to hit in front of the most people." Lee Janzen came fairly close to this when he noted, "When you're hot, you're hot; when you're not, everyone is watching.")

Other aspects of the game were equally bad/unpredictable. I could hit a beautiful seven iron on one shot, a hundred fifty yards straight at the pin with great loft that stopped dead on the green, and absolutely duff the ball the next shot. The ratio of these shots was approximately one of the former to seventy-six of the latter. I was also expert at cutting balls. Not as the pros do, cut a ball around a tree, or cut it on that dogleg right, but cut the ball, deface it, put a "smile" on it, indent it to the point of leaving an indelible mark, render it useless for further play (except when I had to hit it over water – most of my smiling balls wound up somewhere in the deep).

And putting. "In the leather" meant within six feet of the hole for me, because if it didn't go in the first time, I didn't even know what the term meant. For me, reading the green was more like, "Well, it looks kinda like it's sloping left down to the pin. Huh, isn't that interesting."

And a ball with any lie that was not flat? Forget it. Uphill, downhill, sidehill, sand, weeds. They were all going to simply increase the variation in an already widely varying result.

The Day I Hit the Squirrel

I think the day that I realized the great lesson for business in all of this was the day I hit the squirrel.

It was a beautiful spring day and we were playing the North Course at the Woodlands just north of Houston. This is a beautiful and challenging course and, like most courses in and around the Houston area, its fairways are lined with huge pines, old oaks and an occasional pecan. Because of this, and because of the relative safety of a golf course (relative being the operant word-see story below) these courses are havens for hundreds and hundreds of squirrels. So, when I stepped up to the tee box at number twelve and saw that poor little brown squirrel sitting on his haunches under a tree one hundred and eighty yards away on the far left of the fairway munching on some squirrel delicacy, I didn't think any more about it than any of the other hundreds of squirrels I had seen that day all over the course.

A perfect hook, right into the rib cage of that poor unsuspecting squirrel.

But this was to be a day remembered in the short life of that poor little squirrel.

I stepped up to the tee box, placed my ball on the tee, gripped my club the way I always did (that is, like a baseball bat – one hand above the other, thumbs parallel to the ground) and hit the ball as hard as I could. One hundred eighty yards on the fly, never more than two feet off the ground. A perfect hook, right smack into the rib cage of that poor unsuspecting squirrel. If a squirrel could make an "oof" sound, I am certain that this one did. He picked himself off the ground, looked back at me with a contemptuous look that said "duffer" and scampered off into the protection of the trees.

The Lesson of Lessons

A few weeks after this awesome display of incompetence was Father's Day, and my wife (I am not sure whether out of love or pity) presented me a gift of five golf lessons with the local pro.

When I showed up for the first lesson, I naturally assumed that the pro was going to begin with the driver, or at least one of the woods. But of course he was a lot more knowledgeable about golf than I was. We began with the seven iron.

"Show me your grip and how you address the ball," he began.

I demonstrated my baseball grip with my three and a half foot wide stance and my thoroughly bent knees. (I must have looked like Jeff Bagwell with a golf club at the plate.)

The pro (Ron Horton) remarked, "Well, you must have some natural athletic ability," which was probably the only positive thing he could think of to say at the time.

As so we began the grip, the most basic of the basics of the golf swing.

Incidentally (and this is a sidebar, not the real point of this chapter), an interesting analogy about the grip is that, while it is basic, it accommodates variation. If you watch the professional golfers you will note that, while there are some fundamental essentials shared by all golfers, (the hands are placed on the club so that the "V" of the left hand formed by the thumb and forefinger – yes this is how golfer's talk – points toward the right shoulder) there is also variation from golfer to golfer depending on their individual strengths and weaknesses. This is much like the recent usage in interest over benchmarking.

The Golf Swing and Benchmarking

Benchmarking is a wonderful idea. If you can identify a company who is really superior at some aspect of business operations – inventory management, customer service, employee retention, developmental cycle times, delivery accuracy, etc., it makes sense to benchmark this company as a model of excellence.

But there are typically two problems with benchmarking which are similar to the problems encountered when trying to model your swing after a tour professional. The first of these problems is the "gee whiz effect."

A few years ago I attended the Shell Houston Open where I went to the practice range to watch the pros go through their warm up. Watching Fred Couples' unbelievably smooth swing was like watching art in motion, but the golfer who really impressed me was Vijay Singh. (I wrote this before Vijay's string of victories, including a major in 1998.) As his teaching pro took Vijay through the clubs (beginning with his short irons), I was struck by two things: first, the utter predictability with which he hit the ball, and second, as he moved into the long irons and then his woods, the distance, loft and accuracy he generated on each shot.

It was truly an awesome display, but would it help me to videotape Vijay's grip and swing mechanics and model my grip and swing after his? Probably not. He is at least six inches taller than I am, a lot thinner, has thirty years more experience playing golf and still has the flexibility of a young man. I would be better off "benchmarking" the mechanics of an individual who not only hits the ball well, but who is closer to my size and age. (Fuzzy Zoeller comes to mind.)

You cannot take a system that works for one individual or company and implement it wholesale into another. You must adapt rather than adopt.

Adapt Yes, Adopt No

But even then I could not simply adopt that person's grip, stance and swing. Adapt yes. Adopt no.

And that is the first problem that so many companies have with benchmarking. They expect to be able to take a system that works extremely well for one company and implement it wholesale into theirs. It doesn't usually work. Like the mechanics of the swing, these "world class processes" must be adapted rather than adopted. At my age I don't have the flexibility (or let's face it, the athletic ability) to match Fred Couples' 110° shoulder turn. But can I learn from his swing and increase my shoulder turn by ten or twenty degrees so that I can increase my distance by ten or fifteen yards? Of course – with practice (and some stretching exercises)!

The second problem with benchmarking is that companies who do benchmarking often don't go prepared to benchmark but only prepared to visit. They don't bring the questions that need to be answered, they don't ask about problems of implementation, and they don't find out about the resources needed to support these world class processes, so they come away with a sense of admiration but no sense of implementation. It becomes more of a social call than an attempt to find out what works well and why.

Benchmarking, properly conducted, can help companies improve what they do without reinventing the wheel. We informally "benchmark" all the time in golf. We watch what the world class athletes do and try to integrate that into our own game. We tune into the "Golf Channel" and watch professionals provide instruction. We watch Johnny Miller's video on the golf swing. If we are so able to willingly learn from those with acknowledged expertise and skill in golf, why doesn't this extend to business. Why do so many businesses succumb to the "not invented here syndrome" (if we didn't invent the process, then it won't work for us) instead of learning from the best? It often has to do with pride, but golf teaches us otherwise.

However, as I mentioned above, this chapter is not about benchmarking, it is about the lesson to be learned from standardizing a formerly random process. For me, this became overwhelmingly clear as I continued my golf lessons with my teaching pro, Ron Horton.

Standardizing the Swing

Ron is an excellent instructor. He diverts the student from the wistful "let's learn how to use the driver so that I can hit that

260 yard drive straight down the middle," to a focus on the basics of the swing. His goal is to help the student develop consistency in the swing so that every time that the student addresses the ball, he does it with the same grip, the same stance, the same focus, the same backswing, the same downswing, the same release and the same follow through. All of this is integrated into a uniquely individual process dependent upon height, weight, flexibility, age, coordination, strength and other variables specific to that person. (I can't help here, but to retell the old golf joke about addressing the ball: " I have no trouble addressing it, I just don't seem to be able to attach enough stamps.")

At any rate, after three lessons and seven or eight trips to the practice range (notice that I use the term "practice range" rather than the more common "driving range" because I was there to learn and practice a variety of shots, not just hit the drive), I started to feel comfortable with the new grip and the new swing. I was now comfortably hitting the seven iron one hundred forty five to one hundred fifty yards with some loft and some degree of accuracy (and feeling very good about it). There was some consistency to my swing and a sense of purpose and a plan each time I addressed the ball.

The process of hitting a golf ball was no longer a random process. It had structure. There was a sequence of steps, which, though awkward and difficult to remember at first, became increasingly automatic and natural feeling with practice.

As with any new skill, the first hundred or so times that I used these new techniques, I had to really concentrate and it was difficult to remember the fourteen or fifteen elements of a perfect swing and integrate them all at the same time. It was especially difficult to remember to keep some of the body quiet while torquing the rest of it into a spring ready

The process now had some structure – it was no longer totally random.

to be unleashed. But I had a patient coach and that really helped. Practice, practice, practice; coach, improve, practice, practice, practice, which incidentally, is not a bad mode for any corporate training.

After a while, the once random process not only became a predictable sequence of steps, but it became mine. It was my swing, defined in terms of proven fundamentals and the uniqueness of my skill level, dexterity, flexibility, strength, size and coordination. I learned from Ron Horton, from watching Fred Couples and Vijay Singh in person, from reading Harvey Penick and watching Johnny Miller's entertaining video. Finally, it was my swing.

Only when a process is structured, only when it is standardized, can it be improved. The danger is to say, "Now that it is standardized, let's leave it that way forever."

"And your point is?" you may ask.

My point is that now that I have standardized the process of my swing, I can improve it. Now when I hit that errant shot (which I do), I almost never hit two in a row like it. I don't typically hit two in a row because I am able to reflect back on my swing and say, "What did I do wrong? Was the club face open, was I too close to the ball, were my hands closed, did I have too much hip or shoulder turn, was the pace of my backswing out of sequence with my downswing? Was I just plain hurried or not concentrating? What was wrong?" And I can carry out this process of analysis with some degree of certainty that I can make an adjustment at the next opportunity because the process is no longer random, even if it is far from perfect.

Predictability Requires Structure

In short, I can now improve because I have a consistent process that includes enough structure to be predictable but not so much structure as to prevent me from hitting the ball with my skills, knowledge and creativity in order to achieve my goal. I have gone from a random process, which was impossible to improve upon because it was never done the same way, to a consistent process, which encourages improvement.

As a consultant and a trainer I have been in hundreds of different businesses in this country, and the norm (outside the manufacturing floor, although sometimes even there) is random rather than standardized business processes. The way most companies order products, stock their products, interface with customers in conducting the sales process, process goods for delivery, conduct the quotes process, place orders in a queue for production, schedule production, and handle customer complaints is more random than structured, even with intervention of quality standards such as ISO and QS 9000. The great exception to this, of course, has traditionally been the aircraft industry and defense contractors, who often face the opposite problem of being so standardized and so structured that it is nearly impossible to improve their rigidly established and documented systems because the systems become more important than the components that make up the systems. Regrettably, these processes sometimes even prevail when the components that are produced are sometimes defective. Again, this is a leadership issue. Let's not manage a process that produces defects, let's improve the process no matter how many approvals are needed for the change.

(In terms of the golf metaphor, many defense contractors were told by government agencies during the '60s, '70s and '80s, "Here is Fred Couples' swing – imitate it." Things have improved of late.)

Standardizing a Business Process

However, for most companies overly detailed and rigid processes are not the problem. The problem for most businesses is a lack of processes; many companies operate essentially as I did when

I first ventured on the golf course – before my golf lessons. Processes are so random that it is very difficult to determine exactly what went wrong that caused the problem. Thus, many companies revisit the same problem in several different guises over a period of weeks or months with different solutions. Typically, the effectiveness of any one solution is diluted or destroyed because the next time a problem appears a different solution is applied, one that meets the needs of the most vociferous internal or external customer of the process.

There are few more critical processes within a company than responding to an RFQ (request for quote). Yet, this quotations' process (including responding to a request for a price on particularly large orders for a series of assemblies or components) is a classic example of a random process in many businesses. Strangely, this process, so critical to the continuing flow of goods out of the company, often takes a back seat to the interrupting calls taken by sales people all day long from "bad customers" (the eighty percent of customers who produce twenty percent or less of operating profit) looking for a good deal.

The goal is to reduce the number of "urgents" (e.g., reworking a customer order) so that you have time for the "importants" (e.g., improving the process of responding to a quote).

As I began a consulting engagement about five years ago, a company president related to me the following problem. In my experience this problem is not unique to the company where this man was president.

"Don, we have a problem here. We are doing okay with our manufacturing and operations, our sales were over three hundred million last year and our margins are holding steady over the long term, but we just can't seem to respond to a customer's request for special pricing, special parts or special assemblies (anything out of the routine) as fast as our competition. What can you do to help us?" The president of the company then went on to explain how they had invested heavily in technology, that they had made sure that the price of all parts were in the system and available to sales people on a PC at their desk and that even with all this money invested they were still way behind the competition.

I asked what the typical time to respond to any of these quotes was. "The typical response time, that is a good question. We really don't know, on the average I'd say that it is more than four weeks, but less than ten."

I have owned my own company. I know there is individual variation that influences every process. I know this is difficult to control. But four to ten weeks on the average?

Predictably Unpredictable

So, the process of investigating this random process begins, and the process unfolds in all its predictable unpredictability.

In essence, the process looks like this. The customer calls the sales person and asks for a price on a large number of items, or a special order, or a new part, or a new assembly. The salesman, realizing that this is going to be a lengthy process, takes the information down, enters it into the computer, prints it out and places it in a tray for "same day" pickup (anytime that day – even six hours later) to be taken to corporate engineering.

> *"Stop whatever you are working on and..." is an indicator that Mr. Urgent is running the shop.*

When the potential order arrives in engineering, it is put in a queue to wait its time for review. When the time for review comes around, which may be more than forty-eight hours later, the engineer in charge of this quote may have to call the plant engineer for information about sub-assemblies or the availability of parts. As a matter of fact, just as he is about to do this, another engineer walks into the office and says, "Stop whatever you are working on. John (the V.P.,

Sales) says this quote is a hot one and he told the customer he would be back with a price within three days."

So the original quote is put back in the paper queue where it will languish until the "rush" quote is completed. Meanwhile, the specialist in cost and pricing who should have received the normal quote today is sitting in his office playing "Klondike" on his PC or sending his friends e-mail about this coming weekend's golf game. (Of course, what he doesn't know is that this rush quote may just ruin that opportunity.)

When the rush quote is complete, the engineer revisits the previous quote, having to spend considerable time re-aquainting himself with the particulars of this week-old potential order. So now he calls one of the plant engineers who asks him to send a fax so he can take a better look at it.

The plant engineer responds the next day. He says that he will likely need special cost and pricing information, and that he has forwarded it to the cost and pricing specialist who has told the plant engineer that it will be at least two days before he can get to it, because he is working on a rush order for the Vice President of Sales.

And we have not even begun to look at the whirl of approvals that accompanied this process and which typically added two to five days to the overall cycle time. Is it any wonder that this company was losing business to competitors? Is it any wonder that competitors were shipping products before this company was responding to the request for quote?

"Structure" without Discipline Breeds Variation

The process was basically like my golf swing. There was a form to it, and there was some widely varying structure, but there was no discipline to follow a well defined and limited approach. This company's quotes process had so much variation built into it – interruptions, queue times, communication problems, overrides (particularly by the V.P. of Sales and the company President), handoffs, etc. that every RFQ became essentially a special process and every intervention introduced even greater variation into this process.

There were no Band-Aid remedies that could fix this process. The only thing that I could say when this process was explained to me was much the same as my golf pro said to me when he first saw my swing (you might recall that he suggested that I must have some natural athletic ability): "You guys must have excellent products and a first rate sales team" (which they did).

Every request for a quote became a special process unto itself. Leaders find and solve problems with creativity and structure — much like the way you solve the challenge of the "difficult lie."

From the Real to the Ideal

The first step in solving the quotes problem was to get the president's acknowledgment that the current process was not only counterproductive, but that it needed radical surgery if the situation was to be improved. If you don't get this buy in, the improvement typically won't happen. Change is a leadership, not a management, issue.

The solution to this was to take a team made up of people involved in the process (the quotes specialist, a couple of engineers, a manufacturing person, someone from sales) and do two flow diagrams (both done in some detail). The first flow chart was: "What does the process look like today?" The second chart was: "Given today's technology and without any serious investment in personnel or equipment, what should this process look like?"

Now, once these two charts are complete, you change processes to reflect the ideal. When this company made these process changes, they achieved some impressive results.

Average cycle time for an RFQ went from forty working days to seven. Still not fast enough, but a lot better than it was. They did two things, they defined the process and they put discipline into the process. Then they trained everyone involved. Exceptions to the standardized process were reduced, and, because under the old system, nearly every quote had been assigned some thermal quality—hot, very hot, red hot, rush hot—a new system was implemented which said that an order's priority, once determined, would be changed only by the Sales VP, and only under unusual circumstances (e.g., best customer, true emergency situation).

Process Standardization

This process needs to be carried out by most American companies for between twenty and thirty key processes – taking an order, purchasing a product, receiving raw material, producing financials, producing an invoice and especially serving the customer.

Few processes have as much randomness built into them as customer service. If you don't believe me, try this experiment. Have someone call the customer service representatives of your company with a complaint or a difficult problem to solve (or worse yet, to get a price on a given item). Talk to three or four of them—you will typically find tremendous variation.

I did this with an airline. The problem was real. A "Sky Cap" had checked my baggage outside and sent them to Tulsa rather than Tucson. I discovered this with less than thirty minutes before departure time. (I supposedly had preferred status on this airline—I was a "Gold Member.")

First, I took the problem to a gate agent who sent me to someone else who told me that there was nothing that could be done, the bags were probably already loaded on the wrong plane. And her tone said, "I'm too busy for this kind of problem, live with it – and don't argue with me."

So I went to another agent who told me that because the ticket said Tucson, the code should be for Tucson, so the baggage people would probably catch it. Not to worry.

Next, I went to a third agent who said, "I am sorry, sir, this must be very frustrating for you. I am sure that having your luggage arrive where you do is important." (It was, I was doing a presentation the next morning in Tucson, but not with my bags in Tulsa I wasn't; I was near panic.)

She continued, "Let me call my supervisor to get someone to cover my post while I go downstairs and see if I can't locate your bags and get them to the right destination. If you will proceed to the gate, I will call the gate with an update."

I walked down to the gate I was flying out of and checked with the agent. "Dr. Sanders," he said, "Sarah called and said that she has found your bags and changed the baggage tags to Tucson. Here are the numbers." He handed me a slip of paper with a series of numbers.

Extraordinary customer service from this customer service agent? Yes. Responsive to a special need? Yes. Disruptive to the system? No – she called her supervisor to make sure that she had back up. The system had structure, but it accommodated emergencies. The question was, why hadn't the other two been willing to do the same thing?

And the answer is almost always expressed in one of two words: training and consequences. It seems like it is some natural law when we do develop systems and we don't train everyone in those systems. Or, we will develop standards of performance, but we won't train everyone in these standards of performance. Or we train everyone, but don't treat those who don't implement them any different than those who do. And we don't administer nega-

Most poor customer service issues boil down to the absence of two critical practices: proper training and/or predetermined and well implemented consequences.

tive consequences to people who don't bother to follow the training at all (See Vision and Alignment).

Again, airlines are a perfect example (I fly a lot). On any given flight, I give myself about a fifty percent chance of having a flight attendant who is quietly competent (this is okay), about a twenty percent chance of having someone who is really competent and efficient, and about a five to ten percent chance of having someone who is truly customer service oriented, friendly and efficient.

This obviously leaves twenty to twenty-five percent of the time when I expect a flight attendant who is unfriendly (sometimes surly) and neither efficient nor competent. Now let me acknowledge that being a flight attendant is a difficult and demanding job. You deal with people who range from the very young to the very old, from groups of teenagers going on a trip to businessmen who have had a few too many in the bar before boarding. Some folks are obnoxious and others gracious, and you are in the air in a little alloy tube going 550 miles per hour.

The Need for Constant Attention to the Process

But why the variation? Why the variation everywhere in customer service? The answer is found in training and consequences, random processes and the physical law of entropy.

If I don't go to my pro regularly, my game slips back. If I don't pay attention to and implement what he teaches, my scores get worse (the process is called entropy). If you are having problems with customers, if you have reject rates in excess of 2% (I had one client who thought that 6% was acceptable!), if you are experiencing turnover and frustration with your people, begin by looking at your processes. Remember the basics of the golf swing.

REMEMBER:
*YOU CAN'T IMPROVE A **RANDOM** PROCESS.*

How To Play This Hole

1 . Identify twenty to thirty key processes within your company. If you are a department manager, select the five to seven key processes within your department. (If you are not in a management position, this is an opportunity to start leading. Focus on a process. Align that process, work with others. Improve it and report results.)

2. Prioritize this list of processes. Begin with the one that is causing the most problems, costing the most money or generating the most customer complaints.

3. Identify one or two teams to begin working on these processes. A leader should attend the first meeting and present a vision of what the process should achieve and how important it is that this team standardize and improve this process.

4. Make sure that the team leader is a member of management and that team members represent internal customers and suppliers of the process.

5. Exhibit patience. These teams typically take two to three months to produce a process that is truly standardized and improved.

6. Before implementing the newly defined process, train everyone who will be using the process. Get their feedback before full implementation.

7. Six months after implementation, re-visit the process (remember entropy). Is it achieving its desired goals? If yes, what steps can be added or deleted to improve it

further? If no, what needs to be changed so that it can achieve the desired goal?

8. Always have the leader go back and personally thank the team for its contribution to the company, department, plant, etc. This is critical if you want these employees to serve on other teams.

9. Identify another process and begin again.

GOLF TEACHES US

THAT HAVING A KNOWLEDGE

OF THE BASICS

IS A PREREQUISITE TO

IMPROVING

ANY ASPECT OF YOUR GAME.

THE KEY TO IMPROVEMENT

Secrets from the Golf Course
on Keeping an Accurate Score

About Hole #6

The 385 yard hole, "Keeping An Accurate Score" has a par four rating on the leadership course. This hole is rated at 7 for difficulty on this course, more difficult than some to implement, but easier than most. If you are good with your irons and have some discipline about how you approach the game, you can score well here. The challenge on this hole is the tough dogleg right with the fairway sloped left at the dogleg and a row of old pines going down the right side of the course to the turn. Hazards a plenty are found along the way, these include: we don't have time to measure stuff, we look at our profitability, what else counts? If they knew how poorly we were really doing..., and nobody does anything with the information anyway, why keep it?

Introduction

Can you lead without adequate information? Of course you can, but leadership is so much stronger when it is fully informed. Managers have traditionally focused on managing with financial numbers; return on invested capital, sales, profits, margins,

> *The leader is not limited by total reliance on quantitative data.*

RGA. The leader knows this and more. She knows the cost of turnover and the cost of a lost customer. She knows how many people have left the company in the past year and how many customers have taken their business elsewhere—or how many new customers have been added in the last quarter. The leader is not limited by total reliance on quantitative data, she sees where qualitative data can also make a contribution to understanding important trends such as increases or decreases in market share.

Finally, the leader knows that data are as data do, and that a lot of data that is captured by the company is buried in reports that no one understands or bothers to read. The leader is interested in data not as an abstract concept but as an improvement tool and she insists that data be kept accurately. All of this, of course, we can learn from the world of golf.

Golf Is a Game of Numbers (So Is Business)

Golf, like its cousin baseball (white ball struck by a club played on a pasture—perhaps distant cousin would be more accurate), is a game of numbers. There are scores for every hole, scores for the game, yards per hole and yardage markers for the hole. There is the concept of handicap, ratings and slopes for each course and the myriad games within games such as a five point Nassau or Wolf (also called Pig) that are based on numbers. In golf you have woods and irons designed to go a certain yardage and you have measurements such as greens in regulation and average number of putts (including the dreaded four footer).

In addition, today's golf is highlighted by those charts that show how much money is being won or has already been won not only by those on the Men's and Women's Professional tours, but by those on the Senior Tour, the Nike Tour and other lesser tours where excellent golfers labor in relative obscurity hoping to join the elite 150.

All of this attention to numbers has implications for business, obvious implications that are ignored at the peril of those who not only operate the business, but who are stakeholders in its success. Like golf, business is a game of numbers. Typically, there are three problems with these numbers: first, too many companies either don't have any measurements or don't have the right ones; second, even when they have the right ones, they are often kept incorrectly-not dishonestly, just incorrectly; and third, even when the right ones are kept accurately, nothing is done with the resultant data to improve the business.

It is an established rule of business that it is very difficult to manage that which you don't or can't measure. This is also true of golf, of course. If you don't know the average number of putts per hole or the number of greens reached in regulation, it is hard to know where to focus your attention

So, let's begin with how to keep these metrics so that they are helpful in improving your score, then move back to what it is that you need to measure in order to improve your

> *Fewer activities are more frustrating for an employee than to maintain data that are never read or used by anyone in the company.*

game, and then, finally look at what needs to be done to ensure that metrics are integrated into your overall strategic efforts to improve the bottom line.

Not Just a Score, But An Accurate Score

There is a classic story of a young professional golfer who was facing a difficult two hundred twenty-yard shot out of some very short grass. As he waited for the other players to walk to their shots, he began tapping his foot directly behind the ball. After about a minute of this, he turned to his caddie and said, "Well, what do you think? Is it a two iron?"

> *One of the toughest things about playing golf is keeping an accurate score.*

And the caddie replied, "It will be in about another minute, sir."

So what is one of the toughest things about playing golf? It is not just hitting that super shafted titanium headed, oversized driver or that flex shafted oversized offset cavity backed iron. It is not making that dreaded pressure putt with the game on the line. It is certainly not hitting cleanly out of the bunker, or hitting the ball straight (although this is certainly up there).

No, one of the toughest things about playing golf is keeping an accurate score – and this is critically important, as it is the only way to improve.

Oh, I see some of you saying, "What are you talking about? I am absolutely scrupulous about keeping score. I know the rules and I live by them faithfully." And if you do, that is wonderful. You are among the ten percent. You are what might be called a Tom Watson golfer, a purist, a strict constructionist and sportingly honest golfer.

However, having played the game for a few years with many differing personalities, I have come to the conclusion that most people play **situational golf**, yes, situational golf – my score depends on the situation.

Situational Scoring – How We Often (or at Least Sometimes) Keep Score in Golf

The following is a classic example of situational scoring in golf:

> *Two of us were playing golf in late March after some heavy rains. On the three hundred ninety-five yard fourteenth, with both of us making a strong effort to break 85, my partner (who happens to be my brother-in-law) stepped up to the tee box and miss-hit his drive. I forget whether it was*

a slice or a hook (he is equally adept at both), but I do remember it landed on the next fairway and that he muttered the appropriate colorful commentary.

I was next on the tee box and I hit a beautiful drive. This was the kind of drive that weekend golfers dream about. The drive was straight as an arrow, right down the middle of the fairway, two hundred and fifty yards at least and just over a slight hill which – we both knew because we had played this course before – hid a small lake.

My brother-in-law walked over to the next fairway, held up his hand to let the oncoming foursome know he was there and quickly hit a perfect five iron. This shot carried at least one hundred seventy yards; it bounced on the same hill in almost exactly the same spot as my drive had.

We met halfway up the fairway, and it was a strange kind of feeling as we walked the final one hundred twenty yards or so toward our golf balls just over the hill. This feeling goes against everything that the golfer holds dear. The primary feeling was, "I hope I didn't hit it too far." This is indeed a rare feeling for a golfer on a straight shot.

As we crested the hill, our worst fears were realized, both golf balls were nowhere to be seen, there was only one option – those two beautiful shots would wind up as $1.25 golf balls in the big barrel in front of the registration desk.

"Casual water," said my brother in law. "What?" I responded, being rather naive at the time about the nuances of good scoring.

"Casual water." he said again. "The golf ball would be in a decent lie if it hadn't rained so much. According to the rules, it doesn't cost us a stroke."

I looked at the water. The diameter of the lake had increased by about two inches due to the rains, the ground drained really well into the bayou that crisscrossed the course. The balls were nowhere to be seen within those two inches. Casual water?

But this was now a moral decision. If I rejected the casual water theory I now cost not only myself a stroke, but my brother-in-law as well. At least that was my rationalization. The truth was I wanted to break eighty-five on that day and I had shot a forty-two on the front nine. If only I could...

Casual water.

"Yep, that's what it is," I said, "casual water."

Perhaps you have had this experience and perhaps you made a different decision. But sometime in your golfing career you have faced the obvious, but unpleasant truth that the only way to improve the way you play the game is to count every stroke, to keep an accurate score.

This day, this incident, was a turning point in my game. Driving home that day I couldn't think about anything other than "casual water." I realized that the eighty-nine I shot that appeared on my scorecard wasn't "quite accurate." I realized that if I wanted to move from "tween" to competent golfer with a reasonable handicap, I would have to count every stroke. (See Chapter 8-Secrets from the Golf Course on Character).

There are typically ten to fifteen of these decisions of this type to be made each time a person plays golf. A beautiful drive that winds up right behind the tree, the chip that goes three inches, the waggle where you knock the ball off the tee, the first mulligan, the second mulligan, the third mulligan, the "I didn't mean to do that," the out of bounds marker that shouldn't be there, the second shot into the water, the beautiful iron shot that lands in a divot or the putt that rims the hole and wanders three inches away (and it would have been a birdie).

The list could go on and on, given the ancient and honourable rules of golf. The fact is that many golfers keep score depending on the situation – and because of this it is difficult to improve. So what has this got to do with business?

> *There are typically ten to fifteen scoring decisions to be made during each round of golf.*

Situational Statistics – How We Often Keep Score in Business

Situational scoring also occurs in business. It doesn't occur everywhere, but it does occur frequently and the purpose is the same, to make the company look better than it really is. A few years ago, I was working with a large electronics distributor; they had thirty or forty branches along the Gulf Coast. I was helping them set up some statistical measures. I had been called in because they had been receiving an unusually large number of customer complaints, particularly about on-time deliveries. Sales people were reporting that, if improvement couldn't be made, and made soon, some customers would definitely be lost. This is called urgency.

At an early meeting, I asked a group of managers what the company's on time delivery percentage was. "Ninety-four point seven percent," they replied. "And what is your variation around that average," I asked.

"Less than three percentage points either way," they boasted, showing that they knew the basics of attributes control charts.

"Does that mean that you can promise your customers between ninety-one and ninety-eight percent on time delivery," I asked with surprise.

"Yes," they replied, "we have excellent on-time delivery." It needs to be noted that the people in this meeting were all operations people including the managers of Quality Assurance, MIS and Customer Service. The sales people, as is the norm, were too busy selling to spend time in customer service improvement meetings of this type.

"Then why," I asked the group, "do we have all these customer complaints about late delivery?"

It was, we found out after months of investigation, because they were practicing situational score keeping.

Situational Score Keeping in Practice

The process that we uncovered was this. A customer would call and place an order. The Customer Service Representative (CSR) would check inventory and provide a delivery date for the list of items – often ten to twelve lines with one hundred or more items.

As the delivery date approached, the CSR would again check inventory. Whoops, some of those items were back ordered and would definitely not be at the customer's dock on the delivery date. Like the casual water that I hit my drive into, this was not fair, it wasn't the distributor's problem, they had done everything they could to get it there on time. In fact, it was the manufacturer's problem – they had not met their usual delivery date to the distributor. So the CSR determined that this mistake, this late delivery, was not going to count against them. After all, it wasn't the distributor's fault; it wasn't fair for them to be penalized.

So they called the customer, told the customer of the items that were going to be late, gave a new delivery date for the items, changed the delivery date in the system, shipped what they had available to ship and called that number of lines (or number of items depending on which was more favorable) "on time." When the back ordered material came in and was shipped in time to meet the new delivery date, this part of the order was also considered "on time." Sometimes, the manufacturer called to say that the second delivery date couldn't be met either and a new date was given. The CSR again moved the "promised date" in the system to meet the new schedule and the customer was contacted (sometimes by fax). The product was considered on time when it arrived at the customer's dock.

Because it wasn't fair, the CSR's found a way to be blameless for the situation; they called it file maintenance.

The CSR's even had a name for this (in truth, it happened quite frequently). They called it "file maintenance." File maintenance is to business as "casual water" was to my scorecard. It masks how you are really doing. It makes you think you don't have inventory or supplier problems when you really do.

After another month of investigation, we finally got the real number. The on-time delivery rate for this company, based on the original promise date, was seventy-eight percent, with the statistically calculated variation at sixteen percent on either side. So, some customers might be getting ninety-four percent; other orders were coming in at just a little over sixty percent. Suddenly, all those customer complaints made sense. File maintenance was masking the problem.

The management of this company wasn't particularly happy with this data, but at least now they could improve. Oh, and by the way, one other thing. In order to get the real data, we had to offer amnesty to those involved, so that they could tell us the truth about how they were keeping the data without getting in trouble. If you want to find out the truth, you often have to provide amnesty – but I don't know how to provide amnesty on the golf course.

(Incidentally, there is another way that golfers often use the same technique that was being used by these CSR's-it is called "handicap maintenance." High handicappers turn in only their lower scoring scorecards or don't bother to count all their strokes.

Low handicappers, depending on whether they are more concerned with ego or winning, will turn in only those scorecards that help them achieve their goal. In either case, the only way to really know what is going on is to count all your strokes and turn in all your cards.)

How to Keep Score

If keeping an accurate score is difficult in golf and business, knowing what to track is almost as much of a challenge. As a matter of fact, golf provides the perfect metaphor for business in terms of the need to keep score – not just after the game so that you can determine how well you did and how to adjust your handicap, but during the game, the differing elements that need to be measured so that you can not only know how well you are doing on an aggregate basis, but how you are doing with those individual elements that make up the aggregate.

In working with companies across the country, I am amazed at how many of these companies determine their progress solely by keeping a "financial score." This score is typically represented by annual figures for Sales, SG&A, Cost of Goods Sold, Overheads, ROA, Profit/Loss. Some companies (many of them believing that they are "customer-oriented") take measurement to another level. They may measure market share ("We've gone from 17.8% to 21.3%") – somehow believing that these percentages actually reflect something finite and obtainable) or the number of customer complaints – "We have received only eighty-three complaints on this product since its introduction" – uh huh), or repeat sales. ("Seventy-nine percent of the consumers who buy our product would buy it again" – what about the other twenty-one percent?)

All of these measures are important, but like the golf scores that you record at the end of each game, they are necessary but not sufficient. What does it tell you if the last four times you played you scored 77, 84, 91, 82? It tells you what you did shoot, it doesn't tell you what you might have shot, and it certainly doesn't tell you anything about how to improve your game or how to shoot that 77 again. (Who is going to show up, Mr. 77 or Mr. 91?). These scores do not tell you anything about how you are doing; they only tell you how you did. And averaging them often hurts more than helps, especially when you have a fourteen point spread between your high and low score.

The Emphasis on "Lagging Indicators"

Richard Whitely, in his ground breaking book *"The Customer Driven Company,"* published in 1991, calls figures such as annual sales, order volume, and complaint measurement "lagging indicators." A lagging indicator tells you how you have done, rather than how you are doing. A score of 82 simply tells you that, on this day, under these conditions, it took you a total of 82 strokes to complete eighteen holes.

Who is going to show up: Mr. 77 or Mr. 91?

In other words, it tells you how you did; your score is a "lagging indicator." It should also be added that lagging indicators, by definition, both in business and in golf, may suggest trends, but they certainly don't tell you how you are going to do in the future.

Let's return to the golf analogy. Let's say that you wanted to improve your golf game. Where would you start? If you are like most people, you would go to the practice range, the putting green, or the chipping area to work on a specific part of the game.

You might decide that you need to work on your mid-range irons or your bunker play or your driver. You might decide that you need to learn more about course management, the rules of golf, "mental toughness," or hitting the ball from the high grass.

Or you might decide to hire a pro who would watch your swing and provide instruction on how you might improve and then coach you to that point. Or finally, if you were really distraught and were stuck at a plateau score where you did not seem to be improving, you might take drastic action and decide to attend a week-long clinic.

But, in truth, how do you know where to start? Where do you go to get the information you need in order to know what aspect of the game you need to improve?

Actually, because you are the customer of this process, you have to listen to yourself, but the nagging question is "Do you really know where you need to work?" It is not at all unusual to see people who can consistently drive the ball two hundred thirty to two hundred forty yards down the middle, practicing their drive trying to get that extra twenty yards, while they are averaging 2.7 putts per hole (of course they don't know this because they don't have a sophisticated enough measurement system to know how they are really performing – or because it is far more fun and stress relieving to pound that ball with a driver than tap it with a putter.)

So again, how do we know? I submit that it is very difficult with a standard scorecard just as it is in business with a standard financial statement because both reflect lagging indicators of performance.

Like a standard golf score card, standard financials don't give you all the data you need to improve.

For example, you might want to know which product and service characteristics are most important to the customer. You cannot get this from a balance sheet, you must use something like focus groups to obtain this information. Or, you may want to know how your service compares with that of your competitors in terms of those facets of the service process of greatest importance to the customer. Again, a standard financial analysis won't tell you this. If revenues are decreasing, it may point to a problem in the area, but it won't give you the

information you need to improve. To obtain
this data, you may need to structure a customer survey, you may need to use "mystery
shoppers," or you may need to analyze cycle
times within the process.

*Scorecards, like
most financials,
are lagging
indicators.*

The standard scorecard that you play with
on the golf course is also, as noted above, a
lagging indicator; it tells you how you have
scored on each hole and how you have scored
for the entire eighteen holes. It tells you how you have scored in
comparison to the degree of difficulty assigned to each hole
(hardest on the course, easiest on the course, etc.) and to the
standard score for that individual hole (par). Finally, in composite, it helps you determine your competitive position relative to the course (your handicap). However, the information
on the standard scorecard, by itself, doesn't help you improve
your game by a single stroke.

Standard financials are analogous. They may tell you how
you have done on each "hole" – that is for each month, each
quarter or in each division. They may tell you how you have
scored for the entire course – that is, for the entire year. They
may show you how you have done in terms of par – last year's
sales or your competitive position relative to the market (market share), *but they don't show you how to improve.*

Metrics to Improve By or "Why Am I Shooting Ninety-Two?"

So, the question is: "What does?" What kind of measurement
system can help us improve our golf game and what kind of
measures do we need to use to "improve our business game?"

Let's return to keeping score as we play a round of golf. The
average golf scorecard, as noted above, is much like the average
financial report – it is a lagging indicator. In gross figures, it
tells you how you did. It tells you how you did relative to a

Table 1: Scorecard for Improvement Focus

Hole	1	2	3	4	5	6
Par	5	4	3	4	4	4
Yards	585	392	175	414	425	375
Drive	237m	235s	145h	202h	244m	228s
2nd	212	160 5i-s	pw	35 5i	140 4i-s	150 7i-w
3rd	155 6i-s	30		148 7i	50 lw-w	10 sw
Putts	2	3	2	3	1	2
Score	6	4	4	6	6	5

Legend: s= slice, m= middle, h= hook, i= iron, s= sand, w= water, lw=lob wedge

standard set for each of the holes on the course (par) and for the course as a whole. The standard scorecard does not show you where you need to improve. As with business, you may have an intuitive sense of where you need to improve, but don't really know.

In order to identify what is needed for a system of improvement measures let's look at the golf scorecard in Table 1. (It is only covers the first six holes to demonstrate the kind of scoring data you would need to maintain in order to ensure a focus on improvement.)

Obviously, to keep this type of scorecard would take considerably more time than to keep the typical course scorecard and you wouldn't want to fill one out each time particularly if you were walking. It would probably even take some joy out of the game and might even drive you nuts. In addition, to do this right, you would need one of those expensive range finders or you would just be guessing all the time at your yardage. But if you were to discipline yourself to do this, what would it tell you?

It would not only reflect your score per hole but it would also give you your strengths and weaknesses at a glance. This scorecard would tell you if you are consistently hooking or slicing, if you are hitting the three-iron consistently, if you have spent time in the water or sand, and it would actually tell you how many putts you were averaging per hole.

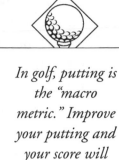

In golf, putting is the "macro metric." Improve your putting and your score will improve. What is your business' macro metric.

For example, the scorecard in Table 1 would tell the player that he or she is getting good distance with the irons, but not much accuracy. Hazards seem to have a special allure. A review of the data suggest the golfer could probably improve dramatically, with more time on the practice putting green.

The Macro Metric

In golf, putting is what is called a "macro metric." It may look the same as all the other indicators on this scorecard, but in the game of golf the ability to putt well and consistently arguably contributes more to the ability to score well than any other single element of the game. (The often repeated statistic that 65% of the average golfer's shots occur within 100 yards of the pin flies in the face of all the emphasis on getting an extra five or ten yards with the driver. Most of us know that hitting the ball farther [increasing sales?] won't improve our score that much but that improving our putting accuracy [less rework?] will. Every company needs to determine what "putting" is for that company.)

When Continental Airlines was trying to pull itself out of bankruptcy for the second time, Gordon Bethune went to the J.D. Power and Associates customer satisfaction study for information. This study indicated that, while there were several factors contributing to customer satisfaction in the airline industry, on-time performance was the prime determinant, the macro metric. By itself, on-time performance was 22% of customer satisfaction; no other element contributed more than 15%. Continental decided to focus on dramatically improving its on time performance, and as the title of Bethune's book says, they went from *Worst to First* in customer satisfaction.

There is another lesson in having a macro metric, a measurement that serves the same purpose as on-time arrival in a given industry. In many companies there is an organizational structure that rewards departmental or divisional performance at the cost of focusing on broad business performance. For example, I sometimes hear a manager saying, "Well, we met our goals, we made our numbers, so don't blame us for the mess the company is in. It must be somebody else who is not carrying the load." The question is, of course, how much does the achievement of your goals contribute to the overall achievement of company goals. It is surprising to find the disconnects that exist between the two.

A business scorecard should help you track a macro metric for your industry just as the golf scorecard above shows you how you are doing with putts. Like the golf scorecard, a business scorecard should act as an improvement tool. It should tell you where you need to improve, it should direct you to an area where you need to focus when you practice. It should also tell you where your strengths are. (This type of scorecard should also help keep your score accurate, but that, as we discussed above, is another story.)

Single data points are not meaningful. To have truly helpful data, trend charts are a minimal requirement and control charts will tell the whole story.

An Industry Scorecard

So, what would a scorecard for your industry look like? It would be a brief summary of data that you could look at to tell you not just how well you are doing in overall measures, but how you are doing in individual measures, particularly your macro metric(s) so that you can improve.

And I need to caution you that a single data point, if not totally meaningless, is certainly not very meaningful. What does a single "hole in one" tell you? Nothing. What does a single 230-yard drive tell you? Nothing. To have a real understanding of the meaning of measures, trend charts are a minimal requirement, and most call for control charts.

So let's look at a corporate scorecard. In order to improve, we need to know where we are (what our scores have been), and how we are tracking our performance (where we are on the course).

Let's begin first with company performance so we can get this out of the way. Measuring company financial performance is like your overall score on the course. It may be a lagging indicator, but you still need it to see how you have done in this game compared to how you have done in the past and to figure your financial "handicap." So you will need:

- Financial statistics linked directly to key success factors
- Financial Measures linked to EVA, MVA or ROI
- Evidence of Past, Present and Predicted Future Performance
- Financials reflecting the true cost of it's products and services including cost of non quality data
- Some financials for the measurement of departmental/ divisional performance

The point here is not to provide a definitive list (for a definitive treatment, see *The Balanced Scorecard* by Kaplan and Norton). Most companies have adequate financial performance indicators (although I recently visited a company that had approximately $150 million in sales last year that had no budget, much less accurate financials!). The point here is that obviously a company needs financials. Each company should identify the measures it needs for financial monitoring and control (those that provide the company with an understanding of its short and long term success and its current status). Once identified, these measures should be continually refined so that the company knows its true financial score, not a "mulligan score" or a "whoops, I didn't mean to hit the ground first," or a "casual water" score.

However, as I noted earlier, there is an equal need for accurate measures of how you play the game. How are you doing at driving, chipping, putting? How many times do you wind up in the rough or the sand? Most companies don't know these things and need to have both departmental and company wide data to see how they are doing.

Basically, a comprehensive system of improvement based metrics includes quarterly reports on varied areas including:

- **Customer Satisfaction Data** – using an internally developed customer satisfaction index that includes data such as lost customers, repeat customer business, customer complaints, returns, and survey data

- **Employee Satisfaction Data** – using data that reflects turnover/retention exit interview data, industry data, and internal surveys

- **Individual Departmental Data** – these vary by department, but should include data linking performance to goals

- **Performance Data** – On time delivery, product returns, key product service indicators

- **Manufacturing Process Data** – Control charts on key product characteristics, cost data, MRB reports

- **Supplier Data** – On time delivery, product quality, rejects, correlation studies, e.g., MRB with suppliers

Obviously, the scope of this book does not allow for a lot of detail on these measurements (anymore than I could present a lesson on how to chip or putt), but I do want to remind you that this list must be improvement-oriented. The presentation and use of the data must also be improvement oriented. Many companies have the data, it is just that they are buried in reports four inches thick, in presentations of black and white numbers in excruciating detail or in seventy page monthly summaries.

In presenting data, many companies get caught up in form over substance.

For example, let's say that I put together an overhead that showed my golf scores for the past three years. Your initial response would probably be, "Huh, what does all this data mean?" (Your second response might well be, "I didn't know you were that bad," but that is not the issue here.)

The point is that the data must be presented in some meaningful way, and don't get caught up in form over substance.

Some years ago I was working with a major defense contractor located in Fort Worth. One of the division vice-presidents, who had about thirty direct reports and supervised a total of more than five hundred fifty employees that reported to him, held a semi-annual review of departmental performance. The presentations were primarily of financial data and this vice-president had a format that he insisted people use.

Grown men and women, some senior managers themselves (many former Army and Air Force officers) literally trembled while waiting to present their data. They were fearful not because of any concern with their data, but because this vice-president had actually stopped people in mid sentence and told them to leave the room until their data was correctly formatted; this was for a typo, a repeated word, a number that didn't match another, columns not perfectly aligned, any small infraction. For these direct reports, it was form over substance. They focused on how to minimize the data so that they minimized the opportunity for error, rather than how to present the data for understanding and improvement. (Incidentally, as we will see in Chapter 7, this vice president had considerable position power and no referent power, he was an accomplished manager, but not a leader. He could order, but he couldn't influence.)

At any rate, any meaningful system of metrics needs to include three types of data: one for customers, one for employees and one for bottom line dollar related results. Within each of these areas appropriate departments should have both long term, (e.g., product/service quality, customer satisfaction) and short term (e.g. scrap rate, customers serviced per day) results.

Measurements Are As Measurements Do

There is really only one reason to maintain data. Measures are there to drive the desired performance; measurements tell you whether you have been successful in linking your strategy to your vision. Measurements indicate whether you need to improve a process or reallocate resources. Data collection by itself, which is what a lot of companies do, is an exercise in futility for many, because month after month, quarter after quarter, year after year, the information is not used to impact the performance of the company. (If you think this notion is unrealistic or exaggerated, conduct an inventory of all the data that is gathered for various purposes. Once the inventory is complete, see how much of the data are actually used as a part of the decision making process. In my experience it is typically less than forty percent.)

I was brought into one company where there was an annual process of determining measurables. Top management got together to determine what they should measure, who should measure it, and how it should be mea-

Measurements, not guesstimates, should drive performance.

sured. The CEO was disappointed with the results, year after year they had the same discussions and the same uninformed decision making. They were experts at "guestimating." What was going wrong, he wondered.

It's frequently easier for an outsider, one who isn't invested in the problem, to see the problem and to suggest a solution. In this case, the data were being collected, but obviously not used. People reported their critical measures data but it was sent to a vice president who collected the data into a forty page document that was issued to all managers on a quarterly basis. It was produced as "green bar." Not surprisingly, no one read the report. This on-going problem led the CEO to form an interdepartmental team which was tasked with the responsibility of analyzing the process for determining, gathering and reporting data. Once they had completed their analysis, they were to make specific recommendations for change. These seven recommendations were made; they have application to most companies.

1. Measurement should drive performance. Decide what you want to accomplish and then determine the measures needed to ensure you will have the information required to achieve the goal.

2. Focus measurement on critical issues, on what is truly important. (One department was measuring productivity as a function of phone calls answered per minute; the issue was satisfied customers – effectiveness—not number of calls answered – efficiency).

3. Departments need individual measures related to overall corporate goals (See Chapter 2-Alignment). The issue of sub-optimization (departments competing against departments in a downward spiral of competitively and intentionally cutting costs and unintentionally cutting service to the customer) can only be understood and dealt with by focusing on the big picture of corporate

goals and results, not the small picture of departmental competition.

4. Financial data are not to be ignored. Financial data must include historical data (how we did last month, last year), current data (how we are doing now) and future data (if trends continue, where will we be 12, 24, 36 months from now).

5. Corporate needs to know how the company is perceived by customers in terms of value; that is, they need to know both the perceived satisfaction with the company's service (numerator) and the perceived fairness of the price charged for the service (denominator).

6. Individual performance data must be reviewed as individual data by the department manager (and linked to company performance), and in aggregate in the report to the vice president.

7. Finally, "differentiation data" need to be maintained. The quality of service provided by this particular company was so far above the competition that the customer paid a premium "price" to obtain overall lower cost. It was critical to continue to maintain this market differentiation.

The team created a new "scorecard" based on these seven recommendations. The scorecard provided meaningful data to management and cut the metrics report to six pages of critical measurements that were discussed in the executive committee and manager meetings. No longer "greenbar", the data told a story that management needed to understand in order to continue to run a profitable business.

How does your company use measures? Do you typically focus just on the short term financial data at the expense of data that would better help you manage and improve the company? The process begins with looking at the data that you need, not the data that you have and then moving from there to "how can we gather and use the data?"

The point here is that in business, as in golf, you cannot improve if you don't know how you are doing, and that the idea is not simply to keep score, but to keep an accurate score.

Once you have determined how to accurately keep score, use that score to: first, let you know how you are really doing (my drive is averaging about 225 yards); second, to give you ideas on how to improve so that the data actually drives your behavior (I am averaging 2.5 putts per hole, I need to reduce that to 2.0, but 2.2 is probably realistic short term); and third, to determine where you will be if you can improve this aspect of your game while holding all other facets of the game steady (I can reduce my average score from 91 to 85.)

> *In business as in golf, you cannot improve if you don't know how you are really doing.*

How to Play This Hole

1. Whether you are a department manager, a division manager or a company president/CEO, begin by taking an inventory of the measures that you are currently maintaining.

2. Once Step 1 is completed, review the data and reports. Which have value? Which ones can be used for improvement? Review the reports and determine those that are no longer needed.

3. Determine the measures that are needed that you are not currently maintaining; add these to your list.

4. Determine what it is that you will need to do to ensure that the data are accurately maintained, that they reflect the rules, not casual water.

5. Differentiate between those measures that are lagging indicators and those that will actually help you improve your processes and results.

6. Assemble all of this into a measurement system that is easy to use, is practical, is compre-hensive, and improvement oriented. Be wary of using yesterday's data to forecast next year's success. (Be especially careful not to base forecasting next year's sales based on last year's sales plus some convenient number, e.g. +12%).

7. Use data to drive improvement in all aspects of the company; monitor the data, let people know that there are consequences for not maintaining accurate data.

GOLF TEACHES US

THAT WE CAN'T IMPROVE

IF WE DON'T KEEP AN

ACCURATE SCORE.

GOLF TEACHES US THAT A DETAILED

SCORECARD DRIVES OUR

IMPROVEMENT FOCUS.

GOLF TEACHES US

THAT, ONLY IF WE LIVE BY

THE RULES, DO WE REALLY

KNOW HOW WE ARE DOING.

IN THE ROUGH

Secrets from the Golf Course
on Judgement, Emotional Intelligence,
Power and the Nature of Leadership

About Hole #7

This four hundred twelve yard par four is a challenge. Its wide fairways let you know that there are many ways to play the hole, but it seems that no matter what you do, you land in the rough. In order to be successful on this hole, you must make informed decisions about how to play when behind a tree, stuck in a fairway bunker, lodged in the high grass or under pressure to make that birdie putt. If you can play this hole well, it makes other holes on the course much easier to par. The key to playing this hole well is knowing your strengths and weaknesses and continuously growing in the knowledge of how to play the game.

Introduction

Having read this far, you are aware of my firmly held belief that the study of leadership has focused far too much on the "name" leaders like Jack Welsh, Andy Grove, Larry Bossidy, and Bill Gates. Focusing the study of leadership on the visible leaders is not unlike focusing all of our attention on the 150 or so golfers on the pro tour. There is much to learn not only from those who have achieved the highest pinnacle in their field, but also from the greater number who have achieved extremely high levels of competence in playing the game whether it be golf or leadership.

There are tens of thousands of excellent golfers, golfers carrying a two, three, six, seven or even ten handicap. Observing these golfers, watching how they play the game, can teach us a lot about golf. Similarly, there are tens of thousands of excellent leaders who have never run a company. We can learn a lot by observing these leaders, categorizing what they do and drawing conclusions for "best practices" based on their performance.

In my career I have had the opportunity to do just this. During the past fifteen years I have had the opportunity to observe and interact with literally hundreds of managers and supervisors. One of the primary lessons of leadership that I have learned by watching those men and women who emerged as real leaders has to do with how they operate under difficult circumstances.

A characteristic of all excellent golfers is competence in course management, and in particular, how well they play from the rough.

In watching these leaders for all these years, one conclusion is apparent. These leaders, as opposed to the managers they work with (including those they may report to) are distinguished by a set of "course management" skills variously referred to as emotional intelligence, inter-personal intelligence, "EQ," and inter-personal awareness. Of all the separate skills that make up what we call interpersonal or emotional intelligence, I believe that one of the most critical is judgement.

There are simply few skills more important to the effective development and execution of leadership than the skill of judgement (yes, judgement is a skill, not an attribute; something to be developed rather than a given). I believe that it is judgment and its close relative per- spicacity (the acute discernment of the inter- action of interpersonal variables), more than vision, alignment, motivation or even the enigmatic characteristic called charisma that distinguishes leaders from would be leaders and managers. Depending on where you are on the leadership development scale, judg- ment is either a baseline skill (you cannot get into the game without it) or a leverage skill (that is, it increases the effectiveness of every- thing else that you do). Mike Benson provides validation for this belief.

Judgement is one of those charac- teristics that frequently distinguishes the effective leader from the efficient manager.

Judgement in Business— The Mike Benson Story

When I first started consulting at the company where Mike worked, Mike was a vice-president in a key division with several managers and supervisors reporting to him. He reported to the second highest ranking person in the company, which at that time was the executive vice-president of sales. Mike was driven, committed, and not afraid of putting in the hours to get the job done (he often worked seventy plus hour weeks). He had risen to his current position, not just because he was bright, articu- late and dedicated but because he had an active mentor (and protector) in the executive vice-president. Then this executive vice-president resigned his position and left the company. It became painfully obvious in a very short period of time that, without the protection of the vice-president, Mike, opinion- ated and driven to achieve his agenda (an agenda which he truly believed was consistent with the best interests of the company), was left badly exposed in terms of his lack of judgement.

I witnessed an example of this lack of judgement in a meet- ing late one Thursday afternoon when he literally caused every jaw in the room to drop as he corrected the president of the company in front of eighteen key managers. The president was discussing anticipated revenues for the next quarter. "Today, we have one hundred eighteen branch offices operating in key cities around the country," the president began.

"One hundred seventeen," said Mike. (This was when the jaw of every person in the room simultaneously dropped about two inches and eyes opened a similar distance.)

"Excuse me," said the president.

"I said that we have one hundred seventeen branch offices, not one hundred eighteen, sir," said Mike.

Now smiling, the president continued: "We now have somewhere between one hundred seventeen and one hundred eighteen offices operating across the country…"

Mike was called into the president's office right after that meeting and asked why he thought that the difference of one office was so critical that he would publicly embarrass the company president. Mike's reply, indicative of a heedless lack of awareness of the interpersonal needs of others was: "I didn't think it would embarrass you, I just thought you would want to be right."

Mike didn't get it then, and, after four years of being reminded by other vice presidents of how to work effectively with others, of being gradually demoted from vice president to general manager to manager he was let go after more than twenty years with the company. He never developed judgment. He never understood that an awareness of the needs of others, an appreciation for the wisdom and experience of others and an understanding of when to talk and when to listen was essential to effective leadership. He never learned that the effective implementation of good ideas, innovative ideas, and creative solutions required collaboration and influence rather than coercion and demands. Mike's experience and willingness to pursue the

untried was an asset to the company; his passion for the unpopular cause was admirable;
however, his unwillingness to accept considered input from others and his lack of appreciation of the importance of persuasion over
pressure eventually led to the end of a prom-
ising career.

> *Are you endorsing
> that wimpy
> approach of "Go
> along to get
> along?" No.*

(At this point I can hear the outcry from
those who have been successful managing
large and small enterprises with coercion, fear
and pressure. "Are you endorsing," they would ask, "that wimpy
approach of 'Go along to get along'?" The answer is no. Going
along to get along is the antithesis of leadership. Consensus often dilutes best solutions and compromise can drown creativity.
However, one of the key distinctions of leadership is, as noted
earlier in the book, "What are they doing when you are away—
and why?" The use of judgement encourages the leader to influence others to continue the task even when unsupervised and
to continue the task for the right reasons. This is the goal of
leadership and one of Mike's failures. After Mike left, one of the
vice presidents of the company said to me, "You know, you had
to admire Mike. He always defended his people. The problem
was, he defended them even when they were at fault. Their work
output deteriorated in quality and quantity because they knew
he would defend them no matter what.")

Judgement involves analyzing a multitude of variables related to a given situation and acting on that analysis. It requires
a knowledge of the motivations and needs of others and a firm
personal set of values. Voltaire first noted that common sense
isn't common. The same can be said of judgement. Good judgement requires interpersonal versatility. You must then demonstrate the appropriate behavior for the situation. This means
sometimes leading and sometimes following. It means knowing
that correcting the president of the company in public is not

appropriate, any more than publicly "chewing out" an employee for a misunderstanding is appropriate. Judgement is all about appropriateness and Mike didn't have it and was unwilling to learn it. Even after the talk with the president he was defending his reasoning and his behavior.

It was ironic but most people in the company liked Mike as a person and when he left there was tremendous regret that twenty years of company history went with him. Most were sad that the patient was unable to follow the prescription. His termination was both a personal and a company loss.

In the Rough

Mike Benson illustrates the reason for the title of this chapter: "In the Rough." Mike was a good manager—solid and knowledgeable in command and control situations. And a few of his own people would have followed him over that proverbial burning bridge—but not all, probably not even most. The tougher times got, the more critical it was that Mike influence and lead rather than cajole and demand; in practice, he couldn't make the distinction. In short, tough times demanded different skills, leadership skills.

Golfers know that it is in those moments when things are not going well, when your drive goes way left or way right, when your five iron puts you in amongst the squirrels, when you over-hit your trusty wedge, or when a host of other "bad" things occur, that the game of golf is either won or lost. How you play when your ball is behind the tree or in the high grass or half buried in the sand against the wall of a seven foot deep bunker often determines your success on the golf course. How do you play when your shot lands on the "hardpan", catches the edge of a green and rolls all the way back down into a gully, or is "bladed" from one side of the green to the other, demonstrates your levels of character and competence. How you play under these conditions usually determines whether the game is won or lost—and it is the same with leadership.

It is not hard to be a leader when things are going smoothly, when there are no problems, when the market conditions or general business conditions just about ensure that you will do well and/or make money. But, of course this seldom happens in business (just as smooth times, those times when you are in a zone and every drive is straight and every putt falls, seldom happen in golf).

This chapter, then is about the skills required to lead in difficult times, in times when the status quo is challenged, when creative solutions are needed, when innovation, novel approaches, team influence and breakthrough problem solving are required—and, in today's climate, this is most of the time.

> *In golf, how well you play from the rough often determines how well you score. In leadership, how well you can play from the rough, how well you can lead people through the tough times, determines your leadership effectiveness.*

We have heard the word "change" so often that we have practically become inured to it. Yet it is a truism that ours is one of the most dynamic business environments in history. Leading in this dynamic environment is different than leading thirty years ago. Today, skills such as judgement and perception, skills I discuss under the rubric of "Leadership EQ," are more important than ever.

Leadership EQ: Nature or Nurture

Have you ever watched a golfer whose swing is nearly fluid, whose posture is perfect, and whose eye sees even the smallest undulations in the green and allows for them on every putt? Have you ever watched the professionals during their time on the practice range and wonder how someone could develop that

> *Leadership is usually the result of some natural talent with lots of practice, or enormous talent with a focused effort to continually improve.*

much grace in hitting a golf ball? We use terms like "natural athletic ability"? and "athletically gifted" to describe this phenomenon and some of it is true. For some golfers, for some athletes, "movement in space" is a natural gift. But for many others it is the result of some natural talent plus thousands of hours of practice. The fluid swing, the perfect posture, the critical eye are as much a result of experience as they are of talent. The same is true of leadership. Leadership is the result of some natural talent and lots of practice or the result of enormous talent and some focused effort to improve. (In the rarest of cases, in the case of the consummate professional golfer or the successful charismatic leader, it is the idiosyncratic combination of enormous natural talent and an unbelievable work ethic.)

All of which is to say that in leadership, as in golf, the opportunity to excel is seized by some and ignored by others. There are managers who had exceptional natural talent and opted not to develop it and those who, because of the desire to excel, took their modest talent, and through diligence and hard work honed their game to a level of excellence. The former are still managers, the latter, leaders.

Leadership "Course Management"

Seven chapters into this book, you know that it is about developing and sharpening skills to become a leader. In earlier chapters, we have looked at different facets of golf—the swing, the skills of pitching and putting, the choice of clubs in a given situation. This chapter is really more about the skills of what golfers call "course management." It is about hitting from the tall grass, from out of and behind the trees, from the edge of the lake. We need leadership course management as well. This is what you do as a leader when confronted with emotional employees, when significant change is made, when there are instant decisions to be made, when the company depends on your judgement to influence the opinions of the many.

Experienced golfers know that good golf is as much about course management as it is about hitting the ball 260 yards (although if you can do both it certainly beats doing either—or neither). Similarly, leadership is as much about influence, judgement and awareness and the judicious use of power as it is about motivation and alignment. This chapter then, is going to help develop your leadership "course management skills"—you cannot truly lead without them. Leadership course management skills begin with an understanding of the concept of emotional intelligence.

> *While IQ is relatively fixed, EQ is amenable to rapid improvement through a process of rigorous self and other feedback.*

Emotional Intelligence

Judgment, prudent risk taking, passion, persistence, self control and advanced interpersonal understanding (compassion) are some of the skills that fall under the heading of what is today being called "Emotional Intelligence" or "EQ." As with all natural intelligences, some of us are born with more and others with less of this critical leadership dimension. However, while IQ is somewhat fixed (it can be improved in only relatively small increments), your emotional intelligence is amenable to significant growth through a regiment of rigorous self and other feedback.

Emotions in the Work Place

There are those who say that emotions have no place in a business environment and that this very concept is totally irrelevant to a discussion of leadership. So, before I review the what and how of emotional intelligence, let me spend a few paragraphs describing how we process information, then share with you the results of a long term study of leaders and the importance of emotion in maintaining a leadership position.

How We Process Information

In the early seventies Dr. Paul MacLean published his seminal work on the vertical structure of the brain called the "Triune Brain." MacLean demonstrated that we have three major information processing centers in the brain. The first of these is the brain stem or "the reptile brain" (animals who have only this system eat their young). This part of the brain is responsible for the coordination and continuation of the primarily unconscious activities required for life, e.g., breathing, maintaining body temperature, moving fluids throughout the system, and maintaining heart rate. The second major area of brain function MacLean called the "limbic system" or emotional brain. This emotional brain overlays the reptile brain and is essential to what we call humanness. Overlaying the limbic system is the largest of the three systems, and the one that we spend the most time focused on in business, this is the neocortex or the thinking brain. The neocortex, the rational, analytical and creative brain, makes up about 55% of our total brain mass.

While this physiology may make sense intuitively and even give rise to the increasing importance of each of these "three brains" as we work from the brain stem to the neocortex, the work of Dr. Joseph LeDoux on the circuitry of our brain, and in particular on the importance of the amygdalae tells us why we cannot ignore the importance of emotion in our personal and professional lives. (It is interesting to note that many of those who suggest that "emotion has no place in the business world," say it with so much emotion!)

Why are these amygdalae (one amygdala in the limbic system on the right side of the brain and one on the left) so important? Because LeDoux's research unmistakably demonstrates that this is where information is processed first! Information entering our brain goes immediately from the thalamus to the amygdala and then to the neo-cortex. Yes, this happens in nanoseconds, but this finding has overwhelming implications for leadership—all information coming from the eyes and ears is processed through our emotional brain before entering our thinking brain! This is why a knowledge of and skill in using emotional intelligence, that is, the understanding of basic human feelings such

Those who say emotion has no business in the workplace, often do so with much emotion.

as passion (and its counterpart impulse control), anger, fear, enthusiasm, joy and other basic human emotional responses, is so essential for effective leadership. Managers ignore emotions, leaders do not. Leaders exhibit emotional intelligence.

Leadership and Emotional Intelligence

Proof for the assertion that leaders exhibit emotional intelligence comes from the work of James Kouzes and Barry Posner. In preparing to write their paradigm breaking book on leadership, "The Leadership Challenge," the authors reviewed over five hundred surveys from various leaders and conducted an additional forty-two in depth interviews with leaders.

　　The results of this effort? Kouzes and Posner noted that the leaders surveyed in this research did not talk about an analytical detachment from their work. Rather they talked about the emotional excitement generated by being involved in the enterprise of leadership. They used words such as passion, elation, caring, kindness, intensity and inspiration. Leaders know that understanding and utilizing emotion is the sine qua non of leadership.

Leaders acknowledge the importance, the critical role, of emotion.

Bam! Once again, a parallel with golf. Great golfers, like all great athletes, understand that passion helps concentration. Great golfers play under a circumstance they call controlled passion, that is, like most successful athletes they let the emotions of enthusiasm and excitement help generate the energy to play well, but they don't (normally) let the "negative" emotions of anger and frustration rule their play. If you let your emotions control you in either golf or business, you lose the balance essential to maximally effective effort. (The possible exception to the rule is enthusiasm, which is a critical part of the energy that leaders transfer to followers and that sustains efforts at change—particularly through the tough times. Enthusiasm is to leadership as grass is to golf.)

In summary, if you play golf or operate in business with a total analytical detachment, focused only on the mechanics of the swing or the "detached analysis" of every decision, you lose the balance needed to be maximally effective: you lose the beneficial effects of emotional intelligence. Leaders leverage thought with passion and compassion to achieve inspired action.

> *Leaders leverage thought with passion and compassion to achieve inspired action.*

Emotional Intelligence: What It Is and What It Isn't

In a nutshell, emotional intelligence is an awareness of both your emotions and those of others. Emotional intelligence is not thoughts about feelings. Thoughts about feelings are often used by managers when dealing with others who are in an emotional state—as in the following example:

> *Manager: "I understand you may be a little upset about not getting that promotion."*

Employee: "A little upset, I am so mad that I am ready to quit and take my whole R & D Department with me."

Manager: "Yes, well, as I said, I do understand why you might be a little mad."

This manager is dealing with the analytical brain (the Neocortex) rather than the emotional brain (the Limbic System). When the employee shows real emotion "I am so mad I am ready to quit..." the manager minimizes the anger with the response, "I understand why you might be a little mad." Put yourself in the place of this employee and see what your next statement might be. Most likely it is just an escalation of the anger. This process will continue until the manager realizes that she has to deal honestly with the anger or until the employee gives up and says to himself, "this is a waste of time and energy, I'll go along to get this over with, then, I'll do what I darn well please.") Clearly the manager in this scenario is not aware of the importance of emotion in effectively leading her people.

Thus, emotional intelligence is not being analytical about feelings. Neither is emotional intelligence about littering the landscape with demeaning and/or artificial, non-specific phrases such as:

"We can talk when you calm down,"

"I feel your pain," ("No you don't you don't have any idea what my pain really is.),

or "Just tell me how you feel about this." (And then not dealing with those feelings.)

What, then, is emotional intelligence? Emotional intelligence is an extremely sophisticated leadership skill that is not directly correlated with IQ or "Rational Intelligence." Emotional intelligence, at its essence, is a combination of percep-

At its essential, emotional intelligence is a skillful combination of perception, understanding, intuition and self control.

tion, understanding and intuition. It unites the knowledge of both your emotions (your understanding of your own emotions) and the knowledge AND acknowledgement of the emotions of others. The skill of judgement that we reviewed earlier in this chapter is a critical component of the larger competency called emotional intelligence. Let's revisit the scenario above and include a response that exhibits emotional intelligence:

Manager: "Jim I know you are really angry about getting passed over for that promotion, I know that you have worked hard for the company and you feel unappreciated and just a bit used."

Employee: "You are damn right I am angry and I am unappreciated. It's like the twenty years I have spent here are worth less than Sheila's eight years. I trained her for crying out loud. I am ready to take my entire R and D staff and move to ...(major competitor)."

Manager: "Jim, I know that you are really angry. I know that it seems unfair to you that you have been passed over for promotion and that Sheila, a person that you trained, has been given that promotion. I would like to present our rationale for that decision to you and then see if we can't problem solve around this decision. You are a very valued employee. In spite of your anger, I'd like to take a few minutes to talk about where we can go from here."

This manager becomes a leader through her use of another advanced emotional intelligence skill called empathy. Using empathy, understanding the employees emotional perspective and acknowledging the right of the employee to feel that way (even when you don't agree with it), this manager is able to move toward influencing the individual toward problem solving. This is leadership.

"I Don't Have Time to Baby Sit"

I hear the objections even as I write. "I don't have time to be a baby sitter, I have a department to run." "This is all well and good for someone who has studied psychology and is good with words, but my strength is my knowledge of how things run around here; I tell, they do. If this guy wants to quit because he didn't get a promotion, let him." "These people are professionals, they can solve their own problems." (Or, as one manager said to me not too long ago, "It is their job to row the boat, I'll steer it.") Perhaps, you are thinking something like, "Don, where is your brain? Business doesn't run like this. Let the guy cool down, then talk to him." Or finally, your response might be, "I don't have time for this kind of touchy-feely stuff, and neither does anyone else in my company."

All of these objections, in a very limited view of what business is, could be considered legitimate. Over the long run, however, they minimize what can be achieved by placing limitations on the potential of both individuals and groups. (For more on unleashing the power of individuals and groups through the judicious use of enthusiasm, read the recently released *"Gung-Ho"* by Ken Blanchard and Sheldon Bowles.)

Thinking that business is just analytical is not unlike the focus of so many companies and executives in the sixties and seventies who thought of business only in terms of quarterly financial results and thus ignored customers, quality and employees to the long term detriment of the company—even, in some cases, to the point of extinction.

The leader knows that finesse with the club is as important as strength with the club.

Thinking that business is only analytical also reflects one of the critical differences between a manager and a leader. When a manager is "in the weeds" or "in the trees" he or she can only hunker down and hit the ball as hard as he or she can and hope for the best. The leader, on the other hand has options. The leader knows what he or she is doing. The leader knows that finesse with the club is as important as strength with the club. Leaders acknowledge emotions. They have emotional intelligence.

Emotional intelligence, like all natural talents, is evenly distributed among the population. And, like all natural talents, what you are born with in terms of emotional intelligence is important, but not the determining factor in how far that talent is eventually taken. Tiger Woods was born with natural athletic talent. But knowing how to improve the skill and acting on that knowledge is the key to attaining the peak of your ability in that area. If Tiger Woods had not spent thousands of hours hitting golf balls, of listening to coaches and working at his craft, we would likely never have heard of him.

All of this is to say that emotional intelligence, one of the keys to effective leadership is an intelligence that can be developed and fine tuned, much like athletic ability.

Recent Developments in Emotional Intelligence

The idea of emotional intelligence has been around for some time. I first ran across some interesting studies by Howard Gardner in the late seventies when doing research for my dissertation. Later I rediscovered Gardner's work in his 1983 book *Frames of Mind*. In this book, Gardner identified seven different types of intelligence. Gardner noted that there were the commonly measured Intelligence Quotient (IQ) the intelligences related to verbal and mathematical/logical talents, plus the spatial intelligence of an architect or artist, the musical intelligence of a Beethoven or Brahms (or a John Lennon), the kinesthetic intelligence of a Michael Jordan, Carl Lewis or Lee Trevino, the interpersonal intelligence of a great therapist like Carl Rogers and the "intrapsychic" intelligence that is developed by those with harmony between the way they live and their deeply held beliefs and feelings.

This concept has recently been popularized by Daniel Goleman in his books *Emotional Intelligence and Working with Emotional Intelligence.* Goleman, building on the work of Jack Block (a psychologist at the University of California at Berkeley) suggests that men who are emotionally intelligent are "socially poised, outgoing and cheerful, not prone to fearfulness or worried ruminations. They have a notable capacity for commitment to people and causes, for taking responsibility,... sympathetic and caring in their relationships." (*Emotional Intelligence,* pp. 44-45)

Emotionally intelligent women exhibit other characteristics such as being assertive and being able to express their feelings directly. Emotionally intelligent women feel positive about themselves and, like emotionally intelligent men, "are able to express their feelings appropriately (rather than, say, in outbursts they will later regret). Both emotionally intelligent men and women are open to new experience, are spontaneous and able to deal with emotions.

Emotional intelligence includes such characteristics as commitment to others and taking personal responsibility.

Contrast this with the characteristics of the pure high IQ type. The high IQ male is seen as ambitious and productive, predictable, condescending, fastidious, critical, uneasy with new experience, and emotionally bland. The high IQ female is seen as intellectually confident, introspective, holding a wide range of intellectual interests, prone to anxiety and unable to express feelings directly.

Can you be both high IQ and highly emotionally intelligent? Of course. It is like asking if you can be a great putter and an outstanding driver. This is what they best do. Those high IQ types who are also emotionally intelligent are excellent leaders because they temper their critical nature with other awareness, their uneasiness with new experience with being open to spontaneous feelings, their anxiety with wisdom. As with so many other characteristics of leadership suggested in this book, the "IQ/EQ debate presents us with the "Tyranny of the Or." Truly emotionally intelligent people realize the "Opportunity of the And." We have already looked at judgement and empathy as fundamental competencies for effective leadership. In the remainder of this chapter we will focus on four other components of the leadership/emotional intelligence interaction: influence, wisdom, referent power and the nature of leadership.

Influence and Emotional Intelligence

Not surprisingly, because people are both rational and emotional, the characteristics of emotional intelligence directly impact the ability of leaders to motivate themselves and influence others. In earlier chapters we have reviewed the concept of motivation— primarily focusing on the motivation that is "other directed." But, in terms of leadership there is an equally if not more important focus that relates to emotional intelligence. What motivates you to exert leadership? What motivates you to want to lead others? People, of course, perceive your true motivation and their perception makes all the difference in the world as to your effectiveness in influencing and leading others.

Late in the fall of 1996, John Matthews, then a Vice-President and Senior Project Manager of a large engineering services firm contacted me. Six months earlier John had been promoted to this position as vice-president and given the chance to head up a project with a new and potentially very large client. He approached the job with vigor, verve and purpose. However, by the time he called me, his people were in near revolt, the client was talking of bolting and his boss was sending internal consultants on weekly visits from Chicago to Atlanta to "problem-solve." Wanting to know the problem and how to correct it, this vice-president asked me to conduct a survey with a mixture of his direct reports, managers from the client company, and a sample of the other employees working for him. We were to go from the survey to solutions and then monitor the implementation of solutions.

As you might have guessed, we never got to solutions. At the end of two days of interviews, I met with John in his glassed-in fifteenth floor office overlooking the river.

The mood was somber; the approach direct. The news was not good. I summarized the results of my survey.

> *"John, if you make it another two weeks, you will be doing well."*

"John, if you make it another two weeks, you will be doing well. Both the client and your own people have asked for you to be replaced. Your boss has hired someone who is working as a consultant who will likely take the reigns if you falter. You have made serious enemies on the client side and with your own people. The internal politics around here are focused on one thing—replacing you at any cost. I'll put it in writing for you, and we can work on solutions, but the situation is tenuous at best."

John was not entirely surprised by this brutally honest report. He knew the consultant that I was talking about and he knew that his clients were disappointed. What he didn't understand was why he wasn't being given more of a chance. And that was the next question he asked. "But why? Why now when we are about to turn a corner? Why now, after ten weeks of putting in eighty plus hours? Why, when I have totally dedicated myself to doing what the company wanted me to do and what they have given me only limited resources to achieve? No one could have achieved more than I have. Why?"

The "Why"—Lack of Wisdom

The "Why" was hard for John to accept. It was not only that he had failed to deliver on promises that he himself had made to the client in the proposal phase, nor that he had been extremely demanding of his immediate staff (to a point where some of his early supporters no longer believed that John could lead the team).

No, the why was that everyone, even John's closest supporters, perceived that John had been seduced by the trappings of position power and prestige and was now managing the project for what it could do for John, not for the company or the client—and certainly not for them. John, of course, denied this. When they pointed out that he had spent more time politicking for the title of vice president than for staffing the project, he was outraged. They didn't know the early mornings and late nights that he had spent on staffing. When they pointed out that he had to have the best office, even if it meant moving someone else out, he was amazed. That's where all senior staff were located. When they pointed out that John had taken credit for projects that the team had completed, he was totally perplexed. Hadn't he identified the team members, attended meetings, provided support? Who else, after all, deserved more credit than John? John had a hard time understanding that he had to consider their perception as well as his own reality.

John Matthews was extremely bright. Even in a world of highly educated engineers and information technology professionals, he could be intellectually intimidating. He had many characteristics of Jack Block's high IQ male. John was used to thinking things through, deciding on the best course to achieve his goals and then pursing that course no matter the obstacles.

In his own mind, he was convinced that what he was doing was in the best interest of everyone. However, in his singular pursuit of what he thought best he betrayed his Achilles heel—lack of self, other and situational awareness, all critical elements of emotional intelligence. Because of this perceived singular pursuit of his own agenda and because of his lack of awareness of how he was being perceived, John relinquished his ability to influence, and therefore, his ability to lead.

Two days after my report to John, his boss came down from Chicago and gave him the choice of resigning and taking a lesser position in the firm or being terminated. There was no mention of a severance package. What had happened?

John cared very deeply about the success of the project, all but his most determined detractors admitted this. However, John's focus on power and the trappings of power dramatically affected his ability to influence others. As the project progressed, and as John became more isolated from the operations of project managers, he became in the minds of his people, the image of the physically, intellectually and emotionally remote boss. He could order, but he could no longer influence.

John's focus on power and the trappings of power spoke volumes to the people he led. Although he truly cared about the project and the people, all they saw was the corner office and the new title.

The people he was working with were looking for a leader, not a boss. At this stage in his career, John, smart, clever, and certainly in his own way caring about others and the project, didn't have the understanding of his employee's need for leadership and vision rather than management and power. At this stage in his career he was lacking one of the critical elements of emotional intelligence that could almost surely have guaranteed his ability to influence – wisdom.

Wisdom and Emotional Intelligence

In his wonderful little novel, *"Miracle on the Seventeenth Green,"* James Patterson (best known for his Alex Cross thrillers, e.g. *Kiss the Girls*) and his co-author Peter De Jonge, tell the story of Travis McKinley, an ordinary man in an ordinary life who experiences something extraordinary beginning one Christmas day on a nearly frozen golf course. Looming just below this extraordinary episode in Travis's life, of course, is the lesson. The tale of Travis McKinley is really all about the development of a multi-faceted aspect of emotional intelligence called "wisdom." Wisdom is one of the most critical skills of a leader and, not surprisingly, because it requires continuous on-going honest self-appraisal, one of the most difficult to develop. Travis McKinley's journey, then, is one of the modern warrior. Like many tales of its type, confronting various demons helps the hero develop courage, and honest self-assessment and the feedback of others gathered during the quest leads to increased wisdom.

Certainly I would recommend this delightful book to anyone who loves golf and even to those who think of it as a "good walk wasted." But let me summarize the story line and take you quickly to the issue of wisdom.

The protagonist, Travis McKinley, is an avid and very talented amateur golfer. Travis is a fifty-something advertising copywriter who is not only bored with his job but about to lose the job and all its perks anyway. His physician wife is disillusioned with him and his three children barely recognize Travis. Understanding this we are introduced to the story of Travis McKinley with these words: "What can I say? Tragedies befall saints. Fortune smiles on cretins. Extraordinary things happen to ordinary people. And this happened to me."

Without giving away the whole story, essentially Travis decides to go to the Senior Tour Qualifying School, qualifies, works his way through daunting circumstances and winds up on the 17th hole at Pebble Beach paired in the Senior Open with Jack

Nicklaus and Raymond Floyd with all the issues of his life staring straight at him. Does
he triumph? I want to say, read the book, it is
wonderful; but I will tell you this, the 17ᵗʰ
green is a metaphor for the crucible of leadership. It is where the wisdom and clarity of vision emerge. How could Travis lose?

> *Leaders must
> overcome both the
> fear of failure and
> the fear of success.*

The story of Travis McKinley is a story in
no small part about the development of wis-
dom, about what it takes to confront personal challenges, to
proceed despite doubt, to laugh at personal follies, to courageously and knowingly overcome both the fear of failure and
the fear of success, and to "follow the line of the heart."

It should come as no surprise that wisdom is a key component of leadership. The Old Testament provides us with some
of our earliest stories, the "wisdom of Solomon" is a common
phrase and sums up the nature of this elusive trait. Wisdom is
understanding all the interactive components of a situation and
making conscious decisions based on that knowledge. It includes courage, empathy, and interpersonal intelli-gence. Judgment and wisdom are closely related qualities. Continued reflection on the exercise of judgment leads to wisdom.

Wisdom in the Workplace

What does wisdom look like in the workplace? It has many different faces, but here is one that I witnessed in 1998. The event
was related to me by the individual as part of a survey I was
conducting. The story involves a mid-sized (four hundred fifty
million dollars annual sales) East Coast firm where Barbara
Lopez, a vice president of administration, needed a commitment from the president of the company.

Barbara's cause was unpopular; it involved hiring temps to
do about forty percent of the work that was going to be caused
by a new acquisition, the third in a twenty-four month period.

Knowing that control was a major issue for the president, she didn't phrase her proposal in terms of either/or.

Her people had been working sixty to seventy hour weeks for much of this time. They were tired and the fatigue was showing in an increasing number of errors and re-work. For those on salary, it was simply a lot of extra work, for the few who were hourly, even the extra money no longer substituted for time with the family. Her challenge was this: how to get the president of the company to commit to spending thousands of dollars on temporary help when he didn't think that there was a problem—he thought that the employees should all be happy to be working for the diner rather than being the dinner.

Her first step was to compile financial data, for example, cost of overtime vs. cost of the temporaries. Next, because some turnover was beginning, she calculated the cost of replacing some key people on staff. She decided not to mention the increasing error rate as that would simply cause him to become angry about all those people "not paying attention to their work." Third, she chose the right time of the day on the right day. She knew that he was more open to suggestion after lunch and that Wednesdays and Thursdays usually found him less stressed. Next, she positioned the issue logically, not emotionally. It wasn't that the president of the company didn't care about the families of the people working these long hours for long stretches, he just didn't see that it made that big of a difference. Finally, she took an open stance, not a closed one. Knowing that control was a major issue for the president, she didn't phrase the issue as one of "either/or", she didn't back him into a corner. Instead with the facts she made a persuasive case and then let him make the call. The temps were hired.

This vice-president showed exceptional wisdom. She understood the nuances of the situation, the pros and cons of her position and the overall goal. She knew that confrontation was dangerous in terms of achieving her goal and that he would respond favorably to well researched financials. Of course, it could have gone the other way, but it didn't, and her ability to lead and influence, her referent power, in that company was greatly enhanced.

Wisdom is not necessarily logical. The wisest know that wisdom is knowledge well leveraged. Leaders know that the logic of any situation is only half of the equation, they know that, in order to lead, to influence, to motivate, they have to tap into that other half of the equation that includes empathy, emotion, intuition, passion, inspiration and heart. When you develop wisdom, you inherit referent power, the next requirement of good course management. Referent power is not a component of emotional intelligence, it is the result of emotional intelligence. Referent power stands in stark contrast to the power that John Matthews was perceived as pursuing. So let's look at power, its types and its impact on your ability to lead.

You can no more play the game of leadership without power than you can play the game of golf without woods and long irons.

Power

It is naive to think that the game of leadership can be played entirely with influence. You can no more play the game of leadership without power than you could play the game of golf without woods. At some point you have to put finesse aside, put your wedges, putter and short irons away and take out a club with which you can hit the ball two hundred forty yards (or further). This may be a driver, a three wood, a two or three iron, but it must deliver power to the ball to take it the distance. The skills discussed in this chapter, skills such as judgment, passion, empathy and wisdom, increase power, but they are no substitute for power. Course management skills help you improve your game by maximizing the impact of each shot, but if you cannot hit your driver, you will be forever struggling with your game.

All of which to say is that power is an essential component of leadership. It is one of the reasons why management skills are a prerequisite to leadership skills.

Power is a neutral attribute and it comes in many forms; the two most often cited being position and referent power. If you exhibit too much position power you knock initiative right out of people. If you want to reduce the initiative and motivation of people, use position power to command or micro-management strategies to control.

As a consultant to hundreds of companies over the past fifteen years, I have observed a range of power behaviors from the consciously Machiavellian to the consciously abdicating. In these fifteen years of meeting with managers of all titles I have witnessed incredibly detailed and chess-like power plays and palace coups. I have also witnessed power vacuums being filled by more aggressive and assertive junior managers. The tendency to run away from power appears to be as common as the eagerness to grab it.

Some potential leaders see power as somehow tainting the purity of their leadership, while others see power as ninety percent of leadership—they simply have to tell and others will obey. Both of these extremes misunderstand the nature of leadership in today's world. Position power, by itself, does not equal leadership, but position power can be wisely used to leverage leadership effectiveness.

Position power by itself does not equal leadership.

A senior manager recently related the following story to me in a very understated, matter of fact tone. This anecdote represents the wise use of position power. This manager was from a Fortune Five Hundred company with diversified business all across the country. He was sent to a plant in the South that had failed to show a profit for the past four years. When he arrived at the plant, he began the process of instilling some business discipline into a plant that had long been neglected. He gathered his top reports into a room during the middle of the second week and told them bluntly that he had been charged with one of two options: first, make the plant profitable; second, if the first could not be achieved, shut the plant down. He then asked the managers of the plant to join him in creating a vision and an alignment plan to make the plant viable.

Note, this leader didn't threaten with termination, he didn't rant and rave. He didn't ascribe blame, didn't look to the past. He simply explained the options and then asked the staff to help him create a profitable plant. He did not pretend to have all the answers, he asked the top managers of the company to help him define the vision and strategy. This is position power wisely used; ignoring the leverage of position power in this situation would have diluted his efforts to turn this plant around (by the way, within three months the plant was profitable, orders were being shipped on time, nagging turnover had slowed and there was a definite improvement in morale).

Remember, as defined in this book, the leader is one who inspires and clarifies a vision, who aligns and motivates his or her people, who ensures that processes are challenged and scores are kept and who models the behavior expected. As we have discussed in this chapter, leaders are those with sound judgment, emotional intelligence and wisdom. Leaders are those who people willingly follow. Again, this view of leadership is based on the need for people "to be involved in an enterprise greater than themselves." This is the art of leadership that has far greater staying power than the strategy of coercion. I am not sure who first said it, but there is a lot of truth to the old adage that most of us "would rather be influenced than coerced."

Referent Power and Course Management

As mentioned earlier in this chapter, there are many kinds of power other than position power; most notably a type of power called referent power. Referent power is the power that comes from knowledge and understanding, that is, from wisdom. It is not dependent on position power but is enhanced by position power. It is the kind of power exhibited by Barbara Lopez. It is not boss's friend power, same last name power, or critical task power. All of these types of power can become referent power through the use of emotional intelligence and are severely limited without it. Having position power without emotional intelligence is like hitting a driver with one hand only.

Hitting into the wind on this course was futile.

A few years ago, I had the opportunity to play at the Lagoons course on the island of Kauai in Hawaii. I played twice; the first day I shot a score of one hundred eight, the second day, a ninety-five. The difference in these two scores? On the first day I used my driver, on the second I did not. For me, hitting into the wind on this course was futile. My ball would soar off into the wind to be blown right and left into the waiting water and weeds. Using my irons the next day, helped me gain control among these same conditions. Simple course management.

Most managers play in the high wind every day without realizing it. Classic management theory describes the role of the manager as one of planning, controlling, problem solving and allocating resources. It is an authoritarian model that suggests that it is the job of the manager to get things done through others and that the manager is "in charge." Thus, most managers rely on "position power,' that is, I have power over you because I have a higher status than you do. My belief is that before you can be an effective leader, you must master the skills of management—but not take on the robes of position power that come with an official title. Good managers can become good leaders if they can develop referent power. However, a knowledge of how to implement these management skills is where many managers stop. They think that the model will make them leaders. It does not. Not everyone can hit their driver in the wind.

For leaders, referent power is at least as important as position power.

Although the traditional command and control model is rarely seen as an effective road to leadership, and although it is frequently discounted in studies of successful leadership, fifteen years of observing managers in large, small and mid-size companies suggests that it is still the dominant model. Middle managers, in particular, because they are called upon to produce results, results, results, (and chewed out if they don't) use this old coercive model of management as their primary tool. As noted earlier in the book, coercive management does produce short term results. But coercive power too often used creates an atmosphere of fear and covering of the backside that is harmful in terms of long term success. Besides, do today's "volunteer workers" really want to work in this environment? Most middle managers are in a unique position to extend the impact of their daily efforts through combining the skills of management and leadership in their individual departments.

The Nature of Leadership

In the early days of golf, specialty clubs were developed in order to hit the ball out of wagon wheel ruts. Pictures of "Old Tom Morris" show both courses and clothing that we would no longer think appropriate for golf. Similarly, just in the past twenty years our view of the nature of leadership has changed. One of the components of that view that has changed, a notion that is frequently reinforced by the media, is that "leaders always lead."

Warren Blank, in his paradigm stretching book, *The Nine Natural Laws of Leadership,* challenges this notion. He states

> *"Leadership is a discontinuous event."*

that "Leadership is a discontinuous event" (with the implication that we should all be ready to seize the leadership moment). He suggests that leadership is not a linear process, rather it is interactive. As a matter of fact sometimes leadership feels like that errant shot that goes into the trees and bounces among them. Oh, it is true that we draw parallel lines when we aim our shot, that we plan strategies based on hitting the ball straight, that we aim to putt the ball on a relatively straight line, but of course, two shots into any game we realize that creative shot making is a requirement. And judgement? Making the right decision is arguably the most difficult skill in golf. Each shot presents five to ten options, which one do you take?

Indeed, we could argue that excellent golf is arguably the result of the ability of the golfer to be outstanding in situations where creative shot making is required and so is leadership. In fact, one of the distinguishing characteristics of a leader vs. a manager is that the leader is flexible and will adapt strategy to meet unexpected contingencies where the manager can or will not.

In a wonderful metaphor told by Roger Enrico of PepsiCo to Noel Tichy and repeated in his book *The Leadership Engine,* Enrico states, "Somewhere along the way, we either told people or they surmised, that it was a paint-by numbers system. It's like, if you use these tools in this sequence, in this way, success is inevitable, as opposed to: these are tools to help you gain an insight into what you are doing, or to help you create a strategy from the insight that you get."

As Roger Enrico says, "leadership is not a paint by numbers system." You cannot wear the mantle of leadership and be assumed to be leading. Picture for example, a meeting of twelve people. Four of the people in this meeting happen to be Jack

Welch, Bill Gates, Jesse Jackson and Elizabeth Dole; Allen Greenspan happens to be in this meeting as well. Who would be the leader?

> *Without followers, the leader is "just another person out for a walk."*

The leader would be the one who could create the interactions that would result in the others following his or her lead. And this would be a discontinuous process—not unlike hitting the best ball in a scramble. Power wouldn't carry that much weight in this meeting, but influence would. Which of these people could provide an agenda that the others saw as worthy of following? Which could detail a vision and show an alignment process (no matter how informal) for achieving that vision? Which one could exhibit flexibility and emotional intelligence? The ones who would demonstrate these skills with continuity of character are the ones who would be the leaders, not those who simply made a power play. The attributes of leadership result in the willingness of others to follow the leader; otherwise, as noted in Chapter 3 "A leader is just another person out for a walk."

How to Play This Hole

As with golfers, leaders spend a lot of time in the rough; events in both golf and business demand well-developed skills for making par when things are tough. In order to succeed when in the tall grass, in amongst the trees, pancaked in a trap or hitting into a howling wind, you must be able to:

1. Understand the concept of judgement and its sister skill perspicacity. Be aware of the intervening variables in any interpersonal equation. Tune your brain to the awareness of the subtle and obvious emotions of the moment. Leadership is dependent upon effective interaction.

2. Consider the results (both short and long term) of what you say and do. While the CEO may want to be right, he does not want to be embarrassed in front of his managers.

3. Acknowledge that not only are emotions present in every interaction, but critical in many. Do not make the mistake of denying the emotional reality of others. Do not insist that emotions have no valid place in business.

4. Become emotionally intelligent. Work to consciously evaluate how well you deal with the emotions of others. Remember that empathy is one of the most powerful communication tools available to the leader.

5. Recognize the power of wisdom. Wisdom demands that we reflect on and learn from our experience. Use each decision to make better decisions.

6. Use power wisely. Power is a neutral construct. It is there to be used to achieve ends that are those of the individual and the group. The overuse of power yields short term results often followed by subtle sabotage. The use of position power without influence causes compliance rather than enthusiasm. Neither should you run away from power; embrace power, use it wisely. It is difficult to lead without position or referent power.

7. Recognize the discontinuity of the leadership process. You do not always have to be the leader. Develop the skills of setting the vision, aligning and motivating and others will follow your lead.

8. Don't be afraid to be passionate about your goals. Passion is essential not to coercion, but to influence. If you truly care about involving your people in an endeavor greater than themselves and let them know that you care, you become the leader.

GOLF TEACHES US

THAT WINNING IS AS

MUCH ABOUT COURSE MANAGEMENT

AS IT IS ABOUT POWER, AS MUCH

ABOUT HOW WE PLAY FROM THE

ROUGH AS HOW WE

PLAY FROM THE FAIRWAY.

IN LEADERSHIP, COURSE MANAGEMENT

EQUATES TO JUDGEMENT,

EMOTIONAL INTELLIGENCE, WISDOM

AND THE CAREFUL USE OF POWER.

PLAY IT WHERE IT LIES

Secrets from the Golf Course on Character

About Hole #8

Hole #8 is a one hundred eighty-seven yard par three that is rated #2 in difficulty to par. This difficulty stems not from the fact that it is a dogleg right or that it is loaded with hazards, but that it requires a one hundred seventy yard carry to an island green which is accessible only by bridge. Hit the ball too hard and it is in the water; hit it too soft and it is in the water. If you land it on the green on the fly, you still have to stop the roll. Character is a tough hole to par.

Introduction

A training room on the fifteenth floor of a downtown Houston office building in mid August. The sun is streaming in the windows fighting a continuing battle with the building's struggling environmental management system. I am speaking about leadership to a group of more than fifty Human Resource professionals, primarily department managers, who have been brought in from around the world to attend three days of training and

"We are playing CEO musical chairs here."

team building. Sitting in groups at their tables, they are somewhat shell shocked; at one and the same time eager and dispirited, trying to do their best to maintain some semblance of HR procedures and to stem a significant tide of turnover in the company.

They inform me that their company has been merged, acquired, and acquiring so often that it has changed names four times in the last six years. The "leadership" of the company, as represented by the person sitting in the president/CEO's office, has changed more often than the name of the company. They no sooner begin to implement the program of the current president/CEO than the company is sold and/or a new person with a new program takes over.

"Don," one participant comments after the first break, "what you are teaching about leadership, the things like vision, alignment, and motivation, makes sense in a stable company. But we are playing CEO musical chairs here, most of the people with whom we interact on a daily basis don't even know the name of the company they are working for, it has changed so often. What relevance does this information have for us in this job?"

What a wonderful question! This question summarizes all that is misunderstood about the nature of leadership. My response, a response that challenged deeply held paradigms of most everyone in the room, was that leadership is not the province of the president or CEO, it is the province of everyone in the company—particularly of those sitting there in that room.

Carl Jaspers wrote a few years ago that we are at "an axial point in history." This point is marked by the pervasive failure of institutions (schools, governments, churches, business, organizations of all kinds) to meet the needs of their constituencies. Carl Jaspers summarized the feelings of many of us who deal with these institutions. These institutions simply do not meet

our needs. The pervasive failure of these institutions to meet our needs is reflected in the
cynicism of all of us about the possibility, not
of change, but of improvement, not of things
being different, but of things being better.
Institutions don't meet our needs today and
we hold out little hope that they ever will.

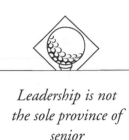

*Leadership is not
the sole province of
senior
management.*

So, what can we do about it? We can do
the same thing that I suggested to the HR
professionals in that room. Remember what it was that was discussed in the previous chapter—Leadership is a discontinuous
process; leadership is not the province of senior management.
Thus the answer to the question is that the individual manager
needs to assume leadership. We can, within our institutions,
accept the responsibility of improvement. By now you have been
reminded in nearly every chapter about my leadership philosophy; that is, that leadership is about influence as much as command, about achieving extraordinary things as a team as much
as individual accomplishment. Every manager, no matter his or
her level in the company, can help every individual feel that
they are part of something greater than themselves; every manager can make his or her people feel that this department, this
region or this plant can be the best in the company. Every manager, every person, can set a vision of greatness for a group he or
she works with and can work with others to change institutions
from the bottom up rather than from the top down.

All it takes is a willingness to step out of a comfort zone and
assume leadership.

"But I'm Not A Leader"

Not surprisingly, my response that the way out of their dilemma
was to assert leadership, was not an answer that delighted everyone in the room. While many were nodding their heads in total

agreement, others were shaking their heads in frustration (and fear—by definition, people don't like leaving comfort zones). One individual who was sitting near the front of the room quietly, almost under her breath, summarized the feelings of many, "but what if you aren't a leader?"

We have touched on this topic in previous chapters in this book, and it would be repetitive to revisit the nature/nurture leadership debate ("Are leaders born or are they created by circumstances?"). However, I have a very strong opinion about the issue. This opinion, not surprisingly, is paralleled by a lesson you can learn on the golf course.

Some years ago, a class participant presented me with a list of "leadership traits" and told me that these traits were possessed by less than one tenth of one percent of the population. Well, I thought, "that's not too bad, given a population of two hundred fifty million, that means that we have more than two hundred fifty thousand potential leaders in this country. That's not so bad."

Of the twenty-six million golfers in this country, how many have touring pro skills? You don't have to be Jack Welch to be a leader.

But further reflection told me it was bad. It meant that there were two hundred forty-nine million seven hundred fifty thousand non-leaders (and some of the leaders were obviously children—this couldn't be.)

The problem was that the traits list reflected the popular belief about the charismatic leader and were based on observations of the very few who are either naturally charismatic or who are imbued with the trait by their constituents (Jack Kennedy was naturally charismatic, FDR was imbued with charisma in a time of crisis). This is not unlike coming up with a list of "golfing traits" based on the skills displayed by Ben Hogan, Arnold Palmer, Tiger Woods, Greg Norman, Fred Couples, Davis Love III, David Duval and other great professionals. Of the more than twenty-six million golfers in this country, how many have "touring pro" skills. Perhaps a thousand, maybe two thousand. Does this keep the guy with the fifteen handicap or the woman with a ten handicap from playing golf? Do these people say, "I have a ten or a fifteen handicap, I am not a golfer. Of course not. You don't have to be Phil Mickelson to be a golfer or Jack Welch to be a leader. You can develop the character it takes to be a leader in the same way that you develop the physical and mental skills it takes to be a golfer.

Leaders are simply those people who choose to influence others to help them make a difference. They may never run a company, lead an orchestra, hold political office, or head a division. They may never have one of those "C" titles (CEO, CFO, CIO etc.), never run a plant, never manage a newspaper. But they have accepted the challenge to develop themselves, to work to influence others, and to make a difference.

The Character/Competence Debate

One of the themes of this book is that leadership has often been portrayed as reflective of elements of character (typically the charismatic or driving image of the leader) or reflective of superior skills and managerial competence (the organized, thoroughly in control, skill driven leader). As I noted in the forward, this need to define leadership as either one thing or the other is simply one more manifestation of the "Tyranny of the Or." In fact, neither image is accurate. Leadership is both character and competence, who you are and what you can do. Much of this book has focused on the competence side of the equation: e.g., vision, alignment, versatility, emotional intelligence, and motivation. While this chapter will look at a few aspects of "intellectual competence" (concentration and focus), Hole #8 will primarily examine the other side of this equation: Character.

Personality Is Not Character

Please notice that the word personality is not used. Personality is a public face reflective of character, but not always consistent with character. Personality, or at least its public dimension, is often a reflection of a collection of skills developed by individuals in order to be more socially effective—it is something we develop as an external reflection of who we are. In other words, personality is often the public persona consciously used to project the right image in any given situation. This public persona can be a learned skill. (Chapter 9, Change, examines the concept of "personality" in more depth.)

As a parallel, you will see people on the golf course with the absolute latest in technology in their bags. Head covers reflect major brand names, the bag is large enough to hold the clubs of every member of the foursome and it sports the logo of a well-known manufacturer. The golfer him or herself looks like golf must be their life; hat, shirt, pants, shoes, not only match perfectly, but are neat and pro shop pure. It is only when the first drive is hit, the second shot duffed and the third shot whiffed that you realize that it is all a show. Show has been substituted for substance. We sometimes find the same conditions in leadership.

Graduating from executive charm school does not make you a leader – it may even endanger your ability to lead by encouraging others to focus on form over substance.

I once worked with a man who had been to executive "charm school." When you met him, he greeted you with a firm hand shake. Simultaneously as he shook your hand, he placed his left hand somewhere between the elbow and shoulder of your right arm. His greeting was strong and friendly. The next time he saw you, he would remember your name. Every ounce of this man's public persona said, "You are the most important person in the world right now." Truly, on first and second impression, the man was impressive.

Regrettably, as you began to know the man over time, you realized that, as Gertrude Stein said about Oakland (a long, long time ago), "There is no there, there." The man had few beliefs he was willing to stand up for and he had no vision beyond that of the book or article he had just read. He constantly sought personal advantage (reminding me of Lily Tomlin's words of wisdom: "If you are a rat and win, you are still a rat."). Those he was supposed to lead soon saw through the purpose of the public persona—it was to hide his lack of deeply held beliefs about who he was and what he stood for. He failed in his leadership role because, in moments of debate, his character was not grounded in principle. *Personality is not character.* Character is who we are and what we stand for when the public persona is stripped away.

> *Personality is not character; character is who we are when the public persona is stripped away.*

The point that I am making is this: like golf, leadership is not the privilege of the few who have incredible natural talent but the option of the many who choose to get out on the course to practice and play. Many of us have leadership capabilities that we choose not to exert because we have been cautioned not to, because we are afraid of success, because we don't want the responsibility, or hundreds of other "reasons." But leadership is a choice: it is character and competence. You can learn the skills and you can develop character.

> *Leadership is a choice...you can learn the skills of leadership and develop the character of a leader others want to follow.*

Play It Where It Lies: Golf and Character

It is the 1998 US Open. The course is the Olympic Club in San Francisco. The course is grueling; the seemingly normal scores for the tour professionals of 65, 67, 68 have been replaced by true pars and more. Scores of 70, 72, 75 and even 77 are common. Payne Stewart, forty-one and playing great golf for three days goes into the last final round with a four stroke lead built on consecutive rounds of 66, 71 and 70.

On the four hundred sixteen yard par 4 twelfth hole, Stewart, then leading Lee Janzen by three strokes, hits a beautiful drive down the middle of the fairway. The ball lands on the grass rolls twenty yards and comes to rest—right in the middle of a sand-filled divot.

Now, if you are not a golfer you probably think one of two things: first, that this isn't fair, he should be allowed to move the ball out of that hole; or second, that landing in a divot is no big deal. If you can hit a ball as well as these pros can, what difference could a little hole in the grass make, particularly a little hole that is filled with sand.

But it does make a difference, a significant difference. It is a harder shot. It changes your club selection and your strategy. It turns an almost sure shot into a much lower percentage shot and it goes back to one of golf's oldest and most deeply held rules—"Play it where it lies."

"Play it where it lies," is all about developing character through the acceptance of personal responsibility. The golfer looking at the perfect drive that wound up in someone else's divot may curse his luck, complain that it isn't fair, and wonder if there isn't some other rule that he can think of to get him or her out of the situation. But basically, the golfer knows that shots happen and the only option is accepting responsibility and getting on with the game.

This is what Payne Stewart did. Stewart struck the ball relatively cleanly out of that divot, wound up two feet short of the green and in a bunker. He took a five on the hole and then bogeyed two out of the next four holes. This shot, this unplanned lie, changed the momentum of the match.

His primary challenger was Lee Janzen. Janzen only birdied one hole after the twelfth, but he wound up winning the tournament by a stroke. A case could be made that the ball landing in the divot, resulting in (no golfer would say, "causing") a missed shot and an extra stroke, cost Stewart the championship. No it wasn't fair, but it is golf. After the loss Stewart said, "I have to deal with the situation...I was in the fairway (on the twelfth hole), but I was in a bunker (the sand divot)...I kept scrambling, I kept trying, I never gave up....The person who deals best with the pressure is the one who becomes successful...(of the sixty golfers today) I came up one short. I can handle that." (USA Today June 22, 1998 7c).[1]

Character Is Golf's Greatest Lesson

Indeed, the character that can be developed while playing the game is probably golf's greatest contribution to the individual golfer. Not surprisingly, this lesson applies directly to the leadership of people. This is not to say that everyone who plays golf has honesty, integrity, predictability, courage of conviction, determination, a sense of personal responsibility, strength of will and an ability to accept unplanned results ("Play it where it lies"). There are obviously some golfers who never learned the lessons of character and, as a result, never achieved their full potential. However, it is to say that, if you let it, golf will teach you these character traits and more.

In terms of leadership and character, golf does teach us about honesty, authenticity, predictability, tenacity, courage, and will. In terms of competency, golf teaches us about the importance of both the physical skills (striking the ball consistently) and the mental skills (maintaining concentration throughout the

---

[1] One year later, at Pinehurst Number 2, Payne Stewart won the US open.

> *The first characteristic that people look for in a leader is honesty.*

swing) needed to win. Let's begin by looking at one of the essential character traits of leaders: honesty.

Honesty

In nearly every survey that is conducted in search of characteristics that people see as essential in a leader *they admire,* honesty is at the top of the list. (There are leaders who are not admired; people grudgingly acknowledge that they may not have ethics, but "neither does the other guy"—better the one we know than the one we don't.)

In the first chapter of Kouzes and Posner's 1993 breakthrough book on the importance of character in leadership, *Credibility,* the top five characteristics that people identified as important in an admired leader were: honest, forward-looking, inspiring, competent and fair minded. As further evidence of the importance of this characteristic, the authors found that efforts to lead change often foundered if people did not believe in the inherent honesty of the leader.

The question is, "Why is honesty so important in a leader, why is it even more important than competence?" Golf provides a hint.

"I will admit that I have occasionally cheated at golf" I sometimes tell my incredulous audience, and then I add, "but, of course it was usually for a very good reason." Bennet Cerf once suggested that the first golf shot took place at nine o'clock in the morning, and the first lie about a shot about five minutes later. In truth, golf without exaggeration would be a different game, but golf well played demands individual honesty.

If there is an underlying theme to the ancient and honorable game of golf, it is one of personal honesty. In my early days of playing golf, before I really understood what the game was all about, I shot a score of 99 without taking a mulligan, without kicking the ball out from behind a tree, without moving the ball out from a divot, without forgetting to add a stroke for putting a ball in the water. In short, I broke one hundred for the first time by counting every single stroke and by playing according to the rules as I then knew and understood them.

"What other kind of 99 is there?"

Shortly after this exciting milestone, I said to a friend who has been playing the game for twenty years and who knew that I had set a goal of breaking one hundred that year, "I shot an honest ninety-nine." His reply wasn't, "good for you," "great, it must feel good to break one hundred," or "now it is time to set your next goal." No, his reply, a summative statement of all that golf is supposed to be, was: "What other kind of ninety-nine is there?"

Golf is played in an environment where individuals have a lot of time away from the people they are playing with. In a normal Saturday morning game, there are no referees to call penalties nor umpires to declare that a ball is "foul." As a result, every golfer has moments of ethical decision making on the course. Your partner doesn't see you muff that chip and hit it three feet, he or she doesn't see you tap the ball unintentionally as you line up to putt, doesn't see you touch your club to the sand before your bunker shot. Golfers must make these decisions for themselves and they must always be wary of rationalizing.

For example, you hit a beautiful six iron that is grabbed by the last branch of the last tree between you and the green. To add insult to injury, this branch flings your ball into the rough under the trees. You and your partner go looking for the ball. It was your best shot of the day. He yells, "Found one, what are you hitting?" Your response could be, " I don't remember, it was white (giving you the option to hit whatever she found) or the more honest "It was a Top Flite 2 with a black dot under

> *Without a covenant between leader and follower based on trust, leadership eventually fails.*

the F." In golf, it is your choice. For the weekend golfer, every game provides ten or twelve decisions of this type. Your communication with yourself on the golf course is: "Am I honest with myself and therefore honest with others?" If you can say yes, it probably carries over to business.

There are those who say that honesty, like any other principle based character trait, is passe in today's business climate, that honesty is situation dependent: "that was my best drive of the day, who put that tree *in the middle* of the fairway, right between my ball and the pin, I think I'll judge nudge it over a few feet."

But honesty is not situational. Not if you want to be a leader. Without honesty there is no trust. Without trust there is no covenant between the leader and the follower. Without this covenant, leadership eventually fails.

Authenticity

Related to honesty is a second critical character trait of the leader called authenticity. Authenticity is best defined as consistency among three elements: what you believe, what you say, and what you do. There are two problems with authenticity: the first is that many of us, due to the influence of all the requirements of cultural norms, have never bothered to learn who we are in terms of important characteristics; the second is that some of us who have discovered who we are labor long and hard to try to be something else.

> *Who you are on the golf course is usually who you are.*

Golf strips all this away. Who you are on the golf course playing a round with three friends is most often who you are. Authenticity demands that you examine what you believe in, it demands that you examine values and principles and that you commit to these beliefs in every-thing you do. Authenticity requires that we practice internal honesty. It requires that we forego bluff and bluster for internal appraisal and external congruence.

This was one of the characteristics that made Arnold Palmer not just a great golfer, but a great merchandiser. Palmer would honestly share the failings of his game with others. If he was being indecisive with his putts, he would acknowledge the flaw and correct it. Because he was able to share this internal to ex-ternal process of authenticity he developed credibility.

Few can achieve 100% authenticity, few of us are perfect, but acting in concert with knowing who you are and what you believe in contributes to an overall sense of predictability, the next essential characteristic of leaders.

Predictability

If the average duffer were asked how good a golfer he or she is, a common answer would be: "It depends on who shows up—Mr. (or Ms.) ninety-five or Mr. (or Ms.) one hundred and five." This is one of those characteristics that separates the tour pro-fessional from the near professional (the excellent golfers who labor on the minor tours) and from the everyday golfer.

Obviously, the professional golfer can shoot sixty-seven one day and seventy-eight the next. He or she can birdie four holes in a row and then bogey the next two. But this is mild in com-parison with the lack of predictability in the average golfer whose scores on a given day might range from a birdie to a quadruple bogey (if all strokes were counted).

One of the most challenging aspects of golf is predictability. In golf, every shot, every lie of the ball dares us to maintain predictability in the face of differing circumstances. Every time we address the ball we are faced with the challenge of consis-tency of approach, swing and follow-through, the three main components of predictability in golf. In leadership we are also faced with the challenge of consistency in three phases: in approach, action and follow through.

> *There are few more valued characteristics of a leader than consistency of approach.*

Approach

In golf, approach includes activities such as the address, the take away and your mental preparation. Golfers know that consistently good golf is dependent upon a consistently good approach. If your hands are not positioned right, if you don't line up correctly and if you don't take the club back consistently, if you don't mentally prepare for each shot, then the best action toward and through the ball won't produce the desired result. Likewise in leadership.

There are few more valued attributes of a leader than consistency of approach. Your people want to know who you are when they need you. They need to have confidence that their approach to you and your approach to them will have a high degree of predictability. Your mental preparation and personal approachability is essential for the rest of your leadership actions to be truly effective.

No one I ever dealt with better exemplified the need for predictability of approach, both in terms of mental preparation and interpersonal accessibility, than Shawn Halston. In 1990 I was engaged by a medium sized manufacturer of tubular products to help them with business process improvement. It was there that I met Shawn.

Shawn was their vice president of sales. Small, compact, intelligent and driven, Shawn exuded confidence from the moment that you met him. He would describe his vision of tomorrow in vivid detail. He would explain to anyone who would listen how his company was going to increase market share by revolutionizing the service side of the business (the product side was seen as a commodity) and thereby increase the value of the product.

He convinced both the president and the vice president of operations that the company needed a total restructuring of their customer service process, and he pioneered a customer satisfaction innovation that included a rebate on a late order that was the responsibility of his company (if the product arrived late because the customer ordered the wrong product or changed his mind, Shawn's company didn't pay).

He also initiated customer visits between the customers' purchasing staff and Shawn's company's customer service representatives. He took his warehouse people on tours of the customers' warehouses so that they would

> *He failed in no small part because of an utter lack of predictability.*

better understand customer's needs before this was common practice in many industries.

Shawn spoke frequently and urgently about the fact that world class customer service was a survival issue. He clarified the vision and in his own way aligned the company.

And he failed.

He failed because his ego overrode his judgement, because people perceived his cause as being too closely related to Shawn's personal agenda (another leader who got ambushed by the trappings of prestige) and not enough to the company's prosperity, and most importantly, because of an utter lack of predictability.

Six months into the project I drove past the gated entrance that led me into corporate headquarters. Shawn and I were meeting to plan the use of a new tool to anticipate potential customer service problems. It was about three o'clock in the afternoon. Twenty feet from his office, the customer service manager stopped me. "You don't want to go in there, today, Don."

I was startled. My reaction was surprise. Surprise not just that she stopped me, but surprise at the implication of her message.

"I'm sure it is okay, Shawn and I have an appointment."

"It's your choice. He has been screaming at people all afternoon. He chewed Kim out so bad she left crying. We lost a customer this morning over a disagreement with an accounts receivable rep over an invoice and he has been screaming at people ever since."

I could hear him now. He was on the phone and everyone knew he was upset. "Does this happen often?" I asked.

"Weekly, sometimes daily," she replied. "Everyone in this department is terrified of him. He is Jekyl and Hyde. He is the most wonderful boss in the world one minute and totally out of control the next. We never know who we are going to get when we walk into that office." Others supported her. Why had it taken me six months to find this out? A new prosperity, a feeling of achievement at the company, an unwillingness to fool with something that seemed to be working and fear of reprisal based on Shawn's utter unpredictability kept others from telling me what it was like to work with Shawn on a day to day basis.

Later, I met with the company president (he had long known of the problem) and we put together a plan to help Shawn become more predictable and easier to work with. For about six months it seemed to be working, then abruptly, Shawn left the company, a disappointed man. He left behind a vision of greatness for all the people he had touched at the company, but in the end, because of his lack of predictability, his leadership was never solid, and his vision was never achieved. The company sunk back into the old ways and was sold some years later.

Obviously, this wasn't all due to the failure of predictability in Shawn, other leaders in the company (and the consultant who learned that you can consult, but you cannot "do") also shared in this responsibility. But it was his Achilles heel. The story would have ended differently had Shawn been predictable in approach.

Action

If Shawn Halston failed in the area of pre-dictability, Janet Bates succeeded—and admirably. With Janet, predictability of approach led to predictability of action. She reflected in an individual leader the principles needed in a company.

> *In leadership, there is a need to maintain an unchanging core in the midst of on-going external change.*

In *Build to Last,* Collins and Porras talk about the necessity of a company maintain-ing an unchangeable core in the face of ongoing external change. This unchanging core is critical for people as well as companies to maintain. Janet exemplified this principle of living core prin-ciples in her role of manager of operations. Given the change that was continuous in her industry and the pervasive change within both her company and her department, Janet demon-strated a bias toward action based on principle. Her consistency was tested by a company president who was almost Machiavel-lian in his strategic moves. But Janet countered these strategies with principle based responses that put her department in an enviable position in terms of resources and growth. Because of this, people saw her as the "go to" person. Her people knew that, on any given issue, her perspective reflected the long term best interests of the company and her decisions consistently sup-ported that perspective.

As a result of her predictability she was one of the few people in the whole company who was respected by both the most senior management and the non-management employees within the company.

This is not to say that Janet wouldn't get upset or that she wouldn't apply disciplinary action. She would. And she was not very tolerant of those who were not well prepared or who had

Because she was consistent in applying those beliefs in moments of choice, Janet was respected as a leader.

not thought through their proposals. She had virtually no tolerance for petty arguments and she avoided office gossip whenever she could.

One day, after the project we were working on was complete, I asked her if she was aware that she represented integrity and predictability of leadership within the company. She answered that the president had grudgingly told her the same thing over a year ago, and that she knew that she was perceived differently from other leaders in the company.

"How do you do it," I asked. "What do you do that is different from other managers here?"

She responded that some time ago she had taken a personal inventory and written down the beliefs that she had and the principles that these were based on. She then made a conscious decision that she was going to base her career on these beliefs. Finally, she determined to live a lifestyle that would allow her the freedom to leave a career if these beliefs were overruled by superiors. That is, she made a conscious decision never to put herself in a position where she couldn't quit her job. That wasn't the hard part though. For her, the hard part was making decisions and living each day consistent with these beliefs. Finally, she said, she knew that every time she made a decision consistent with these beliefs, she knew that she was building a pattern that made the next one ever so slightly easier.

Janet stood for something and she was consistent in applying those beliefs in moments of choice. As a result, she was respected as a leader.

In golf, follow through is at least as important as approach.

Follow Through

Golfers know that the follow through is as important as the approach and the action of hitting the ball. Where you are aimed as you conclude your follow through will often tell you both the expected distance of your shot and where the ball is headed. Follow through determines both the distance of your putt and your shot out of the sand. Follow through determines the accuracy of your seven iron. As a matter of fact, golfers are taught not to hit the ball, but to hit through the ball. That is, golfers are taught to incorporate follow through into action.

There is no predictability without follow through. Your people will watch you to see if you will support proposed actions in face of opposition; they will watch you to see if you will support the team; they will wait for you to "go to bat" for the unpopular idea or the creative individual. Commitments made and not kept destroy the leader's influence. Follow through is yet another critical component of leadership.

Tenacity magnifies talent.

Tenacity and Persistence

"Negative thinking," Bob Rotella notes, "is nearly 100% effective." Thinking that you are going to shoot a ninety when you have a twelve handicap is easy. Resolving to lower that handicap to nine in the next twelve months is the challenge.

We've all heard the adage, "Winners never quit and quitters never win." The absoluteness of that aphorism always bothered me because it suggested that some people "won" not simply because of superior skills or ability but because they just hung in there longer. It also seemed that, because of what these seven words imply in terms of one value, that winning was so much more important than a number of other important values.

But the study of leadership has convinced me that persistence and mental tenacity, choosing the goal and not giving up until it is achieved, is a characteristic of leaders.

We've all witnessed tenacity in action in many different forms. When I was playing varsity baseball in high school, we had one player of above average, not by any means outstanding, talent. Hal would ask anyone on the team to continue to pitch to him *after a two hour practice.* We had about ten baseballs. After he hit the ten, he would run out, round them up and we would start pitching to him all over again. He wound up getting a scholarship and playing in college, getting drafted by a major league team and, after a brief stint in the minor leagues, playing a couple of years in the majors. Tenacity magnified talent.

I find that, like Hal, successful entrepreneurs often have equal amounts of tenacity and talent. This is not to say that they are not often exceptionally bright and skilled in many ways, it is to say that they often succeed because they won't accept failure. They succeed because they are going to find a way to make their vision a reality.

Ryan, in his early fifties, started his company with a small loan from his father, twenty-two years ago. It is now a two hundred million dollar company. I am sitting in a meeting he has called with his senior management as he describes a customer service crisis. "I respect that you have all done as much as you think you can to remedy this situation,"` he says, "and I know that we have made incremental improvements. They are not enough. We must solve this problem within the next thirty days or we will have to begin shutting down some stores. This is unacceptable. Tomorrow morning at 6:00, we will begin to develop a plan. By tomorrow evening we will have a plan. Within forty-five days we will have solved this problem. There is no alternative." And they did. Ryan wouldn't accept anything less. (Incidentally, early morning meetings are almost always a wonderful way to tell everyone, "This is not just important, but critical.")

Tenacity isn't abstract; it isn't having a mental goal and determining how you are going to achieve it. Tenacity isn't saying, "I think I will break 85 this year." Tenacity is saying, "I am going to break 85 this year. It is an important goal. It means hours and hours on the practice range and the putting green and I am going to do it." Tenacity turns plans and goals into reality. It requires prioritizing, values assessment, examining the principles upon which your goal is based and staying the course. But if it is a high enough priority, if it is consistent with your values and it is based on principle, it is tenacity that will convert this vision from a distant goal to a reality achieved.

Courage

Sister to tenacity is courage. If you are going to be a leader, if you are going to influence others to make a difference, it requires courage. You simply cannot talk about leadership character without talking about courage. We will visit courage in more detail when we examine change in Chapter Nine. Books have been written on fear, on the fear of failure and the fear of success. Suffice to say here that courage is not the absence of fear, but is the ability to take action in the face of fear, in the face of both the known and the unknown. If you are to lead, you need to take action in the face of fear.

Concentration

The development of concentration may be golf's greatest lesson.

If you have ever played golf, you have had the following experience. As you are walking toward your ball, which is lying some 240 yards from the tee box and another 168 yards from the green, you are thinking, "Which club, my six or my five?" As you are approaching the ball, you are thinking about all the factors that could influence the success of the shot. Is the lie a good grassy fairway shot straight to the pin? Are there bunkers either side of the green? Is there water between your ball and the hole, water just waiting to reach up and grab the ball?

And now you are walking up to your ball with your trusty six iron in hand. "I can make this shot," you say to yourself, "not only can I make this shot, but I want to put it up and to the left of the pin, which will give me a nice uphill putt against the grain."

So you address your ball, do the obligatory waggle, and place the club face so that it is aligned with your target. As you slowly take your club back, you have this image of the perfect shot. You are so sure that you are going to hit the perfect shot, you are so absolutely positive that it is going to wind up on the green just where you want it to be, that you totally forget to keep your left arm straight and thus unconsciously bend it at the top of the swing so that you can get more distance. You come down hard and hit the big green ball (that is, the earth) first and your ball runs about fifty yards and sinks into the water, not to reappear until it is resurrected for the ball barrel or the driving range.

Of course it can be worse, this same misfortune can befall you because you are thinking about what you are going to get your wife (husband) for her (his) birthday. Or what you are going to say to your son about why you had to take his car away from him. Or why that foursome on the next fairway has to shout and swear with every shot. Or whether you need to apply that mosquito repellant before the next shot. Or whether some marshall might get upset with you because you ran fifty yards parallel to the cart path instead of going back to the cart path and then back out to your ball on a 90° rule day. Or…

It doesn't make any difference, because what you have really done is lose concentration. The greatest business lesson that can be

The greatest business lesson that can be learned from golf is that of continuously maintaining concentration and focus.

learned from golf isn't about processes or keeping score, structuring the deal or even about alignment; it is about concentration and focus. There appear to be hundreds of ways that certain practitioners guarantee you that you can knock five strokes off your game. Most of these surround changing your practice time from the driver to the putter, or from practicing the long irons to practicing the chip.

But, if there is one way that almost infallibly will take strokes off your game, it is to concentrate, to intensely focus on each shot. In his book on the mental aspects of golf, *Golf Is Not a Game of Perfect,* Dr. Bob Rotella tells a story of a time that Tom Kite had just finished playing a round of golf with two members of the University of Texas golf team. They all shot between 69 and 73. When the match was over, one of the students asked Kite why he was (at the time) the all time leading pro tour money winner and they were the number two and three players at the University of Texas. Kite replied, "The difference is that when you guys get in tournaments, the likelihood is that you will lose your concentration on four or five shots every round."

Golf, like business, is about focus. When you approach your shot there is basically one thing you should be thinking about: how you are going to hit that shot. As you hit through the ball, you must have total focus. You need to line up that ball with your target, select the proper club and believe that you can put it where you want to. You must truly believe that you can hit that ball in the sweet spot and lay it softly on the green and you must have so consciously incorporated the mechanics into your unconscious that you essentially have no swing thought.

You simply cannot lose your focus. You must clear your mind of every thought other than the club hitting the ball. You cannot think about your score, your next shot, the back nine. You cannot think about dinner, how good a beer would taste right now, or what to do with your daughter who keeps nagging you for that car she wants you to buy her. You can't even think about

You cannot think about how the ball might go into the water or it most surely will.

how beautiful this particular hole is, or how you just hit the best three wood of your life. All you can think about is the ball, the club and you, coming together at that perfect spot to hit the perfect shot.

You cannot afford to think about the sweat dripping into your eyes, the gnat buzzing around your head, or the sound of a helicopter or leaf blower in the distance. You cannot afford to let your mind wander to the next shot or think about whether you should be playing a Titleist or a Pinnacle. All you can think about is the ball, the club and you, coming together at that perfect spot to hit the perfect shot.

Most of all, you cannot afford to worry about what will happen if you miss, or worse, **when** you miss this shot. You cannot think about how the ball is going to go into the water or it surely will. You cannot afford to think that a bad bounce will put it into the sand trap or it will. You cannot afford to think that the ball will hit that tree instead of all the open space around it or sure as you're thinking about it, that tree will (like the water) reach out and grab your ball.

All you can think about is the ball, the club and you, coming together at that perfect spot to hit the perfect shot that will land precisely where you want it to land.

And isn't the same thing true of business?

In golf, you must live in the present if you are to do well. You must focus on the present moment with total concentration. All of your physical, mental and emotional energy must be focused on that one shot, that one fraction of a second when club strikes ball. It is called the present.

In my years of consulting, I find that most companies have trouble maintaining focus. They are like most golfers; they have focus for a couple of shots, then they lose it. They are focused on the past, the near future, the distant future. They are focused everywhere except the present. They lose an edge when they lose focus. One of the of tasks of leadership is to help the group, the company, the division, the department, maintain focus and concentration. This, of course means that the leader must maintain focus. Even in the most challenging and exciting times, you need to block out the distractions and focus on the goal.

Will

The final characteristic that we will examine in this chapter is will. By will, I mean making the conscious choices that will enable you to lead others. I believe that the characteristics we have discussed earlier in this chapter: predictability, honesty, authenticity, courage, tenacity and concentration, are choices. They are not easy choices, but they are, nevertheless, choices. In my study of leadership and in my experiences with leaders at all levels of

Will is continuously choosing wisely and well and staying the course.

organizations, I find that successful leaders have made and continue to make difficult choices. They consciously choose to be brutally honest with themselves and to be honest with others; they consciously choose to align what they believe with how they act; they consciously choose to face down fear and make the tough call.

Aristotle wrote that "we are what we repeatedly do, therefore excellence is not an act, but a habit." Will means that we continuously choose wisely and well, not the easy path but the right path; it is an internal discipline that can be started at any age, but that produces consistent results. Will requires consistency and discipline and nothing more difficult can be asked of us not so perfect human beings.

Is it difficult? Yes. Is it critical? Yes. Remember the definition of successful people; this definition applies to golf, to business, to life. "Successful people do that which the unsuccessful are unwilling to do."

How to Play This Hole

It is easier to establish and achieve a vision than it is to develop a character that will allow you to lead others. As I noted at the beginning of the chapter, this is a very difficult challenge for most of us. The title of Bob Rotella's book, Golf Is Not A Game Of Perfect, can obviously be applied to the development of the leader's character. Leadership is not a process of perfect, nevertheless, there are some things you can do to build your leadership potential in terms of who you are:

1. Work to continuously evaluate who you are and what you stand for. "Know thyself" was inscribed on the ancient Greek temple at Delphi. Honest self appraisal is the beginning of critical traits such as authenticity and predictability.

2. Remember that personality is not character. People want leaders who show consistency between their deeply held beliefs, their words and their actions.

3. Play it where it lies. Accept personal responsibility for your situation, for your successes and your failures. Obviously, some of us have it easier than others in terms of some types of success, but all of us have the same battle in developing character. Learn to hit the ball from the divot, don't waste time bemoaning the fact that the ball is in the divot.

4. Work to control yourself in terms of approachability, actions and follow through. Remember, your people need to feel comfortable in bringing a wide range of

issues to you. They need to believe in you; belief in you is highly correlated with your predictability.

5. Don't give up or change direction at the first obstacle. If you believe in your vision, commit to it, stick with it. Henry Ford said, "You can't build a reputation on what you are going to do." Tenacity and persistence are traits that will ensure the goal will be achieved.

6. Exert your free will. Make conscious choices that will enable you to lead others.

7. Focus on what you are doing. Work through the stages of competence (unconscious incompetence, conscious incompetence, unconscious competence) until your concentration can be totally focused on your vision because you are not worried about the competencies needed to achieve it, only the marshalling of those competencies to achieve your goal.

8. Change is inevitable. We all change all the time. We learn new things, we have new experiences, we grow in age and (hopefully) wisdom. Take control of this change. Direct it toward the development of leadership character. How to do this is the topic of the next chapter.

GOLF TEACHES US

PERSONAL RESPONSIBILITY;

IT TEACHES US THAT NO ONE WILL HIT

THE BALL FOR US AND THAT WE MUST

BUILD ONWHAT WE ARE GIVEN—WE

MUST PLAY IT WHERE IT LIES.

GOLF TEACHES US

THAT WHOWE ARE IS AS IMPORTANT

AS HOW WELL WE CAN

DRIVE, CHIP AND PUTT.

GOLF TEACHES US

THAT CHARACTER, CONCENTRATION

AND FOCUS ARE ESSENTIAL

TO SUCCESS IN ANY ENDEAVOR.

IMPROVING YOUR GAME

Secrets from the Golf Course
on Personal Change

About Hole #9

This is the signature hole on the course, not the longest, just the most difficult to par. Change is a four hundred thirty-six yard par four that begins with a one hundred ninety yard carry over swamp grass. Hit it straight and two hundred sixty yards and you are in the sand, pull it, and you are in the lateral water that curves left as the hole doglegs in that direction. Worse than this for many golfers is the fact that it leads to "Mulligans," the grill at the turn that always seems to have at least thirty golfers sitting outside on the elevated deck watching you; judging your competency as you hit your approach, critiquing your form as you line up your putt(s).

So, You Want To Be A Leader

So, you want to be a leader. You want to provide the vision, align the group, motivate and influence others. You want to set the direction, accept the challenge, improve the bottom line. You want to implement those skills you have learned. You want to produce the results you know you are capable of producing; you want to influence others to make a difference.

You want to do all of this, yet you have the uneasy feeling that you are not quite ready. You perceive yourself stuck in a rut that you are not sure how to get out of; you want to change your style, but you are not sure how to do this effectively.

If you are not leading now, if you are not one of those very few who naturally assumes leadership, if you are not naturally assertive in implementing your own dreams and ideas, if you are not naturally outgoing and persuasive, how can you become a leader? It is a challenge, but it can be done (and, there is tremendous joy in accepting this challenge). There is a model for becoming a leader. This chapter presents that model, a proven and practical approach to change, discusses the barriers to change and provides a strategy to overcome those barriers.

Mummies

Most of us unconsciously walk around wrapped like mummies (as in Egyptian, not mother). At about the age of five we begin wrapping ourselves in a uniquely patterned fine gauze that we believe we are defining of our own free will. Day after day, week after week, month after month and year after year we continue to wrap this gauze around us. We believe we are creating this mummified state of our own free will, in fact, messages from teachers, parents, relatives, siblings, and friends as well as our own fears and creative imaginations are shaping the pattern that our gauze is taking.

The external and often well meaning messages sent by these sources might include:

"Math will never be your strong suit,"

"Always know your place (implied, we are not as good as they are,)"

Most of us unconsciously walk around like mummies.

"Pride goeth before the fall,"

"You have brains and skill, use them wisely,"

"It is better to stay quiet and be thought a fool than to open your mouth and remove all doubt,"

> At about age 12 we enter the age of fear at full bore.

"Your sister is the outgoing one, you are the quiet one,"

"You are better with things than you are with people,"

"You aren't dumb, just lazy,"

"You always take the path of least resistance,"

"Why don't you ever think about what you are doing?"

"With hard work and dedication, there isn't anything you can't achieve,"

"Money is the root of all evil,"

"The Bigger they are, the Harder they fall," and, of course,

"You will never be able to putt well."

These and literally thousands of other positive and negative reflections on the world and our place in it tend to shape our character, our competence and our sense of control over events. They begin to put shape to the once pliable gauze.

At about age twelve, the speed of the mummification process accelerates. Not only do we believe that we are now more in charge of defining our capabilities ("I am good at Math and Science," "I hate English," "I am good at sports, but I don't want to be Captain of the team"), we also enter the *age of fear* at full bore. Now we are afraid of not fitting in, we are afraid of embarrassing ourselves with the opposite sex, we are afraid of those with more power, of those who seem to be confident and capable. We are afraid of wearing the wrong clothes, afraid of appearing un-cool, afraid to the depth of our being of the disapproval of our peers.

Never in our lives will two major determinants of personality—the need for acceptance and the fear of rejection, be so evident to others (although for the most part, as we pass through it, we are totally unaware of these powerful forces—if you doubt me, ask any teenager if he or she fears the disapproval of friends).

And so, at age twenty we emerge wrapped (some loosely, some rigidly) in gauze that has been defined for most of us both by the opinions of others and by our reflections on those opinions. Thus, we are frequently limited by what we want to avoid, rather than what we want to achieve, limited by problems to escape rather than challenges to seek. We call our unique gauze wrapping, "our personality." Included in this "personality" is both our perception of our leadership aptitude and a related quality called our sense of self-esteem, a combination of our confidence in our abilities and our sense of self worth.

For a few, the gauze of personality is removed and re-wrapped through the experience of college (you become president of your fraternity and find out you do have leadership abilities), the military (suddenly sixty other people are depending on you), marriage or a calamitous event.

At about age 19 or 20 we are defined (and limited) by the image that we have of ourselves.

But for most of us, at around age twenty, we are about ninety percent formed and within this form is our general, often unarticulated, perception of ourselves and our leadership capabilities. For a few, this usually includes those who received primarily positive messages during childhood, and/or those who have had successful leadership experiences in scouts, school, or church related organizations, this perception is a very positive, "I am a leader, I have outstanding leadership capabilities." For most, however, it is just the opposite. For most it is, "I am not a leader, I don't want to be a leader" (with the un-articulated "because I am afraid of ...").

Breaking Out

The first step toward cutting away the gauze of the personality you created as a child is to acknowledge that you created it and what the results of that creation have been. The second step is to use the knife of change. We will look at how to wield this knife of change after I show you that change is not only possible, but a daily occurrence for many. For those of you who have "I am not a leader," written all over the gauze you have wrapped yourself in, the entire purpose of this book is to give you strategies to change the perception that keeps you bound and unwilling to pursue leadership. Please understand that this is all we are really dealing with here: a perception based on the habit of not taking leadership roles and the supporting belief that you—for some reason that often makes sense only to you—are not a leader. But first, let's look at the process of change.

There is a logic to the process of change.

The Transition to Leadership

There is a definite logic to the process of change. For example, if you want to begin the transition to leadership, begin with this: Leadership requires results; results require actions; all actions begin with thoughts, develop thoughts that will produce the results required of a leader, and you are ahead of the 90%

> *Two of the dominant laws of life are that we need (sometimes crave) acceptance and we fear*

who don't have any idea where to begin. Given that this logic is true (and it is) your personal leadership development program begins with thinking, with imagining. The haunting chords of John Lennon's "Imagine" (with your lyrics, your imaginings) can take you to the beginning of your journey to leadership.

Ah, but you are afraid. Of course you are. So was I. So are most of the people who leave the world of comfort to challenge themselves. Phillip McGraw begins his book on purposeful living, *Life Strategies* by pointing out that the two dominant laws of life identified above. We all *need acceptance* and we all *fear rejection*. Whatever your goal, whatever thoughts, beliefs and emotions you are challenging in order to develop your leadership potential, the real task is to leave your comfort zone (known acceptance) and venturing into the unknown (potential rejection). The sane response to this formidable adventure is fear—or excitement.

First let's look at fear, because it is fear that is the dominant emotion in shaping most of what we call "our personality," and it is fear that must be conquered if we are to fully develop any of our potentials—including our leadership potential.

Golf, Fear and Personal Change

There is a wonderful scene in the movie "*Tin Cup*" that summarizes why adult change is so difficult. In this movie, Kevin Costner (Tin Cup) has won a regional competition and earned an opportunity to play at the US Open somewhere in North Carolina (couldn't be Pinehurst No. 2 could it?). Just before arriving at the Open, he has developed a case of the shanks (hitting the ball off the hosel of the club at right angles to the target line). Upon arriving at the course he goes to the practice range where a host of very familiar golf faces greets this unknown "driving range pro" from Salome, Texas. Not only is his nemesis (Don Johnson) hitting practice shots, but so are well known golfers like Johnny Miller, Lee Janzen and Billy Mayfair.

Costner notices the level of competition and the fact that the driving range balls are all brand new Titleists. He steps up to hit his first practice shot and dribbles one off the hosel of his iron (where the heel of the clubhead connects to the shaft). His shot rolls parallel to and right in front of the row of golfers hitting their practice shots.

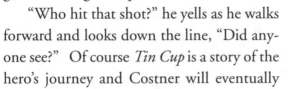

"Who hit that shot? Did anyone see?"

"Who hit that shot?" he yells as he walks forward and looks down the line, "Did anyone see?" Of course *Tin Cup* is a story of the hero's journey and Costner will eventually succeed on his own terms, but this is a defining moment as to why adult change is so difficult.

If you have ever stood on the practice range shanking, hooking or badly slicing shot after shot after shot while trying to learn a new swing, adjust the old swing, or simply "let the club take itself through the swing," you have likely experienced some of the emotion of change. While you are shanking your shots, the golfers on either side of you are hitting beautiful seven irons and perfect two hundred fifty yard drives. While you hit the ground behind the ball (called "hitting the big ball first"), while your pitiful attempts result in forty yard dribbles and hooks so bad they leave the range and wind up in the tee box of the first hole, those on either side of you smile and shake their heads.

However, if you are willing to acknowledge the emotions of fear, anger, embarrassment, and frustration you can improve the distance and accuracy of your shot. If you can risk failure, you can achieve success. If you can leave your comfort zone and accept the potential mortification that comes with learning any new behavior as an adult, you can move to the next plateau in your game. If you are afraid to experience these emotions, if

> *Golf teaches us that change is not only possible, but an expectation.*

you look to practice only when no one is around, or if you give up after only a few tries and go back to your reliable, if less than satisfactory old swing, you probably won't improve.

Golf and a Paradigm for Change

Despite the "Tin Cup" syndrome, golf provides a wonderful paradigm for change. If you are a golfer, you **know** change is not only possible, it is an ongoing expectation. Most golfers do not define themselves by their current handicap. They don't say, "I am a twenty handicapper and I will be for life" or "I finally shot a 90 on a decent course, this is the best I will ever do." No, the serious golfer will say, "I am a twenty handicapper today, but I will be a fifteen within a year" and "All right, now that I have broken ninety, I will set my sights for eighty-five." Golf shows us that change (improvement), is not only possible, it is a continuing theme; a theme that persists despite the impact of continuing modification of equipment and technique.

For example, golf has undergone a dramatic revolution in technology over the past twenty years. The level of invention and technology has gotten so pervasive that some manufacturers are actually advertising the stability of their product. Look at the golfers vocabulary: titanium (club heads and golf balls— titanium golf balls?!), graphite, bubble shafts, Balata balls, (what's Balata, Italian cork?[1]), weighted heads, oversize and undersized heads, diamond faced 60 degree wedges, just to name a few. (In the *Official Rules for Golf* author Paul Dickson quotes William Mead's list of the great technological advances in golf. These

---

[1]Actually, Balata is a relatively soft rubber like outer covering of the ball. It gives more control and feel. Most golf balls are covered with Surlyn, a plastic type material developed by Dupont.

include: "the golf cart, the telescoping ball retriever and the cold drinks cart which circulates around the course on hot days.")

Indeed, there are few things in golf as pervasive as the continuous clamor for change. Watch the "Golf Channel" and you are bombarded by programs and advertisements suggesting that there are better ways to play the game, better ways to hit the ball, better balls to hit and better clubs to hit them with. Open any golf magazine and you encounter a similar clamor with a different slant. Here the ads tend to focus more on training, on workshops and weekends where you can "improve your short game" or "take five strokes off your game by learning the secrets of the power swing."

If you haven't mastered the basics of the swing, if you still regularly duff shots, hit a big slice seventy percent of the time and can't hit the green from forty yards out, balata balls and graphite shafts probably won't help.

The question is, how much lower is your score when you use a bubble shafted driver and graphite shafted copper headed "irons" with titanium golf balls? And here is another parallel with leadership. If you have mastered the basics of the swing, if you have reached a level of competence that allows you to feel confident about your game, these tools will make a difference. Professional and low handicap golfers use Balata balls because it gives them extra "feel" on each shot. However, If you haven't mastered the basics, if you still duff shots, hit seven out of ten drives with a significant slice and can't hit the green with your wedge, much less back the ball up on it, using a titanium ball or a graphite shafted club will likely not make a significant difference in your score.

A Model for Change

In golf nearly everyone feels substandard. After all, the game is based on the concept of a nearly perfect composite score ("par for the course"), a score which very few golfers actually achieve on a regular and on-going basis. The rest of us are left looking at this target and wondering how to get close to it, not necessarily how to achieve it. If par can be thought of as putting the ball in the hole, most of us are satisfied to merely get the ball on the green (break 85) with the hope that we can continually land closer and closer to the hole. This does not apply, of course to those who play competitively at a club or professional level, where there is a constant expectation of making (or breaking) par.

Because we are seldom satisfied with all aspects of our game (including our score) golf provides many lessons on change. Among these are:

- Why Positive, Purposeful Change Is Such a Challenge
- Why We Want To Change In The First Place
- Why Targets And "Overlearning" Are So Important
- Why We Do What We Do, And, of Course,
- The Fundamentals of Change: How to Carry Out Successful Change (The Change Model)

Not surprisingly, we will find that there are many parallels between the process of change used to improve our golf game and the process of change used to improve our "leadership game."

A Clarifier or Two

There are books on the topic of change (actually, many, many books on change). We all know that we are living in one of the most rapidly changing eras in the history of the world. These external changes, a world population of six billion people, revolutions in communication (the Internet being the primary example), weapons of truly awesome and unthinkable proportions, downsizing, rightsizing, reengineering, mergers, and functionally interdependent global economies all force us to change whether we like it or not. In this chapter I am not talking about that kind of forced, external change, change that we must cope with in order to survive. Rather I am talking about conscious efforts to improve an aspect of our lives or our organizations; in this case our ability to lead. This is change to be embraced, not simply coped with. This kind of change is related to our need for hope. The process of consciously becoming a more effective leader, much like the process of practicing to become a better golfer, will bring far more joy to you than simply saying, "I am what I am and that is all I will ever be." Positive, purposeful change is an exciting dimension of human behavior. Let's begin this discussion of change by looking at why change is such a challenge.

> *When I am talking about change, I am talking about a conscious effort to improve some aspect of our lives, in this case, our ability to lead others.*

Why Positive, Purposeful Change Is Such a Challenge

Have you ever tried to change your golf swing? Have you, perhaps, at some time attended a golf school or clinic where you were taught new ways to hit your driver or new ways to chip or putt? The chances are good that you came home from the golf school with great intentions, but after two or three poor rounds of golf trying to incorporate the new techniques, you reverted to your old habits.

Or perhaps, like many Americans, you may have gone on a "diet" during the last few years. If you did go on a diet, or perhaps if you started an exercise plan, the chances are better than nine out of ten that you reverted to your old behavior within twelve to eighteen months (even more depressing, you probably put the weight back on that you lost—and them some).

Why is it that "smoking cessation" programs, three day golf clinics, alcohol and drug treatment programs, exercise programs, and, for that matter, corporate change programs (TQM, re-engineering, Self-Directed Teams) so seldom achieve their goals on a permanent basis?

Half a Brain is Worse Than None When It Comes To Change

It likely will not shock you to learn, based on what we discussed earlier about interpersonal or emotional intelligence, that the reason permanent change is so seldom achieved has to do with how we use our "thinking" and "feeling" brains. In order for change to be effective an alignment of the rational and emotional systems of the brain must be in place. If you can marshal the energy of your thinking brain and the power of your emotional brain, you can effect personal change. If you can marshal the energy of systemic change with the power of vision, you can effect corporate change. This is the reason that "forced change" (often a rational, go/no go process) is seldom effective over the long term. Emotion centered change can have an impact on behavior (fear is a powerful motivator); but the change will always be pursued half-heartedly and will likely disappear with the emotional impetus ("My blood pressure is back to normal, I really don't need to exercise any more."). Only an approach that integrates the rational and emotional will yield permanent change. So the question becomes, "How do we marshal the energy of both brain systems?"

*If you can marshal the energy of your rational brain **and** that of your emotional brain, you can effect change.*

The First Step Toward Change: Dissatisfaction

In order to align our logical and emotional systems for change, we need a starting point. For most of us, this starting point is a disconnect between what is and what is wanted. Whether it is personal change or corporate change, the key initiator of change is dissatisfaction with a current condition. You are dissatisfied with your current handicap, so you

decide to take lessons and spend more time
on the practice range and putting green. You
are dissatisfied with your weight, so you decide to change your eating habits. Your doctor tells you that your cholesterol is above 230
and that your HDL/LDL ratio is hovering
near the danger zone, so you decide that you
will eliminate certain foods from your diet
and begin a regular program of exercise. Your

*All change begins
with dissatisfaction
with the current
state.*

company has found margins falling precipitously, so the company decides to reorganize business units. Your department has
received a number of internal customer complaints so you decide that some re-training in basic customer service skills is
needed.

You might say, "Well, what if you are doing well, what if
your cholesterol isn't bad and your blood pressure is normal and
you start exercising just to feel better and ensure that you stay
healthy." Is this dissatisfaction?

Certainly it is. Essentially you are saying, "I am doing well
and I want to get better." In other words, "I am dissatisfied with
where I am and I want to get better." In short, whether we are
operating from the mode of "It's broken and needs fixing," or
"It's not broken, but it could be better," or "What works today
may not work tomorrow," all change begins with a current or
anticipated dissatisfaction with the status quo. (Incidentally, Paul
Dickson defines improvement in golf as "Missing the ball closer
than before.")

There is, of course, a step beyond dissatisfaction that also
leads to change. This is urgency. Not surprisingly, urgency occurs when dissatisfaction is ignored over the long term. Urgency
is a stronger motivator for change. When a situation has urgency, whether it is personal or organizational, change is the
only option to any condition of entropy which will eventually
lead to significant loss: loss of the company, loss of health, loss
of position, loss of self esteem, loss of hope.

The Leadership Commitment

Thus, the initiator of change for you to increase your effectiveness as a leader is to create a sense not just of dissatisfaction, but of urgency. Look at what will happen if you don't change. If I were a golfer with a twenty-four handicap and I knew that I could easily be a fifteen with focus and practice, I could whip myself into a sense of urgency by focusing on the continued frustration of missing putts, hitting errant seven irons and losing five balls a round to OB and water. To become the leader you can be, you need to do something similar. You need to identify the continuing frustration you experience when your ideas are not accepted, when you are unable to influence others, when you don't receive that promotion, when senior management does not listen to your ideas. You must work yourself to a state where you are saying something like:

> *"I am dissatisfied today with my leadership achievements; the results of my leadership activities have not been what I am capable of producing, nowhere near what I am capable of producing! There is a disconnect between the leader that I am and the leader that I want to be. I have a deep personal commitment to becoming the leader I want to be."*

Sounds nice, how do you get there?

Aligning the Two Systems

Picture a mountain meadow. The grass is full and high, a bubbling creek runs clearly in the not too distant background, and forest surrounds the meadow. Now picture a large deer walking through the meadow, pushing aside the grass as he crosses to the creek. Other deer follow. The grass is gradually broken down and the hoof prints begin to tear into the dirt underlying the grass. The deer continue to use this newly forged trail, more earth is disturbed, more grass broken and uprooted. A narrow trail is formed. Now it begins to rain. Gently at first, then harder. The water finds the path created by the deer and runs through it creating a small rivulet. It continues to rain and the rivulet becomes a gully. Over time the grass broken down by that first deer has become the path of least resistance and the water flows predictably through the meadow to the creek.

> *When you are trying to change years and years of behavior, you are messing with well established neural pathways, your "comfort zone."*

My apologies to those who labor in the fields of neurochemistry, neurobiology and neurology in general, but this metaphor describes the basic process (oversimplified that it is) that humans go through in establishing the ways we behave—the habits we often unconsciously engage in on a daily basis. Habits of the golf swing, habits of eating, habits of managing others, habits of being more or less assertive in dealing with others, habits of drinking, smoking, church going and fidelity, all basically begin as one time behaviors (breaking down the grass) and become entrenched habits as they are repeated time and again and literally burned into the neural pathways of our brains. It is these neural pathways, these electrical/chemical paths of least resistance and the synapses that must be bridged that you are impacting as you are trying to change. It is these neural pathways that create the gauze we wrap ourselves in. This is why change is so difficult and why it requires such a commitment. When you are trying to change a behavior, you are essentially trying to change years and years of neural communication that has resulted in the "ruts of behavior;" we call these ruts of behavior, "Our Comfort Zone."

Breaking Out of the Comfort Zone

Yes, we call it the "comfort zone." It is a place of relative emotional and physical predictability. Like our favorite chair, it requires little else of us other than that we stay there to experience a certain unexamined sense of resigned acceptance of the world as it is. We experience little fear of failure, little anger, and only minor dread of inadequacy or embarrassment. But in the comfort zone we do not experience the jolting joy of a challenge met, a dream achieved. We don't experience the pure sensation of hitting the perfect shot on the golf course, or leading others to purposeful achievement in business. In the comfort zone, we feel little at all—it is one of the things that keeps us there. In fact the comfort zone for many of us may be explained by noting the fact that on many Sunday afternoons, more "golfers" may be found watching golf than playing it.

Let me describe a "comfort zone" day for a lot of Americans. You arise in the morning with thoughts of all those things you have to do. After getting ready for work, you turn on the TV and watch the bad news from the day before. You eat a breakfast that is either too starchy, too heavy, too sugary, too something (so you feel some degree of guilt). You drive to work and listen to the radio, switching stations and picking up more bad news. Arriving at work, you meet your friend who shares inside information on what is happening and all the problems existing at the company. You not only commiserate, you share your own insights into what is wrong with the company and why things are never really going to change around here. Arriving at your desk, you notice that you have three voice mails and twelve e-mails all of which ask you to respond. You grab a cup of coffee, sigh and start responding to the requests.

At 10:00 you have your first meeting of the day (three more to follow). You have been working all morning on your responses to people, so you aren't really prepared for the meeting. As usual, Bob dominates the meeting. You wonder why you are there. After two more meetings like this, you return to your office to find two more voice mails, three more e-mails and all of them appear urgent. At three o'clock in the afternoon you finally get time to begin working on your project when your boss calls to see if you have compiled that information she asked for last

week. You put your project aside and begin
gathering the data she needs. After putting
the information in spread sheet form and presenting it to her, you return to your office to
find another three e-mails. After responding
to these, you get your coat, go to your car,
drive home listening to the bad news of today on the radio and arrive home to your energized children. You spend a few minutes
with the kids, gobble down another meal that
makes you feel guilty and sit down to watch
your favorite team run up and down the basketball court or
your favorite evening news hour, soap opera, detective show,
etc.

Breaking out of the comfort zone is essential for most of us to achieve our leadership potential.

You do this until you finally fall into bed tired from your
exhausting day of reacting to the needs of others, feeling guilty
and sensing that you really accomplished nothing except another day done, another day in the comfort zone.

Looking at a day like this in the comfort zone clarifies it for
what it is: a comfortable couch that deadens us to our own potentials, whether it is in leadership development, family or health
issues, or a host of other personal growth issues that we might
want to attend to. More than this the comfort zone breeds cynicism about the success of others and a sense of hopelessness that
things will never get better. This is why breaking out of that
comfort zone is so critical to development as a leader and as a
fully functioning human being—and, it can be done.

The Logic of Change—The Need for Autonomy

So, how do you break out of the comfort zone? Predictably, in
order to break out of the comfort zone, you need to redirect the
neural pathways that control both logic and emotion. Let's first
look at the role of logic in the process of change.

As mentioned earlier in this chapter, the first question is, "Why?" Why do you want to become more of a leader? Why do you want to lose weight? Why do you want to spend less time at work and more time with the family? Why do you want to lower your handicap? In other words, you have to create that sense of dissatisfaction and urgency, you must give the brain a strong reason to change. The answer to the question of "why" will either increase the likelihood that your change effort will be successful or will almost assuredly condemn your change effort to failure.

Your answer to the question "why" will indicate whether internal or external forces are propelling your sense of urgency and dissatisfaction, whether you are driven by an autonomous or extrinsic impetus. Your effort to change will likely succeed or fail based on the autonomy of the reasons—its degree of personal volition as opposed to its degree of outer control. Even when we know that the change is a product of urgency, we must *will* the change.

Psychologists have demonstrated beyond discussion that a fundamental human need is the need to feel autonomous, that is, to feel that the actions we take are taken out of choice rather than coercion. If we feel that our actions are our own choice, if we feel autonomous, then we feel involved and integrated, and we are more in harmony with our environment. Thus, the need for personal autonomy is one of the critical keys to effective change.

Putting the concept of autonomy in concrete terms, frame a question beginning with "why" for something you want to change in your life. A common example in American life today is, "Why do I want to lose weight?" An autonomous response is, "Because I want to feel and look better for myself." An au-

A fundamental need for all humans is that of feeling autonomous, of taking action out of choice rather than coercion.

tonomous response is, "My health is a high priority for me and I know that my current weight is not healthy." An autonomous response is, "I really don't want to have to buy a whole new wardrobe."

Autonomous or coercive? The answer lies in the "why."

Coercive or controlling reasons are those that reflect society's or someone else's priorities for your behavior. Controlling responses for losing weight include; "My doctor told me to", "My husband or wife thinks I weigh too much, "All those models are thin," and "If I lose some weight, I will be more attractive to the opposite sex." (Or the one that almost always leads to failure: "I really **should** lose some weight"— *shoulds* are poor motivators for change. Internally based *"I wants"* are powerful motivators for change.)

The key here is not the language but the reason behind the language. Two people could say, "I want to lose weight so I can look better." If the reason that one person wants to look better is because then he feels better about himself, the rationale is autonomous—he is going to lose weight because he wants to. However, another person could use the same language and her real motivation would be that she wants to look better *in the eyes of others, she wants the approval of others, she wants people to tell her that she looks better with the weight loss.* This is coercive, it is giving control of our environment over to external forces, and it is much less likely to engender successful long term motivation.

Let's take an example that relates to this book. Why do you want to improve your leadership skills? Autonomous responses would include: "Because I have a contribution to make and my present skill level doesn't allow it," or "Because I want to feel more a part of the team," or "Because I feel challenged by the opportunity to make a real contribution to this company," or "Leading people gives me a chance to operate at the top level of my ability, I am excited and energized by the opportunity to lead."

Answers that reflect external control include: "My boss told me that, if I didn't increase my leadership skills, no more promotions," "My parents (wife, husband etc.) are disappointed that I haven't progressed up the ladder faster," and "The only way to make money in this society is through leadership—I intend for this leadership stuff to pay for itself."

The same control issue applies to golf. Why do you want to lower your handicap? If you responded that playing well and scoring well increases your enjoyment of the game, your answer reflects an autonomous choice. If you responded that you are tired of losing and looking foolish to others, you are giving up autonomy by giving control to others.

In order to successfully achieve your change goal you must dispassionately determine your primary motivation.

Our reasons for change are rarely as clear cut as just for autonomy or just because of external force. Most decisions to change reflect a combination. So the real question is not so much what is your motivation, but what is your primary motivation?

The secret is to consciously frame your motivation. Which is more important? That you make a contribution that will then help you get a promotion or making more money will allow you to more effectively influence others. In order to successfully achieve your change goal, you must dispassionately determine your primary motivation.

The bottom line on the logic of change is this: If you are changing a behavior for consciously considered primarily autonomous reasons, the change is likely to be pursued with joy and successfully achieved. If you are changing a behavior for external, coercive, non-autonomous reasons, you are more likely to grudgingly pursue this change and the change is far less likely to occur. By the way, things: bigger and more expensive cars, bigger houses, vacation homes, bigger and better toys, are all external coercive motivators. It is the reason that there is so much truth in the old adage, "Money won't buy you happiness" (even though it makes a good down payment). However, as we noted above, the logic of change, the need for autonomy is only half of the process. The other half has to do with feelings, with the emotion of change.

The Emotion of Change—Accepting The Risk

In his breakthrough book on human motivation, *Why We Do What We Do,* Edward Deci highlights the importance of the emotions in change. "To be ready to change…people have to reach the point where they are willing to allow the feelings that (current) behaviors are blocking." In addition, Deci says, people must be willing to "feel different" than those people who not only are not changing, but who will belittle those trying to change.

During the late eighties and early nineties, trying to undo decades of denying the role of emotion in everyday life, we typically went overboard in asserting the importance of emotion. Suddenly, many of us began focusing on the "negative emotions" as part of our identity. It was not uncommon to hear, "I am angry," and "I am hurt" as pronunciations of people whose emotions seemed to take on an identity of their own. Even our president was heard to say, "I feel your pain."

Today, the pendulum is swinging back to balance. Change involves acknowledging the emotions of fear and joy. It also requires that we stay in a conscious, rational mode; dealing with problems not as though they were de-

> *You must be ready to allow the feelings that current behaviors are blocking (this includes fear, anger and joy.)*

signed to hurt us, but as opportunities designed to challenge us and thereby help us grow.

Watching Tiger Woods win a tournament in June 1999 in preparation for the coming US Open at Pinehurst No. 2, illustrated in a five minute span why the balance between logic and emotion is so important.

It is the 18th hole. Tiger knows that he must get down in two to win the tournament. His ball is in the high grass about twelve feet beyond the green. His first shot from that position is a shot that every duffer makes. He takes a full swing and lifts the ball out of the deep grass eight feet into the air and five feet further into more deep grass.

He has one more shot. Now picture this. Tiger Woods is standing twelve feet from the green with his wedge still in his hand. He has to be angry with himself, he has to know that he likely just lost the opportunity to win this tournament. Now he looks over his next shot. He is still seven feet from the green, he is still in high grass and the green slopes down to water. Hit this shot wrong and he could easily wind up in the water, lose another stroke and perhaps finish third or fourth, rather than first or second. But he tames these emotions, he tames the anger, he tames the fear, he tames the frustration he must have felt at missing a relatively easy shot for a pro golfer. His logical mind controls these emotions, he embraces the philosophy of Curtis Strange who said, "Never let your emotions interfere with your ability to make smart decisions." Tiger Woods becomes pure focus, pure concentration. He hits the ball, it bounces on the green and roles into the cup; the tournament is his. Then we see the emotion of joy, the familiar right arm swung up in a three quarter position again and again. It is balance.[2]

"Never let your emotions interfere with your ability to make smart decisions."

Becoming a leader, exerting yourself in order to influence others, means acknowledging the emotions and consciously taking the risk. You will naturally progress through the four stages of competence (unconscious incompetence, conscious incompetence, conscious competence, unconscious competence) as you leave your comfort zone and implement the change.

Commitment is not a feeling.

You can lose momentum in achieving this change because you sense that "something is wrong." That something is typically an inability to recognize and rationally deal with the feelings that occur whenever we leave the comfort zone. So, be prepared for strong feelings of fear: fear of rejection, fear of other's reaction, fear of failure. Be prepared to feel lonely (leadership is often a lonely role), to feel inadequate, to feel terror. But, like Tiger Woods on the 18th green, know that you can control these fears through concentration and focus. Don't deny them, just don't let them take over your life.

Then be prepared to experience the emotions of joy and elation that result from knowing that you have reached the level of conscious competence as a leader. This is your goal and you will only achieve it if you dare to leave that comfort zone and confront the feelings (particularly fear) that have contributed to your staying cozy but dissatisfied in that comfort zone.

---

[2]It is interesting to note that two weeks later at the US Open, Tiger had a bad first round (for him) and he was shown taking an angry half swing at a missed putt, throwing up his arms at another missed shot and generally losing the concentration that makes him such a great golfer. With all this, he wound up losing to Payne Stewart (yes, the one who lost the previous year "playing it where it lies) by just two strokes.

Commitment: Logic or Emotion?

There is one final word that requires consideration before moving on to some models for change. This word is *commitment*. Commitment is often seen in our society as a feeling; we will say, "yes, I feel committed to this project (or this person)." But commitment is not a feeling. Commitment is a thought that leads to action. Commitment must be both volitional and rational to be effective. If you say, "I feel committed to this process of becoming a leader," you won't be as effective in your pursuit of it as if you had said, "I am committed to becoming a leader."

Nowhere is this definition of commitment more evident than in the life of Bill Pinkey, the third American (and first African American) to solo-circumnavigate the globe. Having endured incredible hardships and life threatening situations that he could easily have turned away from and thus failed to reach his goal, he said this about commitment:

> *"Commitment is more than a word; it means **I will…in spite of what happens.**"*

Commitment is part of the cycle of change. You begin with urgency and dissatisfaction which leads you to a commitment to change; you encounter problems, you remember and renew your commitment, you change the problems into challenges and you overcome them. Your confidence is increased, your commitment becomes even greater. The process continues. But without commitment, without "I will…in spite of what happens" your chances of success are severely reduced.

A Model for Change

Let's now look at how a model of a change process might work for a golfer who is sick and tired of coming in fourth with his Saturday foursome. He decides he wants to improve his consistency, reduce his handicap and beat his friends. His goal is set.

He *wants* to win his club tournament twelve weeks from today (no *should* here—he *wants* to).

(A note on personal goals. We all have a minimum of four areas of high value in our lives: family, spiritual, career and physical. We can seldom handle more than two major change goals at a time and these must be selected from different priority areas. For example, you might be able to handle a spiritual goal and physical goal, but not two physical goals. I have tried to lose weight and improve my golf game at the same time [while maintaining family, spiritual and career values]. It doesn't work. Every time I am practicing golf, I am thinking, "I *should* be running." Every time I am running, I am thinking, "I *want to* be practicing my chipping." So don't put yourself in this framework. If you are constantly being forced to choose between competing priorities, you will always feel guilty about one or the other and guilt is a powerful "demotivator." Eventually you will quit both. So decide on one and commit. In my case I need to choose one or the other or convince myself that losing weight and getting in shape will help improve my golf game, so that I don't feel guilty no matter what I do.)

Back to our golfer. Now, for some of you, losing a few rounds of golf at your local club would not be a sufficient motivator for change, but for our mythical (mystical?) golfer, losing is reason enough to create *an urgency* for change. Let's look at what he is going to do to improve his chances of winning at the next tournament twelve weeks from today now that he has set his goal:

- Review His Current State
- Develop A Deep Personal Commitment to Change
- Create A Vision (Of Himself Winning The Tournament)
- Align All His Internal Systems Toward Achieving That Goal
- Learn and/or Perfect New Skills On The Practice Tee, Green or Chipping Area (Overlearn)

- Take Action
- Stay the Course Until He Has Achieved His Vision

Review Your Current State

The first step is to review your current state. Our golfer is going to make an honest assessment of his strengths and weaknesses. What is he good at? Where does he need additional skill development? (Or, what is he not so good at?) He is going to do this not by thinking but by gathering data. He is going to count drives on the fairway, greens in regulation, putts made; he is going to determine the accuracy of his second shots, how well he hits out of the sand and the rough, how he does from thirty yards in (See Hole # 6, "Keeping an Accurate Score"). This will give him his focus.

Develop a Deep Personal Commitment to Change

Once he has identified the skills he needs to develop, he is going to truly commit—or he won't begin at all. He is going to anticipate those things that can get in the way of his improving these skills (weather, demands of family and work, money, time) and decide if he really can make this a priority. For the purposes of this exercise, let's say that he determines how he can handle the barriers to achieving his goal of winning the tournament; in essence, he can manage the commitment.

In order for change to be successful, you must develop a deep personal commitment to the change you wish to achieve " "I will, in spite of what happens."

Create A Vision

Vision without action is a waste of time; action without vision is spinning your wheels. I once had a friend tell me that his favorite motivational method was to go to sleep listening to a subliminal tape titled "Sleep and Grow Rich." (It didn't work. And neither will a vision if you don't take action.) What a vision does is galvanize action. It creates focus and concentration. When you envision yourself winning that tournament, when you see yourself sinking that final putt and raising your arms in victory, you aren't just sending a pleasure picture to your emotional brain. You are sending a message of focus to your rational brain; you are creating urgency.

If you watched Mark McGwire in the on deck circle during the final twenty games of his 1998 seventy home run season, you knew he was in a vision state. He was seeing himself connect for another homerun. While he was in that state he was so focused he couldn't hear the roar of 50,000 people.

Our golfer is also going to learn to put himself into a vision state. How? He is first going to create an image rich picture of himself. For example, he might see himself smiling as he picks up the club trophy and feels the weight of it in his hands. He sees the smiles and frowns on the faces of his friends, he sees himself shaking hands with the club pro as he experiences the joy of winning the club championship. Once he has developed this vision in sufficient detail, he is going to write it down and he is going to regularly (at least once a day) envision himself winning that tournament.

I cannot emphasize the following enough in terms of change. Our images of the future significantly influence what we achieve and how successful we are. Our dominant thoughts, our dominant mind pictures of who we are and what we want to become most often become "self-fulfilling prophesies." This is true for both "I can" and "I can't." So choose the positive, fill your mind with pictures of you achieving your vision, achieving your goals, achieving the leadership role you aspire to.

Align Internal Systems Toward Achieving The Vision

Aligning systems to achieve a personal goal is similar to aligning to achieve a corporate goal. It means taking an honest inventory of the barriers to achieving that goal or vision and then planning a strategy to overcome them. For our golfer, an honest inventory tells him that his driving is okay. But his review of his current state produced unmistakable data regarding his game from 60 yards in; this is where his major problems are. Why doesn't he do well from 60 yards in? The primary barrier is not lack of knowledge, but lack of skill. He knows how, he just doesn't execute. Another barrier he faces is that he dislikes practicing his pitching and chipping; finally, while there is a practice range with a putting green a few miles away from his home, there is no place close to practice pitching and chipping to a raised green from the rough.

> *Whatever it is that will interfere with achieving the goal must be brought into alignment with the goal.*

He knows that these barriers will have to be overcome if he is to achieve his vision. He will need to commit to practice, set aside the time to practice and then practice, practice, practice.

There may be other alignment issues. For example, family agreement that this is a priority, equipment issues, confidence issues and others. Whatever it is that will interfere with achieving the goal must be brought into alignment with your goal. Another alignment issue is ensuring that you are properly motivated. For some of us this means sharing the plan with others, for some us writing down a plan, for still others, affirmations of success. Whatever your strategy, do it!

Learn and/or Perfect New Skills

"Practice is one of the greatest inventions in human history," says Steve Chandler in *Reinventing Yourself,* and in *"Everyone's a Coach,"* Don Shula points out the fact that one of the hallmarks of his great Miami teams was their "overlearning."

Our golfer will need to overlearn the skills of pitching and chipping. Realistically, this cannot be done in twelve weeks, or even twenty-four, but he can improve. Changing any behavior requires intensive repetition of the new behavior—remember, you are undoing the effects of years and years of neural connections if it is an old behavior you are changing or creating new pathways if the behavior is something you are just learning. One of the most challenging aspects of developing leadership is identifying, developing and mastering the skills required to lead effectively.

This is where commitment comes in. Remember, commitment is "I will, in spite of what happens." For our golfer, this may mean getting up at six o'clock on a Saturday when he would rather sleep in, forgoing his regular Saturday foursome, driving fifteen miles to find the best place to practice, or investing in a new wedge.

But here's what it means for sure. It means practicing way past the time when he thinks he has mastered the skill. It means willing himself to practice when he is tired of practicing, it means hitting twenty more shots from ten different lies and learning from each one of them. It means gaining such skill in chipping and pitching that his attitude when faced with any one of these shots in a real game is, "no problem, I can do that."

"They can who think they can."

Overlearning builds self-confidence. When you overlearn a skill you send a message to your brain of mastery. The confidence will often be unconscious, but it is there when you need it if you have overlearned. That those who have self confidence built of skill will succeed is not a new idea, but a proven one. Virgil wrote, "They can who think they can." Thinking you can gets a real boost when you prove you can. This is the reason for overlearning.

Take Action

Watching a video of Bill Pinkey rounding the Cape of Good Hope in his small sailboat as twenty to thirty foot waves assault him from every direction, I was amazed at his personal courage. To see him standing at the helm of the "Commitment" with tons of water washing over the little boat, I was again reminded of the indomitable spirit required to face danger. But Bill Pinkey doesn't see it that way. He points out that navigating those waves was simply about skill; "courage," he says, "is deciding to leave the dock."

So now it is the moment of choice, the moment to leave the dock, the moment of courage. You have decided where you are going, you have learned and overlearned the new skills needed to be successful, now you have to leave the dock, you have to take action. Taking action overcomes fear and changes your beliefs about you. "There are times," says Steven Chandler, "when you really have a chance to go for it. (It is at these times) when you realize that you are not who you think you are, times when you can be anyone you want."

So take your own power and go for it. Our golfer will walk confidently to that lob he has to hit over the bunker and put it on the green. He won't chip around the bunker, he won't panic, back away from it or try and figure out some way not to have to take this shot. No. He will take action. Remember that it takes as much energy to avoid a problem as to solve it. Change your neural pathways by taking action.

Stay the Course Until the Vision Is Achieved

One hole does not make a course. You cannot quit after one shot or success at one hole (or even failure at one hole). You have to keep coming back for more, you must keep taking the action until you achieve your vision.

Remember that the vision of our golfer was not to hit the ball well; it was not to improve his chipping. It was to win the tournament. The rest was simply the means to achieve this end.

So stay the course. If he didn't win this tournament, he would need to keep practicing and playing until his goal was achieved.

Remember commitment? The emphasis on commitment pertains to golf, to leadership and to life. Stay the course. We will look at how to apply these lessons to leadership when we make the turn at Mulligans.

> *Stay the course—the toughest part of change is not starting, but finishing.*

A Final Lesson From Golf on Change

As a consultant and speaker one of the most common themes I hear in response to this presentation goes something like, "It doesn't make any sense for me to change until my boss, (the department, the company, my spouse, etc.) changes."

This is a misconception that spells doom for many change efforts; golf provides an insight into why this is so. For the most part golf is an individual sport. It is true that there are sometimes scrambles and other team events in golf, but for the most part it is an individual event. As such, golf teaches us the importance of personal change—not of changing others, or changing departments or bosses, but changing ourselves. Golf teaches us that improving our own game is really the only thing we have control over. It does no good to wish others would improve if we don't improve ourselves. Ghandi said, "Be the change you wish to see in others." Whether it is leading a team, leading a department or leading a company, begin the change process by accepting personal responsibility for change. Change yourself and others will follow.

Summary

There is a reason that change is the signature hole. Strangely, it is easier to establish a vision for our department or company, to align, to motivate and to keep an accurate score than it is to leave the comfort zone we have created, the gauze we have wrapped ourselves in, and become a leader. The process of change, conscious, autonomous, permanent and positive is one of the toughest challenges we face.

But if you are a golfer, you know that change is possible. If you are a golfer you likely do not define yourself by your current handicap, but by the handicap you know you are capable of achieving. The process of change to becoming a competent golfer is parallel to the process of becoming an accomplished leader.

The process of change, stepping away from the dock and committing to conquering the fear that has held us back is one of the great joys of life. Whether it is breaking 80 or becoming the leader we were never sure we could be, the gradual achievement of a goal in any field is one of joy and hope. To begin this journey, to "Go for the Green" simply requires action, it means cutting away the layers and layers of the finely woven gauze we have wrapped ourselves in. It is often not others who keep us back but the comfort zone we have created for ourselves. As Steven Chandler writes, "Hypnotized by who we are, we cannot see who we can be." So, set your sights, make the commitment, stay the course.

How to Play this Hole

The most difficult step on the road to leadership is to leave whatever road you are now on and commit to the changes required to take that new path. Remember, if you keep doing what you are doing, you will keep getting what you are getting. How to play this hole.

1. From the day we could understand, our personality began to be shaped by external messages and internal reflections. Thus, we created that which we call our personality and we can change it.

2. We all need to feel accepted and we all fear rejection. These needs not only help shape our personality, but underlie why the process of change is so difficult.

3. Change begins with dissatisfaction. If you are not a leader and you want to become one, you must create dissatisfaction with your current state; the greater the dissatisfaction, the greater the urgency. Urgent dissatisfaction leads to change.

4. Golf provides a wonderful model for personal change. In golf we know we are not defined by our current handicap, we know that improvement is possible. In the same way that we seek improvement in our game, we can seek improvement in our ability to lead and influence others.

5. Positive, purposeful change requires that you align your emotional and analytical systems toward the goal of achieving that change.

6. Most of us are prevented from changing by our "comfort zone." This comfort zone requires that we do little, but at the same time the rewards for staying in the comfort zone, of failing to grow emotionally, intellectually and spiritually are minimal.

7. If change is to be effective it must be carried out for autonomous reasons. If a change process is undertaken because of external pressures, it is far less likely to have a permanent effect.

8. Change is risky. Leaving that comfort zone and proceeding into the unknown requires courage and commitment. Commitment means "I will, in spite of what happens."

9. In the seven-step change model that is presented in this chapter, the most difficult step is staying the course. Many start a change process, far fewer complete it.

10. Change begins with self and not others. You cannot control the behavior of anyone but yourself (and that is hard enough). Focus on changing yourself; Ghandi said, "Be the change you wish to see in others."

GOLF TEACHES US
THAT, IF YOU KEEP DOING
WHAT YOU ARE DOING,
YOU WILL KEEP GETTING
WHAT YOU ARE GETTING.
GOLF TEACHES US
THAT POSITIVE CHANGE
IS NOT ONLY POSSIBLE
BUT EXPECTED.
GOLF PROVIDES A MODEL FOR
CHANGE THAT SAYS YOU CAN
IMPROVE IF YOU WILL ONLY COMMIT.

AT THE TURN
Mulligans

About Mulligans

Most public and private golf courses have a restaurant or a bar and grill of some sort. They range from the classy to the plain, from a walk up window where you can get a hot dog and hard boiled eggs to a sit down restaurant where eggs benedict are served in the morning and steak Diane at night. Whatever the décor, the purpose is the same; to review, either at the turn (after nine) or at the conclusion of the match, how well you did and what you would do differently the next time you play.

In my experience, these establishments, a place where you can sit with your favorite beverage and review the game, are often called "The 19ᵗʰ Hole", Mulligans, or some other Gaelic name. I have chosen Mulligans because golf is the only game I know that has given an official name to an "oops" shot, to a "do-over," and even though everyone knows there is no such thing as a Mulligan, you can still buy them at anywhere from five to twenty dollars at most charity scrambles. (On the other hand, in defense of golf, Sam Snead once noted that when a golfer hits a foul ball, he or she has to go out and play it.)

At the "Mulligans" at the turn of "Go For The Green" you have an added advantage; you have a coach with a checklist on how best to play each hole. This checklist serves the purpose of providing you with a series to steps to improve your game. So, let's sit down with your coach and see how you did—and more importantly, what you would do differently if you had the "Front Nine" to play again.

Hole #1: Vision

How did you do on this hole? Sitting in your chair at Mulligans with a companionable beverage and some favorite sustenance, it is time to review your play. Did you establish both a personal and organizational vision? Remember Harvey Penick's words – "Take Dead Aim." Winners have goals, they have targets. It's the old saw about "How do you know if you have arrived if you never knew where you were going?" Every leader needs two pins and two flags: the first personal, the second for the department, region, division, organization or company being led.

If you did not par or birdie this hole, if you still do not have a written vision for yourself and your organization. Here is how to par it the next time.

1. Understand that the purpose of this vision is to galvanize action in achieving it. It isn't a "wouldn't it be nice wish list." It is a call to arms.

2. Review your values, beliefs and goals. The vision should reflect your personal and/or the organization's core values.

3. Draft the vision statement, then take a pen to it and edit it down to the basic, essential message. It should be no more than a page or so and it should reflect ideas that can be pared down to one or two paragraphs.

4. Make sure that the statement creates personal and organizational urgency. "We cannot continue as we have been; we have no choice but to embark on this new course."

5. If it is a company or organizational vision, present it to the executive committee and obtain not just "buy-in" but enthusiastic support. If you are fired upon by those who don't understand the urgency, be the leader you need to be. Explain why the vision is essential; articulate the lack of alternatives.

6. If it is a departmental or regional vision, make certain that it is consistent with the larger goals of the organization. If it is your personal vision, make sure you can make the commitment over the long term.

7. Organizational visions need to be boldly presented to the organization. In smaller organizations this should be done personally; in larger organizations, the leader should make as many personal presentations as possible, and then rely on electronic and visual media (video conferencing, tapes) to take the message to everyone. The leader must practice presenting this vision until he or she is totally comfortable with the message. It must be presented with controlled emotion.

8. Personal visions should be reduced to a paragraph and reviewed on a daily basis. Every day the leader should ask him or herself, "Is what I am doing this day, this minute, helping me to achieve my vision?" If the answer is "no," then you need to change the behavior or the vision. (Hopefully, you will change the behavior!)

9. Remember that you will have obstacles. Somebody once noted that hazards on the golf course were there to "spice it up." This may be true but you do not need spice when pursing your vision. Anticipate that there will be blockers, that there will be cynicism and apathy. In the same manner that you practice getting out of the sand so that you will know how to be effective with a sand

shot in a real game, anticipate how you will deal with cynicism, apathy and obstructionism. Know in advance what the consequences will be.

10. All of this needs to be undertaken with a great deal of preparation. Don't rush into a personal or organizational vision. Take the necessary time. Particularly in terms of an organizational vision, you may not get a second opportunity. So prepare, prepare, prepare. And then align.

Hole #2: Alignment

Establishing the vision is only twenty percent of the battle. Achieving the vision is the other eighty percent—the real challenge. In order to achieve the vision, you must align the entire organization (or to achieve an individual vision, you must ensure that all your potential personal barriers are anticipated and conquered).

Alignment was actually a golf term before it was part of the leadership lexicon. Great golfers have always aligned their shot with the target; probably no one was better at this than Jack Nicklaus. Nicklaus not only knew where he was going; he knew how we were going to get there.

Before we review what you could do to surpass your first round score on this hole, please remember the critical distinction. A visionary leader must align the entire company; a visionary leader by himself or herself will achieve some results. However, if a visionary leader can transfer the vision to the entire organization and thus create a visionary company, the company can achieve the vision. How do you align to achieve the vision?

1. Look down the fairway and identify the obstacles.

2. Based on your assessment of your strengths, analyze the risks and define a strategy. Make realistic "stretch" as-

sessments of how to avoid the hazards and play your game.

3. Ensure that your alignment process is comprehensive. Barriers to achieving a vision that are often overlooked include policies, procedures, cultural norms, promotion and compensation policies, tactical and strategic planning, and job descriptions. In short, to effectively align the company, you must consider everything within the company. Even something as small as the way the phones are answered can impact your ability to achieve the vision.

4. Implement a comprehensive alignment model which will ensure that the flow from vision to corporate goals to departmental objectives to individual and team tasks/ projects is targeted.

5. Empower employees to act in accordance with the vision. Coach them when their actions aren't in keeping with the vision.

6. Visions don't just happen so make sure that you identify and activate a guidance team whose responsibility is to track the process of achieving the vision and report the results to the senior leader (or the executive team).

7. Ensure that you use the tried and true SMART formula when setting corporate goals and that your detailed objectives flow from these goals.

8. Influence and insist, establish consequences for noncompliance, but do not intimidate into submission. Pounding on the table and demanding results will pay short term dividends and will cause long term problems. Alignment is a comprehensive, cooperative and coordinated effort to achieve the vision.

9. Stay the course. If your first shot should go into the water, know what you can do to still make par (and remember, not all bogeys are bad). Develop and implement a structure that is at one and the same time dynamic and flexible and well enough defined to ensure achieving the vision.

If you didn't do well on this hole, these nine recommendations provide an excellent reference for improving your score on the next round. Now lets look at some of the activities that enable you to achieve the vision with a minimum of stops and starts, of interruptions and attitudinal problems. Let's begin with determining how best to motivate your people to want to achieve the vision.

Hole #3: Motivation

You remember motivation; not the toughest hole on the course, just the longest. The challenge of this hole is the need to adapt your natural style to the unique features of the course—in motivation, one size does not fit all. Remember, motivation is not about making people feel good, it is about results. If you can establish those conditions under which people feel motivated, they will produce at a higher level. Motivation is good business. So, what are the secrets of playing this hole well?

1. While it is true that, in the end, none of us can really motivate someone else to improve or change a behavior, we can certainly establish conditions under which an individual is much more likely to discern agreement between our goals and his or her behavior and to act on that discernment. (In other words, although psychologists say we cannot really motivate anyone, in the real world we can.)

2. Understand that not all people respond to the same "motivators." You need to be aware of an individual's level of competence and his or her self-confidence in order to properly motivate the individual.

3. The reasons that we play golf can be adapted to the workplace and used to motivate people. Why do we play golf? We play because of the challenge, because of the continuing opportunity to improve, because each shot brings hope of the perfect.

4. We play golf for many reasons, all of them motivational. We play golf because the bar is always being raised, if we do well today, we expect to do incrementally better tomorrow. We play golf because it demands our best every time we play, because the course is littered with creative opportunities, and because there is "joy in the effort." If you understand why people play golf, you can transfer many of these lessons to the workplace.

5. Money is a motivator of limited effect. Money will produce short-term results, but once an individual makes as much as others who do similar work, the motivational impact of more money is greatly diminished. Management often believes that more money is the answer to motivational issues while employees are looking for a good place to work and a manager who respects, praises and challenges them. People look for managers who will motivate them through constructive, improvement oriented feedback and coaching rather than opinionated, destructive, "you did it wrong," ego destroying statements.

6. An important motivator for most people is the sense that they are engaged "in an enterprise greater than themselves," and that they have some influence on the suc-

cess of that enterprise. Incidentally, a vision statement at any level (department, division, company) should define beyond any reasonable doubt, that this organization is doing something vital, important and worthy of directed effort.

7. Motivating employees is good business. Unwanted turnover is an enormous hidden cost is most businesses today. A positive management style, an important mission and a chance to contribute all dramatically impact employee loyalty. Dr. Nathaniel Branden proved the correlation between productive employees and employee self-esteem. Enhance self-esteem and you increase productivity (and vice-versa).

8. Other important motivators include meaningful work, achievement oriented (stretch) goals, personal autonomy and some control over the decisions that directly impact the employee. Company stories that demonstrate how success was achieved through the implementation of the core values of the company serve as a motivator for all employees. Everyone is motivated when they are accorded respect.

9. The most dangerous motivator is fear. Fear often produces short-term results at the expense of long term dissatisfaction, cynicism and sometimes even sabotage. Fear as a motivator should be saved for emergencies.

10. Managers often say they are too busy to motivate, that a paycheck is ample motivation. Leaders know that behaviors such as paying attention to people, showing respect for their opinions, providing immediate sincere and specific recognition and creating challenging opportunities are well worth the time and effort required. True motivation is good business.

So the application of effective motivational strategies is one of those distinguishing characteristics between managers and leaders. Leaders understand the nature and importance of individual motivation, and they ensure that the motivation is effective through the use of purposeful communication. Communication just happens to be the next hole on the course.

Hole #4: Communication

Everyone can communicate, right? The question begs the answer. The fact that nearly everyone can talk does not mean that everyone can communicate. In golf there is a time when an individual finally feels that he or she has mastered the basics of the swing, understands the concept of course management, and has some degree of competence with the driver, the wedge and the putter. In other words, once the individual has attained a certain degree of confidence in his or her skill level, the term "golfer" assumes a more comfortable fit.

People used to ask me, "Are you a golfer?" In my own analytical way I would respond, "Well, yes, I play golf." Today, even though I carry a twenty handicap, I feel as though I at least have a sense of where the drive, iron, wedge, or putt is going. With this skill level I can reply, "yes, I am a golfer" (I am not Greg Norman, you understand, but I can play an occasional round in less than ninety and even occasionally break eighty-five – I don't say this, of course, but I think it.).

The point is, of course, without skills you can be neither a golfer nor a communicator. So how do you play this hole? If you tend to bogey or double bogey "communication", here are some tips to bring you back to par.

1. Listening is more difficult than talking. Leaders can only get the information they need from their people by listening. Active listening is hard work. Listening to others is not a sign of weakness.

2. "You cannot lead from the rear of the battle," noted General James Longstreet. Laissez-Faire leadership, not communicating because you don't want to offend someone, is more dangerous than the dominating style of leadership. Effective leadership requires balance between telling and listening. (Research shows that effective leaders talk about 40% of the time and listen about 60%.)

3. If you are good with your driver, and not as confident in your putting, work on your putting. Challenge your communication style. Make an honest assessment of your strengths and weaknesses in this area and discipline yourself to build on your strengths and improve in your weak areas.

4. The skill of paraphrasing has been trivialized through overuse. Used wisely it is an effective tool for clarifying communication. Used poorly it smacks of management "charm school."

5. The skill of empathy can be used to help the individual realize that his or her interests are in line with those of the company. It can also be used to defuse highly emotional situations. Learn to "tune in" to the emotions of the person you are communicating with. Remember that all information is first processed in the emotional center of the brain.

6. How many clubs in your bag? Probably fourteen plus your telescoping ball retriever. If it requires that many clubs to win at golf, why would you expect to carry any fewer to win at communication? The people reporting to you have different interaction styles; learn to understand these styles and to be effective in communicating with each of the different styles.

7. The key question related to motivation and communication is this: "What do your people do when you are not there—and why?" If your people take the attitude, "the boss is away, now we can play," or the attitude, "if we get caught not working we are in deep trouble," you are managing and not leading. Remember the leader influences the team to want to accomplish the task; pride, not fear, drives the leader's team.

8. Many managers fail to develop leadership because they are afraid of conflict; they will tell you that they "hate being involved in any kind of conflict." Leaders know that conflict comes with the territory. You can manage conflict through the use of paraphrasing, empathy and judgement. The two extremes of conflict management are "My way or the highway" and "You can have whatever you want." Leaders use judgement and communication to negotiate the best solution.

9. You can be obeyed into bankruptcy. Leaders learn to listen and to ask the probing questions that determine the validity of information. The goal of communication is that the resulting product is greater than either of the individuals would have had by themselves. True communication is synergistic.

10. Non-verbal communication is often stronger than verbal communication. The most important message you can send your people is your sense of credibility, your modeling of the expectations you have of them.

Hole #5: Process Improvement

Leadership is about results. It might be (and has been) argued that maintaining a process leads to the desired result; but in leadership, as in golf, it is process improvement, not process maintenance, that leads to improved results.

One of the premises of this book is that capable leaders are also competent managers, essentially that management skills are a prerequisite to effective leadership skills. It is only when you understand a process that you can challenge it. Golfers are never satisfied with their game. They are always seeking to improve. They may change their swing, their stance, their approach to course management. But they can only change from something; they must understand what they did before in order to improve it.

Many leaders don't want to "get into the weeds" of process improvement. As a result, they often "take a double or triple' on this hole. They essentially live with the unpredictability of the novice golfer. Thus the question: If you don't do well on process improvement, what can you do to improve your score?

1. Identify the processes in your department or division. Today, with ISO and QS 9000 in so many companies, many, but not all of these processes are already well defined. Remember that there are effective models, but no one best way—even among the pros you seldom see two swings or putting strokes that are identical. The important thing is that these swings and putting strokes are effective at achieving the objective and have a high degree of repeatability.

2. If you are just designing processes, ensure that the basics are in place. Remember that the golf pro will not start you out with the driver; he or she will work with you on the basics of the swing with a mid range iron. Once you master the basics you can move on to more challenging processes.

3. Benchmarking saves time and energy when developing and improving processes. Why reinvent the wheel when you can learn from already world class models. Visit

companies whose processes are world class. Adapt them to fit the needs of your company.

4. Seldom should a non-manufacturing process be so rigid that it allows no flexibility in its implementation. Effective processes, like effective golf swings, are grounded in fundamentals, yet allow the individual some leeway for imagination and creativity (for example in customer service or inside sales) in their implementation. Processes that are too inflexible often result in a negative rather than positive customer service. (There are few things more difficult for the customer to hear than, "Our procedures do not allow me to do that.")

5. Once you have identified key processes, move on to those that are less critical, but do not overproceduralize. Remember, while you cannot improve a random process, too many procedures drive enthusiasm out of the individual.

6. Be wary of accepting the procedure as "The Procedure." Focus on improving the effectiveness of procedures. Work with teams to move the procedure from the real to the ideal.

7. The process of improving processes is continuous. When you have written or improved one procedure, thank the team, find another, and begin again.

8. Process improvement is not the glamour job of leadership. However, it is a vital role. Remember that when you are experiencing wide variation in how tasks are being completed and/or in the results achieved, it probably points to an unstable process. Don's Dictum, based on hitting an innocent squirrel at 180 yards is: "You Cannot Improve a Random Process."

Hole #6: Keep An Accurate Score

Keeping an accurate score would appear to be another management function. Leaders don't worry about the score do they? Yes, they do, more than that, they make certain that the score is accurate and balanced; they make sure that the numbers don't just reflect the results achieved (the score for the game), but more importantly, how the game was played (greens in regulation, length and accuracy of the drive, putting accuracy, effectiveness of the short game).

Leaders also know that data gathered, but buried in reports, is often worse than no data at all. Data need to be turned into information that is used in decision making. The leader also knows that there are many ways to interpret numbers; if there are several ways to present the information, the leader needs to ensure that negative as well as positive aspects are covered.

If you didn't do well in playing this hole, what can you do to improve your score the next round?

1. Review all the data that is currently being kept for use in your department, division or company. Be aware of the 12-inch thick "greenbar" report that no one understands or uses. Remember that data only becomes useful when it can be translated to useful information.

2. Remember that situational *scoring* provides a false sense of how you are really doing. Insist that there be a basis (an operational definition) for maintaining the data. Base this definition on customer service, a financial or improvement goal whenever possible. Don't just set up a measurement that can be manipulated to "show how good we are doing."

3. Lagging indicators tell you how well you have done in the past and are not necessarily correlated with how well you will do in the future. Some companies rely too heavily on lagging indicators such as annual sales, an-

nual revenue and complaints received. To know how you are doing today and how you can improve for tomorrow use customer focus groups, mystery shoppers and well designed surveys.

4. Define a "macro metric" that is industry or company specific; this is typically the factor that contributes the most to customer satisfaction (other than price). In golf, there is usually a strong correlation between putting and scoring. Find a macro metric and define a goal for this metric for your company; publicize your progress in achieving this goal throughout the company.

5. Install a system of metrics that includes: customer satisfaction data, employee satisfaction data, individual department data, performance data and supplier data.

6. Use the measurement data to improve performance. Ensure that people know that the data they keep are being used for a purpose, not that these activities are simple busywork.

7. Dr. W. Edwards Deming popularized the concept of costs that were "unknown and unknowable." Make sure that any measurement system looks beyond raw numbers to implications of the numbers. Look at data on lost customers, reduced business with customers, and shifting demographics in your customer base as evidence of costs unknown and unknowable. Data never tell the whole story. Data are critical, but more important is judgment in using the data.

Hole #7: Judgment, Emotional Intelligence, Power and the Nature of Leadership

A woman tour professional was interviewed while leading a major tournament. She was asked by the interviewer how she could be leading when other golfers were far stronger off the tee than she. "It's true," she replied, "some are more than 80 yards longer than I am. You just have to know your game and play it."

So it is with leadership. There is no one best way to be a leader; no one technique you can master that will enable you to lead at all times. But the best leaders know their strengths and weaknesses and play their game. Almost universally, two of these strengths are sound judgment and emotional intelligence. These two are the putting and chipping of leadership; you simply cannot win big without them.

If you typically have not been scoring well in this area, here are some tips to improve your game.

1. Many are under the misunderstanding that good judgment is something you are born with. In fact, judgment is a skill to be continuously developed. It begins with a rigorous self-evaluation of how you are seen by others (an honest, amnesty based 360 degree feedback process is a good way to begin). Part of the self-analysis must include how you play from the rough. Business rough includes angry employees, needed change, and obstacles and hazards to your success that you consider unfair and/or unreasonable.

2. Judgment involves analyzing several interacting variables and the impact of these variables on all the parties involved. Good judgement is then taking the proper action based on this analysis. For example, working with a big ego: tread softly but firmly, with a timid personality: be forceful, but not intimidating. The Mike Benson story illustrates that "being right" at the expense of publicly embarrassing a superior demonstrates a serious lack of judgment.

3. As a leader, you have two choices. You can run over people or you can influence them. Understanding per-

sonal non-monetary motivators is critical to your ability to influence.

4. Developing judgment and emotional intelligence is much like perfecting your short irons. With your irons you go to the range, take you stance, hit the ball, evaluate the result and then change your stance or your swing to improve the result. The same is true for interactions with people. If you have a difficult interaction with a colleague, a superior, or a direct report, take time to evaluate how effective you were in achieving your goal. What might you have done differently? "Tune into" the non-verbal response of people to your communication style.

5. Do not ignore the importance of emotion in processing and analyzing interpersonal interactions. The two big mistakes of managers are to assume that everything can be handled logically and that a paycheck is motivation. Leaders do not make these assumptions.

6. Leaders play with controlled passion. They care. "Leaders leverage thought with passion and compassion to achieve inspired action."

7. Emotional intelligence, wisdom and judgment are closely related and equally important. Interestingly you develop emotional intelligence through the rational analysis of both your emotional response and that of others. Emotional intelligence combines perception, understanding and intuition. Continued reflection on the results of judgment leads to wisdom.

8. Power is a necessary but not sufficient component of leadership. Leadership depends on influence but does not shirk away from the wise use of power. Total reli-

ance on power, particularly position power, produces passive compliance rather than active agreement.

9. Leadership is a discontinuous process. Few, if any, are in a leadership position at all times. Leadership depends on the interaction of individuals and the needs of the situation.

10. Leadership is not a "paint by numbers" process. Each leader, as with each golfer, must define his or her own personal style. This leadership style will include judgment, emotional intelligence, controlled passion and the wise use of power.

Hole #8: Character

Who we are as a leader is more important than what we say as a leader. Leadership is both character and competence, both who you are and what you can do. But the medium is the message, and in the case of leadership you are the medium.

Character can be developed and there is no better game in the world through which to learn character than golf. In golf there are no umpires and no referees, no linesman, no back judge. Only at the highest professional level are there judges. For the great majority of us, we must play according to the rules and there is often no one there to make sure we do—thus character.

If you think of a leader as a charismatic, hard charging, visionary individual you are focusing in on a very small percentage of the population. As we mentioned in the forward this is not unlike thinking that all great golfers are long drivers (they are not). The classic traits of leadership are "inborn" in less than one tenth of one percent of the population—we need more leaders than this. Remember, leaders are those who actively and consciously seek to influence others to want to do—and do—that which the leader has determined needs to be done. So, how do you develop the leadership character that supports your success in influencing others? If you have not been scoring well on this hole, what can you do to improve your results?

1. Understand that personality is not character; personality is an external reflection of who we *think* we are. Character goes beyond persona to what we stand for, to what we believe in and value—to who we really are.

2. Management "charm school" behaviors can mask character to some extent, but sooner or later character is revealed. The validity of the old saying that "Who we are shouts louder than what we say" is proven when would-be leaders with technique, but without character, attempt to influence others.

3. "Play It Where It Lies" summarizes in the game of golf so much of what is essential for leaders to understand about leadership. "Play It Where It Lies" says that, while not every situation is under our control, our response to each situation is. It says that the world isn't fair, even on a great shot, but that it makes no difference. It says don't kick the ball out of the divot because no one is watching, or because it is a tough shot. "Play It Where It Lies" says that we are not victims of circumstance, but rather in charge of taking what is given to us and doing the best we can. "Play It Where It Lies" says that we all must accept personal responsibility. It is, of course, a metaphor for leadership.

4. Personal and professional honesty is the most frequently cited character trait for a leader that people admire. Efforts to lead change flounder if those being led do not believe in the personal honesty of the leader. Honesty is not situational.

5. Authenticity, congruence between what we value, what we say and what we do, is a second character trait essen-

tial to leadership. Authenticity is based on candid self-appraisal and external behavior that fit with that internal appraisal.

6. A third critical character trait is predictability. Your people must know that you are who you are. They need to know that it isn't Dr. Jekyl one moment and Mr. Hyde the next. Predictability includes consistency in approach, in action and follow through. This need for consistency of behavior is one of the most challenging aspects of the leadership game. George Macdonald wrote, "It is better to be trusted than loved." This is certainly true for leaders.

7. Tenacity and Persistence are also required of the leader. He or she who persists can have what they will. Persistence and tenacity magnify talent. Golf says ""Stay the course." Tenacity is mental toughness that says you don't quit when things are difficult.

8. Concentration seems like a skill, but it really is a part of character. Lack of focus derails leadership efforts. Remember that we become that which we think about. Focus on becoming a leader, give it your concentrated effort. Discipline your character to focus rather than to become preoccupied with irrelevant and unimportant distractions.

9. The final character trait to be developed is will; making the conscious choices that enable you to lead. Don't let others make these choices for you, use your own volition, your own free will.

Hole #9: Change

If you do not think of yourself now as a leader, and you desire to become one, this book is a beginning; the beginning blueprint from which you will construct your leadership structure. This structure will be unique to you; like the golf swing, everyone's leadership style has common elements and wide variation. The measure of the effectiveness of your structure is found in the results achieved and your personal harmony with the process.

For most of us becoming a leader means changing some of the ways we approach both people and situations. How to change is the subject of hundreds of books, this final chapter of "The Front Nine" provides a summary of some of the most recent findings in the field and presents a model that you can use to improve your leadership effectiveness. It begins by looking at this highly individualized package we have created for ourselves called personality.

What we know about personality is that each of us creates our own, and because we create it, we can change it—not easily, but it can be done. This chapter, then, is about personal change; a process of metamorphosis that can be haphazard or purposeful; that can be dynamic and exciting or static and enervating. Some kind of change will happen whether we like it or not, the only question is: how hard will you word to direct that change. How hard will you work based only on faith and the word of others that the results, even if they don't create your dream, are worth the effort.

If you have typically not done well at personal change efforts, if your habits seem to be stronger than your will to change them, review the steps presented here and ask yourself how they can be better integrated into your leadership plan. Change is truly the opportunity of a lifetime.

1. Think back to some of the salient events that created your personality. Think of the successes and failures, the messages and the moments that shaped how you think about you. In particular examine the fears that helped shape the fragile gauze we call personality.

2. This is a difficult but essential step. Acknowledge that this personality is of your own creation. You made it, you can change it!

3. All actions begin with thoughts (words and pictures). If you imagine a direction for yourself and continually re-visit that thought, you have taken the first step on your way to achieving that goal.

4. The two dominant realities of people are the need to be accepted and the fear that we might be rejected; these two combine to make personal change, particularly adult personal change, a real challenge. Tin Cup shouts "who hit that shot," to ward off rejection and to ask for acceptance. To change is to risk losing acceptance and experience rejection, but it is a risk you must take to become a leader.

5. Golfers know that change is a given, the only choice is how much of it will you control. Thus golf provides a model for how to embrace effective change.

6. Change begins with dissatisfaction. If the need for change involves urgency, then it is more likely to happen, but all change begins with a disconnect between what is currently being experienced and what is wanted.

7. Change begins with dissatisfaction and continues with commitment. Commitment combines a rational knowledge of the skills required with an emotional resolution to overcome the fear being faced in order to achieve the goal. Commitment is "leaving the dock" knowing that the twenty foot waves are out there waiting for your skill to challenge them.

8. Successful change is usually autonomous, that is, the change is undertaken because "I want to" rather than "I have to."

9. Change is not simply related to external physical appearance or mental attitude. Successful personal change is physiological—it creates or is created by altering the neural pathways of your brain.

10. For most people the primary barrier to change is fear; fear of leaving a place where we are comfortable even if we aren't particularly successful, fear of failure, fear of embarrassment, fear of rejection. Successful change, then, involves conquering the emotions that present the barriers to change. Take your inventory of reasons why you haven't been more effective as a leader. Make an in-depth personal assessment of what has held you back. The rational brain is stronger than the emotional brain; use that brain to free you from fear and to focus on the emotions that accompany achieving a goal or solving a problem.

11. Take action. Action overcomes fear; it may sound like double talk, but the truth is that when you act, your brain begins to believe that you can do, that you can overcome the resistance to taking that action. The next action thus becomes easier to take. "Look ma, no hands."

12. Begin now. Leadership is the opportunity of the many rather than the privilege of the few. Stay the course, play all eighteen; don't quit until you have achieved your personal leadership vision. "Be the change you wish to see in others." *Go for the Green!*

GOLF TEACHES US

THAT AVERAGE EFFORTS

PRODUCE AVERAGE RESULTS.

GOLF TEACHESUS

THE LESSONS OF LIFE

AND LEADERSHIP

EVERY TIME WE VENTURE

FORTH TO

PLAY THE GAME.

Bibliography

Warren Bennis, *On Becoming a Leader*, (Reading Massachusetts: Addison Wesley, 1989).

Warren Bennis and Burt Nanus, *Leaders,* (New York: Harper and Row, 1985).

Kenneth Blanchard, Patricia Zigarmi and Drea Zigarmi, *Leadership and the One Minute Manager*, (New York: William Morrow and Company, 1985).

Warren Blank, *The 9 Natural Laws of Leadership*, (New York: AMACOM, 1995).

Nathaniel Branden, the Psychology of Self-Esteem, (New York: Bantam Books, 1969).

Steven M. Chandler, *ReInventing Yourself,* (New York: Career Press, 1998).

James C. Collins and Jerry I. Porras, *Built to Last,* (New York: Harper Business Books, 1994).

Dennis Deaton, *Mind Management,* (Mesa, Arizona: MMI Publishing, 1994)

E. L. Deci, *Why We Do What We Do*, (New York: Penguin Books, 1995).

Paul Dickson, *The "Official Rules" for Golfers*, (New York: Barnes and Noble, 1997)

Lee Eisenberg, *Breaking Eighty*, (New York: Hyperion Books, 1997).

Daniel Goleman, *Emotional Intelligence*, (New York: Bantam Books, 1995).

Robert Greene and Joost Elffers, *The 48 Laws of Power*, (New York: Viking Press, 1998).

Robert S. Kaplan and David P. Norton, *The Balanced Scorecard, (Boston: Harvard Business School Press, 1996).*

John Kotter, *Leading Change*, (Boston: Harvard Business School Press, 1996).

James M. Kouzes and Barry Z. Posner, *The Leadership Challenge* (San Francisco: Jossey-Bass Press, 1995).

James M. Kouzes and Barry Z. Posner, *Credibility*, (San Francisco: Jossey-Bass Press, 1993).

Gary McCord, *Golf for Dummies*, (Foster City, California: IDG Books, 1996).

Phillip C. McGraw, *Life Strategies*, (New York: Hyperion Books, 1999).

James Patterson and Peter de Jonge, *Miracle on the 17th Green*, (Boston: Little Brown and Company, 1996).

Harvey Penick with Bud Shrake, *Harvey Penick's Little Red Book*, (New York, Simon and Shuster, 1992).

Frederick F. Reichheld, *The Loyalty Effect*, (Boston, Harvard Business School Press, 1996).

Bob Rotella with Bob Cullen, *Golf Is Not a Game of Perfect*, (New York: Simon and Shuster, 1995).

Alan Shapiro, *Golf's Mental Hazards*, (New York: Fireside, 1996).

Noel M. Tichy, *The Leadership Engine*, (New York: Harper Business Books, 1997)

John Updike, *Golf Dreams*, (New York: Random House, 1996)

Richard C. Whitely, *The Customer Driven Company*, (Reading, Massachusetts: Addison Wesley, 1991).